Palgrave Historical Studies in Witchcraft and Magic
Series Editors: **Jonathan Barry, Willem de Blécourt** and **Owen Davies**

Series Foreword

The history of European witchcraft and magic continues to fascinate and challenge students and scholars. There is certainly no shortage of books on the subject. Several general surveys of the witch trials and numerous regional and micro studies have been published for an English-speaking readership. While the quality of publications on witchcraft has been high, some regions and topics have received less attention over the years. The aim of this series is to help illuminate these lesser known or little studied aspects of the history of witchcraft and magic. It will also encourage the development of a broader corpus of work in other related areas of magic and the supernatural, such as angels, devils, spirits, ghosts, folk healing and divination. To help further our understanding and interest in this wider history of beliefs and practices, the series will include research that looks beyond the usual focus on Western Europe and that also explores their relevance and influence from the medieval to the modern period.

Titles include:

Palgrave Historical Studies in Witchcraft and Magic
Series Standing Order ISBN 978–1403–99566–7 Hardback
978–1403–99567–4 Paperback
(*outside North America only*)

You can receive future titles in this series as they are published by placing a standing order. Please contact your bookseller or, in case of difficulty, write to us at the address below with your name and address, the title of the series and the ISBN quoted above.

Customer Services Department, Macmillan Distribution Ltd, Houndmills, Basingstoke, Hampshire RG21 6XS, England.

Agents of Witchcraft in Early Modern Italy and Denmark

Louise Nyholm Kallestrup
University of Southern Denmark, Odense

First published 2015 by
PALGRAVE MACMILLAN

Palgrave Macmillan in the UK is an imprint of Macmillan Publishers Limited, registered in England, company number 785998, of Houndmills, Basingstoke, Hampshire RG21 6XS.

Palgrave Macmillan in the US is a division of St Martin's Press LLC, 175 Fifth Avenue, New York, NY 10010.

Palgrave Macmillan is the global academic imprint of the above companies and has companies and representatives throughout the world.

Palgrave® and Macmillan® are registered trademarks in the United States, the United Kingdom, Europe and other countries.

ISBN 978–0–230–30071–2

This book is printed on paper suitable for recycling and made from fully managed and sustained forest sources. Logging, pulping and manufacturing processes are expected to conform to the environmental regulations of the country of origin.

A catalogue record for this book is available from the British Library.

Library of Congress Cataloging-in-Publication Data
Kallestrup, Louise Nyholm, 1975–
Agents of witchcraft in early modern Italy and Denmark / Louise Nyholm Kallestrup, University of Southern Denmark, Odense.
pages cm. — (Palgrave historical studies in witchcraft and magic)
Includes bibliographical references.
ISBN 978–0–230–30071–2
1. Witchcraft—Italy—History—17th century. 2. Witchcraft—Denmark—History—17th century. 3. Trials (Witchcraft)—Italy. 4. Trials (Witchcraft)—Denmark. I. Title.
BF1584.I8K345 2015
133.4′3094509032—dc23

2015002373

Typeset by MPS Limited, Chennai, India.

To my family
In memory of my father

Contents

List of Tables

Acknowledgements

Finishing a book feels like completing a long journey. A lot of people have helped me on mine, and I feel indebted to them all. Without their encouragements, comments and inspiration, I would never have come this far. First and foremost I wish to thank Stephen Mitchell and Matteo Duni. Stephen Mitchell for the many inspiring discussions, the provision of constructive comments and questions to the manuscript, and for his continuous encouragement during the past five years. Matteo Duni for thoroughly reading and commenting on the manuscript, and for his interest in my comparative approach. I also wish to thank Elizabeth S. Cohen and Gunnar W. Knutsen and my series editor at Palgrave Macmillan, Willem de Blécourt, for reading final versions of the manuscript and offering me their valuable specialist comments.

I thank Gustav Henningsen and the late Alex Wittendorff, from whose remarks I have learned a great deal. Their works continue to be a source of inspiration. I am grateful to have been given the opportunity to study at the Archivio della Congregazione per la Dottrina della Santa Fede. When I was first admitted to the archive more than a decade ago, I was still a young, naïve PhD fellow, who had no idea of the challenges I would face. I am grateful that Oscar Di Simplicio helped point me in the direction of the Orbetello trial records, as he himself was working on his books on the Siena Tribunal. Daniel Ponziani and the rest of the staff at the ACDF have always been kind and helpful, despite my modest spoken Italian skills. During my work in Italian archives, I stayed at the Danish Academy in Rome, and I am grateful for the various directors' readiness to accommodate me, sometimes at short notice. During my visits to Danish archives, namely the Danish Archive for Folklore (Dansk Folkemindesamling), the National Archive (Rigsarkivet) and the provincial archives in Viborg and Odense, I have been met with kindness and helpfulness. Also the Department of History, especially the Centre for Medieval Studies at the University of Southern Denmark, deserves my gratitude. The Faculty of Humanities at University of Southern Denmark and Knudsen's Foundation has made the translation of this book possible, and I am grateful for John Mason's language revision and that Tine Dam Bendtsen and Roger Rees took on the task of proofreading. Jens Christian Vesterskov Johansen, Helge Gamrath, Rune Hagen and Torben Kjersgaard Nielsen all read earlier versions of the text and provided me with valuable comments for improvement.

I am equally indebted to a number of colleagues, many of them having become friends over the years: Charlotte Appel, Raisa Maria Toivo, Richard Kieckhefer and Johannes Dillinger; Lars Bisgaard for never giving up on trying to answer my many questions on Danish Church history; Per Seesko for the numerous nerdy discussions on Ribe and its early modern residents; Janus Møller Jensen for sharing my interest in witches, vampires and other supernatural creatures; Nils Arne Sørensen and Jesper Majbom Madsen for sharing my passion for Italy, Camilla Schjerning for discussions about angry and offensive women of the early modern world, and Per Grau Møller for drawing the maps. I also owe thanks to Deborah Simonton for introducing me to good colleagues in the research network 'Gender in the European Town'; to colleagues in the Nordic network 'Religious Belief and Practice in the Danish-Norwegian Kingdom'; Michaela Valente for her efforts to track down inquisitor Pedrosa of Orbetello, and Erling Sandmo for being a continuous inspiration as well as for taking care of a speedy book deliverance when needed the most. I owe special gratitude to three dear friends and colleagues, Nina Koefoed, Anne Magnussen and Kirstine Sinclair. I am grateful for your comments on my studies and I cherish your continuous encouragements and reminders never to settle for less. Despite all the aid I have received, the responsibility for all faults is of course mine alone.

Ultimately, I wish to thank my family. Morten, I am forever grateful for your patience and for untiringly engaging in conversations about wicked women, devils and magic of the 17th century, and to Dicte and Anna for insisting that the present is more important than the past.

Nyborg, December 2014

Maps

Map 1   Early modern Italy

Map 2   Orbetello and its surroundings

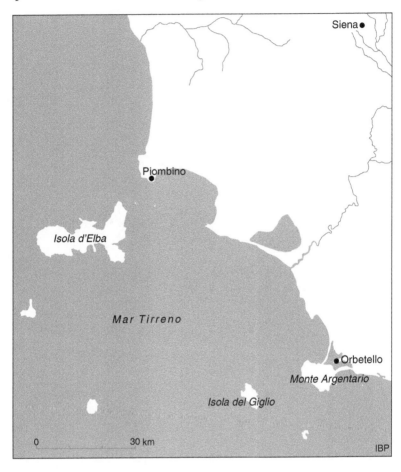

Map 3   Jutland

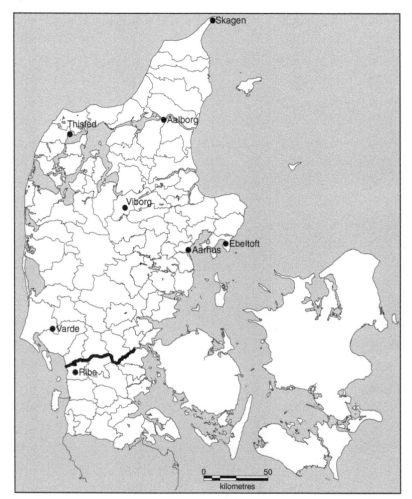

1
Introduction

In 1650, the Roman Inquisition in the Tuscan town of Orbetello convicted Fra Stefano Tommei of witchcraft (*sortilegio*). Stefano was sentenced to arbitrary imprisonment and a fine of 500 *scudi*.[1] In 1620, the provincial court in Viborg in Jutland convicted Johanne Pedersdatter from Sejlflod in Denmark for witchcraft (*trolddom*). She was sentenced to death and to be burned alive at the stake.[2]

The two penalties reflect how diverse the outcome of a witchcraft case could be in 17th century Europe. Arbitrary imprisonment and a fine of 500 *scudi* were among the harshest sentences imposed by the inquisitor in Orbetello, as opposed to Lutheran Denmark where execution by burning was the standard penalty in a guilty sentence for witchcraft. In Italy,[3] several of the pre-Reformation witch-hunts had ended in capital punishment, but from the last quarter of the 16th century, the Roman Inquisition put a halt to executions for witchcraft. In Denmark-Norway, the number of death penalties after the Reformation is estimated to amount to about 1,000 executions out of a total of approximately 2,000 trials.[4] About 650 of these trials were conducted in Jutland. Digging a bit deeper, one discovers that the two trials also represent other and less evident differences as well as similarities. Both culprits had a reputation for practising witchcraft for several years, and in both cases the initial accusations started from below, as they were both denounced by their neighbours. Stefano Tommei was denounced for having used a magical book in rituals for love magic, and Johanne Pedersdatter was accused of having bewitched the vicar.[5]

Despite being prosecuted for – and found guilty of – the same offence, witchcraft, Stefano Tommei and Johanne Pedersdatter were sentenced by the two courts to two very different penalties. Being a *crimen mixti fori*, European cases of witchcraft could be tried by lay as well as religious courts depending on regional power relations and statutes. In Italy, cases of witchcraft were placed in the hands of the Roman Inquisition in most parts of the peninsula from the second half of the 16th century. The inquisition was organized in 35 tribunals acting as representatives of their superiors at the

Congregation of the Holy Office and ultimately answering to the Pope himself.[6] The inquisitor to sentence Stefano was sent from the tribunal of Siena.[7]

A case before the inquisition was first and foremost a conflict between the individual and the Roman Catholic faith. The inquisitor represented and defended the faith; he was the one formally to press charges, to investigate, to interrogate and to sentence. Still, at the same time, he was the one holding the key to forgiveness through abjuration and penance. He was usually a trained canonist or theologian, and in addition to his own experience, he was obliged to consult and inform his superiors at the Tribunal, and in severe cases the Congregation in Rome, on the course of trials. After the verdict had been pronounced, the inquisition submitted the culprit to lay authorities for corporal punishment.

As with all suspects of witchcraft in post-Reformation Denmark, Johanne Pedersdatter had been prosecuted in a lay court. Initially one or more witchcraft accusations against a person were brought to the local lower court, and if a guilty verdict was sentenced, a trial of appeal was mandatory at the provincial court (*Landstinget*). In 1600, there were about 200 lower courts and four provincial courts in Denmark. The bailiff (*herredsfogeden*) was head of the lower courts. He was officially the king's representative in local society, although in practice he was merely a peasant appointed by the king's vassal, and he had no legal training. In court, the bailiff was accompanied by a number of legal witnesses (*stokkemænd*), who were commissioned to witness the course of the trials. At the provincial court, judges remained lay, but they were more educated, and were recruited from the nobility. In the Danish lower courts as well as the provincial courts, the trials were led according to a system which must be characterized as accusatorial, but with elements of inquisitorial procedures.[8] In cases of witchcraft, the accusers were private individuals, mostly the victims themselves or their families, and the trial itself a 'theatre of power'[9] in which the stronger party won, and where the judge assessed who had the stronger case.

In short, since witchcraft was a *crimen mixti fori*, two essentially different courts representing two very different judicial systems could conduct the trials against Stefano Tommei and Johanne Pedersdatter. When comparing cases for witchcraft in Italian and Danish courts, it becomes clear that what historians term the 'prosecution of witchcraft' has multiple meanings depending on the court and country referred to.[10] It is the purpose of this book to shed light on how and why prosecutions for witchcraft were so different in Italy and Denmark. In order to do so, a number of questions must be answered. Here, the key word is 'witchcraft'. What did the authorities and the people involved in the cases consider as witchcraft? Which rituals and practices were to be identified as witchcraft? What were the learned and popular arguments for prosecution, and how were they interconnected? And not least: how did people respond to accusations of witchcraft when confronted in court?

The concept and the semantic field surrounding witchcraft vary greatly. In his closing sentence, Stefano Tommei's inquisitor pronounced him 'vehemently suspected of heresy and apostasy'.[11] In this sense, Stefano Tommei's offence – *sortilegio* – was explicitly linked to sin and the inquisitors declared him an offender against the faith. The verdict over Johanne Pedersdatter contains the phrases (true) 'witch' (*troldkone*), 'threatening with evil' (*love ondt*) and 'rumoured to be a witch' (*havde et trolddomsrygte*), which indicates the court's different understanding of the offence. The term 'semantic field' is applied to the pattern or the networks of concepts, in which the key concept, witchcraft, interacts with other related concepts. In this study the semantic field includes among others heresy, magic, the Devil and acts such as the diabolic pact, worshipping, the practice of rituals and threatening.[12]

Terms such as 'witch', 'sorcery' and 'magic' are used frequently and commonly today, but differ from academic use and meaning. As is mandatory in a book on witchcraft, these concepts need further specification. In English, 'witchcraft' is the term commonly used by scholars. This is far from comprehensive as a term, but it is nevertheless applied here as the overarching expression. A direct Danish translation would be *hekseri*, from the German word *hexerei*, but that term is attested in Danish only in the late 17th century, and earlier legal cases as well as theological texts applied the word *trolddom*. The people involved in the Italian cases applied the term *sortilegio*, as did the inquisitor, who also often used the broader term *superstitione* (superstition). Directly translated, *sortilegio* means 'sorcery', whereas witchcraft would be translated as *stregoneria*. As this book will demonstrate, the examples given above are covered by the Danish term *trolddom* and the Italian *sortilegio* which correspond well to the scholarly use of the English term 'witchcraft' and to a lesser extent to 'sorcery'. The term *stregoneria* is not commonly used in Orbetello, and in this book it is referred to as 'diabolical witchcraft'. In this study, the term 'witchcraft' can therefore be considered as a working concept and as such it does not take into account its various nuances and connotations. Where such nuances are important, they will, of course, be highlighted.

Comparing witchcraft

This comparative study is triggered by a curiosity regarding what caused two courts to punish the offence of witchcraft so differently. The comparative approach owes much to the French historian Marc Bloch, who in his 1928 article, 'Toward a Comparative History of European Societies', outlined a number of points and aims for comparative studies.[13] Bloch was one of the first historians to argue in favour of comparative studies. He stressed that the building blocks for trans-European comparison always consisted of local studies, but that comparative studies would contribute with new and fruitful interpretations for local studies. According to Bloch, the comparative approach can be applied in various ways – none being superior – and historians are advised to engage in comparative analyses of different or similar societies.[14] If one wanted to search for similarities in the witch trials, an obvious pair of cases to compare would be Jutland with Slesvig or Skåne as they too were part of the Danish monarchy in the 16th century and part of the 17th century.[15] For the Roman Inquisition, the obvious point of comparison would probably be the Spanish Inquisition. However, the strategy of comparison chosen for this study has been to single out two very different cases in order to reveal, along with the differences, similarities not apparent to contemporaries.

Recent years have offered interesting comparative works on witchcraft, of which three must be highlighted in the present context. In 2011, Stephen Mitchell, himself a folklorist, published a comprehensive study of witchcraft and magic in the Nordic Middle Ages. Based on a wide range of sources, Mitchell broke with a traditional view prevalent at least among Danish witchcraft scholars that the Middle Ages were a historical blind spot about which it was difficult to make any qualified assertions. Through a systematic reading of sagas, high and late medieval literature and through a study of the laws and the few medieval cases that have been preserved, Mitchell's study confirms that the ways in which notions of witchcraft developed in Europe – becoming incorporated into theological writings and into court proceedings, as first suggested by Richard Kieckhefer – were paralleled in Denmark. In the Nordic judicial courts, medieval cases for witchcraft focused predominantly on personal conflicts, in which the harm caused by the witch was the centre of the offence. Mitchell points to a further important consideration regarding the perception of women as particularly wicked and vengeful. Through a close reading of late medieval moralistic texts and other elements of medieval culture, Mitchell determines how a popular tradition of wicked women challenging male authorities, corresponded very well with the misogyny of demonological writing of the 15th century.[16] I will return to this narrative of the evil woman during the course of this book.

Wicked people also play leading parts in Johannes Dillinger's comparative study of Swabian Austria and the Electorate of Trier. Dillinger launches the 'evil people principle', which refers to the tense environment created by witch-hunts. By naming it the 'evil people principle', Dillinger directs attention towards the main argument of his book, namely that the cases were sparked from below by people, mostly villagers, attempting to protect themselves against witches. In both Swabian Austria and the Electorate of Trier, the existing tension meant that every conflict held a potential accusation of witchcraft against the opposite party. Fear of a neighbour being an ally of the Devil lay at the heart of witch-hunts both in Swabian Austria and Trier and other territories in the region. Generally, the authorities experienced pressure from below to initiate cases, and in both territories, popular ideas of witchcraft combined with learned demonology were spurring on fear of witches.[17]

As with the Danish cases studied in this book, those examined by Dillinger concerned malevolent magic, as opposed to the cases in Italy, which mostly dealt with acquisitive magic, that is, magical rituals for personal gain, but with no explicit desire to harm. A similar difference prevailed in the comparative study by Gunnar Knutsen on the Spanish Inquisitions in Catalonia and Valencia. These cases were based on a charge that was typically termed 'superstition', a charge commonly employed by the Roman Inquisition. These cases encompassed both witchcraft and simpler forms of magic. In this important study, Knutsen shows how the Catalan tribunal mainly prosecuted cases for forms of witchcraft marked by maleficent magic and worship of the Devil. In Valencia in eastern Spain, most cases related to acquisitive magic, that is, the gain of either love or money.

In the present context, Knutsen's emphasis on demographic diversity as an explanatory factor is very compelling. Drawing on the argument that rural areas and small village communities provided fertile ground for witch-hunts, Knutsen suggests that demonological ideas did not gain ground with the Morisco population inhabiting the rural areas of Valencia. Instead, cases for witchcraft in this region took place mostly in urban areas. These cases were related to magical offences traditionally linked to urban cultures, namely love magic and magical rituals for gaining wealth. Such magical practices were more in line with the urban 'Old Christian' population inhabiting the towns. In Catalonia on the other hand, the rural population was under the strong influence of French immigrants, which Knutsen sees as a factor contributing to the inclusion of demonological features in local cases.[18]

The present study has developed from the thesis that Italy and Denmark, two societies polarized by religion, culture and geography, nevertheless had one vital thing in common: they were Christian and had until very recently been Christians of the same sort, sharing the same doctrines. Regardless of the Protestant break with Rome, the two societies shared a fundamental condemnation of witchcraft and magical rituals generally, which gave rise to the prosecutions of the 15th–17th centuries. Both regions issued strict laws and regulations, and theologians published demonological treatises and writings against witchcraft and magic. In addition, many of the same demonological writings of the period circulated on both sides of the confessional border.[19]

A modern breakthrough

In the past four decades, witchcraft studies have been a growing field of research. Comparing two so geographically different socio-historical cases as Italy and Denmark means bringing together different research traditions. In 1976, Richard Kieckhefer published his ground-breaking study of medieval witch cases. Along with Norman Cohn's *Europe's Inner Demons*, Kieckhefer's studies erased the idea of a medieval witch-hunt, at least among scholars of witchcraft. But Kieckhefer's book was also a contribution to the ongoing debate about subjecting witch cases to anthropological methods in order to decode popular beliefs. Kieckhefer took a sceptical position here in arguing that torture and judicial coercion made it difficult, if not impossible, to distinguish between stereotypically learned ideas and popular ideas.[20] In his 1966 *I benandanti*, Carlo Ginzburg argued for a less sceptical approach for the use of inquisitorial cases in the search for popular culture and beliefs. The conditions under which the documents had been produced, that is, in the courtroom and during interrogation from a superior judge, provided the sources with a filter, which we as historians could to some extent remove. By close reading, including taking into consideration the unequal balance of power in the courtroom, the historian was, according to Ginzburg, able to decode fragments of popular ideas from the transcripts of oral testimonies. This viewpoint was also dominant in his more famous *The Cheese and the Worms* (Italian edition published in 1976) and further stressed in the article 'L'inquisitore come antropologo'. The inquisitor may not have allowed an exchange of views, but the interrogations could nevertheless be read as transcripts of a dialogue revealing at least fragments of popular beliefs. When the inquisitor came upon beliefs unfamiliar to his stereotypical categories, such as the *benandanti*, the transcripts were particularly useful.[21]

Throughout the 1980s and 1990s, international and Italian scholars alike hotly debated Ginzburg's results. In her studies of the Roman Inquisition in Modena, Mary O'Neil dismissed Ginzburg's portrayal of an inquisition unable to comprehend popular beliefs, and in an early article from 1983, the Italian historian and leading expert on the Roman Inquisition, Andrea Del Col, argued against the plausibility of extracting popular culture from inquisitorial cases. Like Kieckhefer, Del Col was sceptical about the use of trial records for extracting popular ideas. Del Col also directed attention towards the origin of the source material, arguing that inquisitors always had a clear agenda for an interrogation and that this agenda determined the course of events as well as the statements given in court. Every inquisitorial case was marked by a strategy of having the offender accept orthodox beliefs. Inquisitorial protocols were intended solely for internal purposes, mainly in order to demonstrate the eradication of heterodoxy. According to Del Col, historians should never mistake reading court records for anthropological fieldwork.[22]

Generally speaking, current discussion concerning witch trials and the overall use of court records has taken many different directions. In Italian witchcraft studies, it is possible to trace a renewed view on the Roman Inquisition. Whereas part of the debate following Ginzburg revolved around the Roman Inquisition as a progressive and in legal senses almost modern court sceptical about the reality of diabolical witches, one current trend is moving in a different direction. Rainer Decker has argued that although the

Roman Inquisition may have been sceptical about the reality of diabolical witches, it did prosecute, sentence and execute hundreds for the invocation of demons. Giovanni Romeo has emphasized the cooperation between the inquisition and local authorities in order to implement church reforms. To ensure this cooperation, inquisitors would sometimes turn a blind eye to executions of witches sanctioned by local secular courts.[23]

This study is inspired by these works, although my interest and my reading of the court records have focused more on testimonies from witnesses as stories: what Guido Ruggiero would call 'tales'.[24] In the present study, I aim at reading the cases as texts with multiple layers and in mixed genres. As Natalie Davis has argued in *Fiction in the Archives* (1987), French pardon letters formed letters of pardon aimed at authorities, accounts of events and stories simultaneously.[25] If applied to the trials in the present study, that is, to those parts of a case where people were given a voice, we must focus on denunciations and accusations, and also on the testimonies of suspects. These texts are also of mixed genres. First, denunciations and accusations were statements intended to identify a suspected witch to the judge, and as such were part of a judicial investigation that was sometimes even regarded as evidence; secondly, testimonies from defendants could serve as confessions in a judicial as well as in a religious sense, and third, these texts also contain an account of a course of events, in which particular narratives about witches, gender, the good and the bad, and so on, were applied.

When reading these accounts as stories, we have a tool for identifying the good and the bad characters, or as in the present context, mostly good or bad women. What actions did they commit and when and why were they considered wicked or evil? What reputation did they carry in local society? All of this will be considered in relation to the offence of witchcraft. Through the reading of trial records as stories, we can determine behaviour and beliefs outside the courtroom, albeit only with due caution and critical sense. Although this book addresses popular beliefs and actions outside the courtroom, it does so only to investigate what is going on inside the courtroom. My interest is mainly centred on how these beliefs were applied and negotiated within the courtroom.

The close reading of cases in the second and third part of this book can be seen as peeling layers off the testimonies. In doing so, it is possible to determine the narratives about the witch that were presented in the testimonies, and how these narratives were applied in court. In this book, I focus especially on the denunciations of witnesses and the initial interrogation of the suspect. Throughout the book, I incorporate cases from initial allegation to sentence, although my main priority has been to focus on the accusations and denunciations and, in the inquisitorial cases, on the initial interrogation of suspects. During the initial part of a trial, the outcome was as yet unknown, judicial coercion was at its minimum, and torture had not yet been applied. At the same time, it was a common feature of accusations, denunciations and testimonies from suspects that we as historians can read them as texts of self-representation. They were, in the words of Elizabeth Cohen, 'conceived strategically to represent their speakers and to negotiate more complex meanings'.[26] In the courtroom, whether inquisitorial or lay, series of acts were presented, and at the same time they were measured up against both written and unwritten norms. The construction of the accused and the accusation were closely linked to ideas of how certain individuals or groups behaved.[27] When denouncing a person, an accuser may have made up stories about the suspect, but these stories were necessarily full of cultural truths; they needed to be plausible in order to convince the judge.

Tales of magic: reading the court records

The collection of inquisitorial cases from the Tribunal of Siena at the Archivio per la Congregazione della Dottrina della Santa Fede is one of the most complete collections of inquisitorial cases preserved in Italian archives. With only few lacunae, the archive contains almost 150 years of cases conducted by inquisitors sent from the tribunal in Siena.[28] So far, the Italian Oscar Di Simplicio is the only historian to have studied these cases.[29] Part of the Siena archive consists of a collection of about 2,000 pages of protocols from Orbetello, a small town in southern Tuscany. It is these cases that form the basis of the local Italian study of this book.

The early cases from 1612–1613 together with a few of the later ones are distributed across various volumes, while the cases from the mid-17th century are preserved in two separate volumes.[30] Some cases contain extracts from other trials, usually testimonies containing information relevant to the present cases. These extracts are distinguishable by being written by another notary and are marked copy (*copia*). As was common for the inquisition, many cases are simply a collection of denunciations or what we could call preliminary investigations, during which the suspect was never formally charged or even brought in for questioning. All of the protocols are kept in chronological order and there is no register. Most of the cases are written in a combination of Latin and Italian. In those cases where a thorough investigation was initiated and the suspect ended up being formally charged, the cases also include correspondence between the inquisitor and his superiors in Siena. These letters are mostly in Latin. The transcripts of interrogations are recorded as if the inquisitor had posed his question in Latin, and the defendant or witness had answered in Italian, although most likely the inquisitor too posed his questions in Italian, and the notary subsequently translated them into Latin.[31] As was standard for inquisitorial cases, the testimonies are recorded *in extenso*, and the accounts of witnesses and defendant are in a sense an oral culture put into writing. With only a few exceptions, all of the cases derive from a denunciation by a local lay-person with some relation, social or professional, to the suspect. Most often the cases include many denunciations before the suspect was brought into custody. In these cases the protocol also includes correspondence having taken place parallel to the interrogations of the suspect and the final sentence and abjuration. The cases vary in length from a single denunciation of a few pages to extensive collections of documents of several hundred folios.

The Danish cases studies here are kept at the Provincial Archive in Viborg in northern Jutland.[32] The court kept three parallel protocols of sentences sorted by geographical area. Protocols are preserved from 1609, although with interruptions. Sometimes all three protocols are missing, but in most cases at least one has been preserved.[33] The protocols contain various kinds of offences originally settled by the lower courts, and now brought to the appellate court in Viborg. As with the Italian, the Danish cases vary from a few pages to more voluminous trials, although rarely more than 15–20 folios. A case consisted of testimonies from witnesses, with one or more of these statements presented as a detailed formal accusation. Testimonies from witnesses, as well as denunciations of the suspected witch, appear in a different form than in the inquisitorial cases, since they were written as summaries of events, not as interrogations. Some testimonies were presented as written statements, usually those from clergymen. One or more individuals acted as prosecutors by formally charging the suspect. These prosecutors were usually co-villagers and in most cases themselves, their family or their livestock, victims of the suspect's evil deeds.[34] The sentence and its justification are always found at the end of the case material.

Moving between scales: the structure of the book

This book is based on the notion that the micro-historical approach is fruitful only when combined with a macro-historical contextualization. The book is divided into three parts. Part I, The Prosecutors, presents a macro-study of the courts and draws on legal texts, theological writings and witchcraft manuals. It examines the legal and ideological basis for Danish lay and Roman inquisitorial courts separately (chapters 2 and 3) before a comparative discussion of the procedures in chapter 4.

Part II, The Prosecuted, is devoted to the people involved in the cases, drawing on two case studies from the Roman Inquisition in Orbetello and its Danish counterpart, the Provincial court in Viborg. For this part of the book, several thousand folios of trial records involving hundreds of people have been examined. This second part of the book takes as its point of departure a general description of the two case studies. In chapter 5, through a thorough presentation of the two trials, the reader is introduced to the differences and similarities of the material, which leads to a methodological discussion of the close reading of court narratives. In chapter 6, the various categories of witchcraft applied by scholars are questioned and discussed to propose an analytical categorization, which is on the one hand not too narrow and on the other still useful for further analysis. The focus of chapter 7 is the initial phase of an inquisitorial case, the denunciation, and the allegations found in testimonies in the Danish cases. The intention is to establish what eventually led to formal accusation. In chapter 8, various kinds of allegations of witchcraft are examined to determine the popular ideas that formed the bases for magical rituals and to isolate what powers provided these rituals with their effect.

Fully aware of the inadequacy of the dichotomy of elite/popular, the final part of the book intends to bring into line the perceptions of witchcraft as seen by the judges and by the individuals on trial. This part investigates and compares the ideas of the witch held by witnesses and suspects as these are drawn upon when addressing the judges. Furthermore, the chapter explores the suspect's options in defending herself, and seeks to clarify the response from the judges in court.

A selection of cases will be referred to more regularly throughout the book with the intention to demonstrate to the reader the many layers in these texts. Secondly, as it poses a challenge, even for the author, to maintain an overview of names, dates and places, reference to only a limited number of cases should minimize confusion and so help the reader acquire some familiarity with the many individuals represented in them. With the material presented in this way, I hope the reader will better identify with the men and women who entered the courtrooms of Italy and Denmark 400 years ago.

Part I
The Prosecutors

2
Marking the limits of transgression

The early Christian Church

One could argue that theologians in the 16th century attributed all things either to God or to the Devil. What was good was entirely God's work. Good people were good only as a result of their trust in God, their devotion to him and the strength of their faith. Their goodness would entitle them to eternal life in Heaven. The Devil by whatever name – Satan, the fallen angel, Beelzebub, Lucifer – represented all evil. His followers would be condemned to an afterlife in eternal agony. According to the book of Revelation, God had cast out Satan, the great dragon, and in his fall Satan had taken the host of fallen angels with him. The Devil had declared war against God and against all Christians, with the intention of toppling the entire Christian world. Everything that was morally wrong originated in the Devil. He would constantly try to tempt man in his efforts to recruit new allies for his final confrontation with God.

This dualistic way of thinking had not come from the early Church. The insistence of both the post-Tridentine Catholic Church and the Lutheran-Protestant Church on a connection between the Devil and all kinds of magic was due to centuries of theological discussion about sorcery and about practitioners of magical rituals. These debates were rooted in the early Church, and their underlying theological positions were under continuous development. The early Church was no centralized organization, and it presented no official policy. It is, however, possible to shed light on some of the principal tendencies that suggest a general consensus in the views held by the Church, and these played their part in shaping the post-Tridentine understanding of witchcraft as an offence and a sin.

For the post-Tridentine inquisitors, the connection between magic and heresy was fundamental, and to seek its origin we need to go back to the beginnings of organized Christianity. The early Church was continuously confronted by challenges from other forms of religion and beliefs. Such pagans urged the early Church to define itself, to formulate a dogma that could clarify its doctrines to its own followers and determine how their faith should be practised. It was essential to such self-definition that the limits to the powers and the claims of the Church be determined, both externally and internally, and that it should be clear which religious practices were to be prohibited. Groups and individuals that interpreted Christianity in ways that conflicted with the resulting dogma became a standing challenge. In the Middle Ages the magical rituals practised by learned and semi-learned people, usually referred to as 'ritual magic', had given rise to substantial problems. The question was not whether magic existed, for the Bible was itself filled with magic and magicians, for instance the magicians of Pharaoh or the woman known as the 'witch of Endor'. Differences arose from the need to decide what kinds of ritual could be permitted, which individuals could be allowed to experiment with magical rituals and for what purpose.

The word 'magic' comes from the Latin *magus* (magician), and in the Acts of the Apostles (8:9–24) we hear of Simon of Samaria (Simon the Magician), who was a sorcerer in the land of Samaria. When the apostles Peter and John came to the town and gave the Holy Spirit to the newly baptized people through the laying on of hands, Simon saw it and thought the practice could enhance his own magical powers. Simon then offered money to St. Peter, but Peter immediately saw that Simon was not in his heart Christian, so he scolded him for thinking he could buy such divine powers for himself. Simon was not motivated by piety but by a selfish ambition to strengthen his own magical powers. From the second century AD the tale of Simon the Magician had made him the first heretic.[35]

The Church Fathers continued to debate the themes of magic and heresy in the centuries that followed. In the fourth and fifth centuries St. Augustine of Hippo (d. 430), one of the Fathers of the Church, questioned the notions of magic and magicians by discussing specific examples. Augustine considered that heathen gods were, in fact, demons. He was convinced that Christianity was the only true faith, which meant that logically the gods of other religions had to be demons in disguise. The work of these demons was to weave illusions, and to trust in such demons was accordingly regarded as superstition.[36] In Italy, Augustine had heard of a group of innkeepers who performed witchcraft on their guests. According to the account, these innkeepers would offer the travellers an unusual kind of cheese, which would transform them into beasts of burden. After completing the onerous tasks given them by the innkeepers, they would be restored intact to their original shape and, despite having gone through this metamorphosis, their minds would return to being rational and human, except that they would have no recollection of their transformation or of what they had done during it.

Another example cited by Augustine concerned a man who claimed to have been in a trance for several days after eating a poisoned cheese, which had left him the victim of some form of bewitchment. After waking up from the trance, the man had explained that he had been transformed into a horse and as a horse had transported grain from one place to another. All the time he was supposed to have been transformed into a horse and working hard, his body had been in bed, as if asleep. The man's description of the transportation of grain was allegedly substantiated by independent witnesses, and this meant that his bewitchment had indeed caused a metamorphosis and indicated that the soul could leave the body.[37] Needless to say, Christian dogma asserted that the human body could only be separated from the soul in death. Augustine had several examples of individuals who claimed that their souls had left the body and had then returned, but his reaction to these accounts was always the same. Such accounts could not be conceived as being real, since the soul could only leave the body in death. In this sense, Augustine dismisses any notion that the metamorphosis might come to pass in practice. Augustine argued that the innkeepers must have used demons to make people believe that they were beasts of burden, but demons did not have the powers to make the soul leave the body. The bewitched cheese could not generate a metamorphosis. Augustine accepted that diabolic activities could take place, but that the effect of these was to be regarded as illusionary. Humans had to beware of the Devil and to avoid falling under his power. By experimenting with witchcraft, people would actually be engaging in dealings with Satan himself. Augustine concluded by stating that the Devil was an imitator and all of his work was to be considered illusion. It was God alone who had the real power to perform the actions that the Devil could only pretend to do, but for all that the Devil was a talented charlatan and impostor.[38]

From Augustine to Thomas Aquinas

The teachings of Augustine confirm that even at an early stage the Church was concerned with defining magicians and their powers, and that by doing so it was defining its own identity. In this sense the Church indirectly sought to ensure the proper practice of the Christian faith. In the early Middle Ages, the teachings of Augustine were reinforced by the *Canon Episcopi*.[39] According to this text, any person found guilty of any kind of magical practice was to be condemned and banished from the Christian Church. There are two points in the *Canon Episcopi* that should be particularly noted here. The first is the description of magicians as individuals tempted by the Devil to worship him, and as people riding through the night with the Roman goddess Diana. These people were primarily women, and they considered Diana to be their mistress. Such worshippers of Diana had necessarily abandoned their Christian faith, they were prey to the delusions of the Devil, and the *Canon Episcopi* made the heathen goddess into an instrument of the Devil. Such combination of the beliefs of ancient Rome and of Christianity can be considered as an example of how the early Church was confronted with a matrix of heresy and paganism. It was heresy in that these people had allowed themselves to join the cult of the Devil;

it was paganism in that they were being led by a heathen goddess, Diana. The *Canon Episcopi* did not discuss the matter further, but made it clear that the Church had 'to be cleansed of this plague'.[40] This plague analogy is the second interesting point in the text. According to the *Canon Episcopi* the effect that Diana's disciples had on their surroundings was equal to a contagious disease. Many were drawn to follow these women and their belief that other divine creatures apart from God the Almighty existed, which is why the Church had to direct its efforts towards demarcating the spiritual limits of God's fold. The metaphor of the Body of Christ permitted the banning of such people, the excision of the infection they brought with them. For if one was infected, more would follow. This kind of rhetoric was not exclusive to the *Canon Episcopi* but became characteristic of the Church and its efforts to eradicate heresy in the medieval and early modern period. By referring to heresy as contagious the authors demonstrate that in the early Middle Ages paganism and heresy continued to be intertwined and that for the Christian Church they remained two sides of the same coin.

The *Canon Episcopi* confirmed Augustine's doctrine that the separation of body from soul was only possible in death. Tales of people riding the sky at night had to be attributed to dreams or illusions, for who had not seen mystical objects and visions in sleep that would not be possible when awake?[41] And such dreams or illusions of man turning into beast had to be considered figments of the human mind.

During the Middle Ages the Church would gradually come to regard such magical events as described by Augustine as real. It is not possible, however, to point towards a specific text or episode as the decisive factor in this development. By the high Middle Ages the writings of the Dominican St. Thomas Aquinas (d. 1274) had systematized medieval thought on magic and its purveyors. However, the magicians Thomas Aquinas was aiming at in his writings were not illiterate villagers performing everyday magic in order to secure their harvest or to foretell a marriage. The debate on magic in the Middle Ages focussed first and foremost on learned and semi-learned individuals regarded by the Church as rotten apples, who practised magical rituals, referred to as ritual magic, using magical books like the *The Key of Solomon* (*Clavicula Salomonis*).[42] The central issue here is that Thomas Aquinas was attempting to define magicians' position in relation to God and the Devil. In this sense he was continuing the attempt to identify the Church's position on the matter. The doctrines of Thomas Aquinas would prove to be crucial for the inquisition's prosecution of popular magic in the 16th and 17th centuries. Thomas Aquinas' teachings on the source of magic and on the powers of the Devil and his demons in sorcery became integrated into the Italian inquisitors' handling of the witch trials.

Thomas Aquinas' overall concern was the relationship between God and man, and in several texts he discusses man's use of magic in the context of the Devil and demons.[43] Like Augustine, St. Thomas believed that magical experimentation was being instigated by demons. Augustine had argued that the Devil and demons did not create anything real,[44] but Thomas Aquinas took precisely the opposite view. This he laid out in his teachings on miracles.[45] The Devil and the demons were indeed capable of generating great wonders, which could be similar to miracles in appearance. Still, it was the trickery of demons and, irrespective of how wonderful and glorious it might appear, it was never a true miracle.[46] A woman's love produced through magical rituals was not true love. The demons could create something that resembled love, but it was still the work of demons and therefore a deception, and a demon's trickery would always be fatal to the human soul.

Many practitioners of magic did not believe their actions were in any way linked to the Devil. They believed that their rituals involved divine powers. Thomas Aquinas argued against this. The power had to come from the person or the thing that the magician had addressed. In his eyes magical rituals were characterized by the practitioner having addressed something outside human nature. He had summoned a power superior to himself – he had summoned demons. When these demons appeared, they would obediently follow commands. This, however, was only to entice the magician ever further into sin.[47] To Thomas Aquinas, the conclusion was that witchcraft *only* happened through the medium of the Devil and his demons. The remedies of the magician, especially words and formulas, possessed no powers on their own. It was the Devil who would make the magical rituals effective. To obtain the help of the Devil, the practitioner had to agree to a pact. The Devil did not provide his assistance for nothing. Any contact with the Devil and his demons was a sign and proof enough that such a pact had been made. The pact could be made *explicitly*, which meant that the magician had been aware of his diabolical connection. A pact could, however, also be made without the magician knowing it. Thomas Aquinas called a pact that was made in ignorance an *implicit* pact with the Devil. Such a pact would be made when the magician might think that he was calling upon divine powers in his rituals but when he would, in fact, be summoning demons. Here Thomas Aquinas would have been countering the perception of many magicians, who thought that God was the power that made the magical rituals work. According to this, magicians were simple folk who were tempted into sin. They were simple in the sense that they believed their magical rituals to be shortcuts to wealth or happiness. For Thomas Aquinas, the purpose of the rituals played a vital part. Their aims would often be malicious or selfish and as a result the power could not stem from something good. For that reason the Devil must be behind the effect. God would never participate in anything selfish or malicious. When magicians copied church rituals such as kneeling or making the sign of the cross, what exposed them as subjects of Satan was their egotistical intention. On this point Thomas Aquinas was in complete agreement with Augustine.[48] Church rituals were instituted by God alone and ought only to be performed in devotion to God and not for personal selfish reasons. Thomas Aquinas, therefore, rejected any suggestion that magical rituals could be performed by summoning God.

Defining witchcraft for the 16th century

During the centuries before the Protestant reformation, the Roman Curia issued a number of statements that indicate the extent to which magical rituals and their practitioners were in the spotlight at regular intervals. Letters, declarations and bulls targeted heretics or the use of ritual magic by the learned and semi-learned. In 1258, Alexander IV responded to a group of inquisitors that no inquisitor could prosecute a person for sorcery unless it was also heresy.[49] In 1376, the former inquisitor Nicolau Eymeric wrote the inquisitorial manual *Directorium Inquisitorum*.[50] Here Eymeric dealt primarily with idolatry in the practice of magic. His concern centred on whether the magician was guilty of apostasy or not. The diabolic witch, defined as the witch who had engaged in a pact with the Devil, attended the sabbath and caused harm by her supernatural powers had yet to be invented in the 15th century. The manual became one of the most authoritative of its kind for post-Tridentine inquisitors and in 1578 it was revised by the Spanish canonist and theologian Francisco Peña.[51] In 1434 Pope Eugene IV presented a wider and rather unusual interpretation of heresy. Heresy had as a rule only been found amongst members of the Christian Church, but Eugene IV now included those Jews who used various forms of magical practices, such as spells and invocations of the Devil.[52] All these rituals would now be considered heretical.

Two crucial papal bulls of 1484 and 1585 show how everyday magic as practised by the populace is gradually included in the Church's frame of reference. Papal bulls were normally issued to address some more or less acute problem for the Church and expressed the official position of the Holy See. As a consequence, they often appear rather haphazard and need to be placed in their context, which the next two sections will attempt to do.

Innocent VIII's bull of 1484 has previously been assigned considerable importance in research into the Catholic Church's approach to the problem of witchcraft. However, as we shall see, this bull should rather be viewed as a statement of power politics than as a testament to the Pope's insistence on extensive witch trials.

The *Witches Bull* of Innocent VIII, 1484

Pope Innocent VIII's *Summis desiderantes affectibus*, now infamous as the *Witches Bull*,[53] was occasioned by the southern German inquisitor Heinrich Krämer (Institoris) who was met by local opposition towards prosecution of witchcraft from the population, the local church and the German Courts.[54] After an urgent appeal from Krämer, Pope Innocent VIII used his *Summis*

desiderantes to stress that the jurisdiction of witch trials was solely the preserve of the inquisitor.

Summis desiderantes differs on one particular point from the line the
Church had previously held. It is these deviations from earlier decrees that
have made it notorious. It has been nicknamed the *Witches Bull* because it
was incorporated in the even more infamous *Malleus maleficarum*, which
has been published in many editions since the *princeps* in 1486.[55] Interest in
the controversial content of *Malleus maleficarum* has led to the bull being
allotted far greater and very different significance by witchcraft researchers
in the first part of the 20th century than it would have had in its own time.

Summis desiderantes was the first papal document to submit the population at large to suspicions of practising diabolical witchcraft. Its propagandist qualities can be clearly detected in its description of witches and their
actions. Witches were vulgar and evil by nature; they had renounced their
baptismal vows and had committed themselves to the Devil. They had even
engaged in sexual relations with him. Their witchcraft was aimed at causing
harm to people, livestock, crops and property. They inflicted disease, made
men impotent and women infertile. They mocked God, conspired against
him, and had no scruples in committing these gruesome deeds. They were,
in short, the primary enemy of Christian society. This damning description
of the witches and their practices left no doubt that the Pope had to invest
everything in the prosecution of these fiends.

The *Summis desiderantes* contained information about witches and magicians based on Catholic theology, but it differed from previous arguments.
The magician was no longer the practitioner of ritual magic demanding the
Devil's assistance. The pact with the Devil continued to form the basis for
the performance of magical rituals, but it had taken a new form. The magician worshipped the Devil and had sexual relations with her master. *Summis
desiderantes* referred to both male and female magicians, while *Malleus maleficarum* focussed entirely on the female sex. It is equally worth noting that
the selfish motives of the magician have now been replaced by the idea that
witches harmed their surroundings without any particular reason except out
of evil. The role of the Devil had also shifted. Whereas he had previously
been the passive figure to be summoned and commanded, now he became
an active and initiating beast constantly seeking to recruit allies in his war
against God.[56]

Summis desiderantes is the only official statement from the Catholic Church
that described the diabolical witch as, for example, someone who committed herself to the Devil and caused harm with her witchcraft purely for her
own pleasure. The bull should not be regarded a document that initiated the
pre-Reformation witch-hunt. Rather, it was an official expression of certain
tendencies in demonology in the second half of the 15th century. Until
then, the Church's debate on the connection between practitioners of ritual
magic and the Devil had led them to focus on a more socially elevated group

and not on illiterate villagers. The *Summis desiderantes* was issuing a warning not against learned or semi-learned people but against individuals secreted even in the most remote corners of the countryside. Performers of magical rituals were no longer seen exclusively as learned, manipulative males who used magic for personal advantage. They were also illiterate villagers, whose witchcraft had the sole intention of harming for the sake of the harm itself.

Since the inquisition was a court handling offences committed against the faith, witchcraft needed to be defined as a sin and an offence against God, as it became in Innocence VIII's bull. Still, the bull has to be considered primarily as a political document. It employed propagandist and emotive language to ensure that in cases concerning witchcraft, the jurisdiction lay firmly in the hands of the two inquisitors, Heinrich Krämer and Jacob Sprenger. By adopting a consistent stance in this conflict between the population and papal representatives, it signalled both the Pope's will and his power. It was a direct manifestation from the highest ecclesiastical authority.[57] Rather than expressing perceptions of witches and magicians commonly held within the Curia, the *Summis desiderantes* was a demonstration of the political will of papal power to eradicate the crime of witchcraft.

In this respect the *Malleus maleficarum* expressed a controversial viewpoint, namely that witchcraft can occur without heresy. Heresy involved a false interpretation of the true Christian faith, and witchcraft did not necessarily derive from such a misinterpretation. The author of *Malleus maleficarum* was applying Thomas Aquinas' argument that the magician's sin was one of idolatry, in the sense that he considered witches to be worshippers of the Devil. Idolatry in itself should not be mistaken for heresy. This position meant that, in deciding whether the individual case of witchcraft involved heresy or not, an assessment of intention was crucial.

Summis desiderantes did not include *Malleus maleficarum's* distinction between heretical and non-heretical witchcraft, but it marked an important change in attitude towards witchcraft. As the 16th century approached, the Catholic Church had been provided with a frame of reference that categorized as heresy the magical rituals performed by lay people in order to heal their cow or foretell the harvest. Such activity was, therefore, a case for the inquisition and for no other court of law.

Sixtus V and the *Coeli et terrae*

Almost a century would pass before a pope issued a bull relating to magical practices again. During this period, the Church had gone through what must be characterized as the most profound upheaval and transformation in its history. Despite its internal efforts to reform the Christian Church, Protestantism appeared to be the shock that forced Rome to execute reforms. The Council of Trent (1545–1563) produced the decrees that lay the foundations for reform on ecclesiastical discipline and doctrinal decrees.[58] Parallel to the sessions at Trent, the Roman Inquisition initiated its efforts to eradicate heresy on the Peninsula. In the middle of the 16th century, the main concern was related to Protestant and Valdensian heresy, but from the 1570s and especially the 1580s, inquisitors had an increasing focus on magic and superstition among the illiterate. In 1586 Sixtus V Peretti issued the bull *Coeli et terrae*. The text included condemnation of all kinds of magical rituals, divination and astrology.[59] The Roman Inquisition had been reorganized in 1542, and several parts of Europe had now converted to Protestantism. In the decades following the reorganization of the Roman Inquisition, the main focus of attention had been Protestant heretics, but in the 1580s witchcraft once again became the inquisitors' primary focus. Before becoming pope in 1585, Sixtus had worked as an inquisitor in Venice. Here he had led an active campaign against heresy. During the second half of the 16th century, the Holy Office had been acknowledged for taking a moderate line in its approach to witchcraft, and Sixtus V pursued this policy of moderation, although in his career as an inquisitor he had been an avid prosecutor of heresy.[60] It is likely that the bull reflected Sixtus' personal experiences as inquisitor, but this is hard to prove, since so few trials from the mid-16th century have been preserved in the Venetian archives.[61] The general picture of activities in the Roman Inquisition during the middle of the 16th century remains unclear, since many trials and documents have been lost. The most useful data comes from Modena where seventeen people were accused of 'superstition and magic' between 1550 and 1565; in comparison in the same location 73 trials were held between 1590 and 1600.[62] As in Modena, the number of witch trials conducted in Venice had probably fallen to a relatively modest number when approaching the mid-16th century.

Sixtus distanced himself from the *Witches Bull* by returning to the Catholic Church's more 'traditional' focus on ritual magic, particularly in condemning astrology and divination. Sixtus warned against several specific types of magical rituals, saying that the practice of these would only be possible through a pact with the Devil. The bull listed the signs that indicated that a person could be practising witchcraft. These might be circles, diabolical letters, the abuse of sacraments and church symbols, and the fact that the intention was always selfish. Soothsayers would cast dice or beans to predict the future, but the information thus gleaned would come with a malediction. The source of it would be the Devil himself. In accordance with the teachings of Thomas Aquinas, the bull viewed the magicians' use of rituals as an attempt to obtain an insight that would normally be beyond human capabilities. The only answer to this request for insight would come from demons, and the answers would therefore always be false. Regardless of the nature of their rituals, practitioners had made a pact with the Devil that would consume their soul. The relationship between the magician and the Devil in terms of power was unequivocal. It was ultimately the Devil who commanded the magician and took on the authority over his soul that should be given to God. The Evil One had to be summoned before it would appear, but the magician would also bid it welcome by praying, lighting candles, making sacrifices and performing religious rituals in its honour. There could be no doubt that the magician was trading his or her soul to obtain the services of the Devil.

Adriano Prosperi has noted that the publication of *Coeli et terrae* was an expression of Sixtus' personal engagement in *la guerra contro indovini e astrologi* (the war against diviners and astrologers).[63] After the publication of the bull, there was a massive increase in the number of witch trials at the Italian inquisition tribunals, but the number of executions for magical offences remained low and for several years there were virtually none.[64] In most places executions culminated in around 1600.[65] It can be argued that the increase was brought about by the publication of Sixtus' bull. This bull, however, has also to be seen to mirror the general attitude that had been prevalent within the papal headquarters in Rome. Sixtus V has been characterized as an avid opponent of heresy. Many of the post-Tridentine popes had served as inquisitors before entering the Curia.[66] This would have meant that in the highest echelons of the Congregation there were both a dedication to the tribunals and their activities and a comprehension of the difficulties the average inquisitor would face in his daily work. Astrology and divination belonged to a grey area where the inquisitors lacked a doctrinal frame of interpretation, something that the issuing of *Coeli et terrae* solved as well as giving the inquisition the power to proceed in cases that were not directly heretical (*sortilegi semplici*).[67]

Post-Tridentine inquisitorial manuals and instructions

The theological teachings in conjunction with the decrees from the Holy See expressed the official viewpoint of the Catholic Church on the issue of witchcraft. The inquisitors, however, needed more comprehensive guidance in transferring fundamental theological principles to their practical work. Even though Sixtus V's bull included bans on the practice of certain types of magical rituals, it completely left out any mention of procedures, that is to say how the inquisitors were to tackle the offences in practice. Usually an inquisitor was skilled in canon law, sometimes in theology. In addition to this academic background, he would have been given a number of instructions in support of his investigation.[68] These guidelines or manuals were to assist the inquisitor in identifying violations of the Christian faith as well as to provide him with information on details of correct procedure. The intention was to secure consistent and professional treatment of the people who came into contact with the inquisition.

In the present book, I have examined three texts for their guidelines on procedures in trials of witchcraft. Each of these bears testimony to the Roman Inquisition's sober approach to accusations of witchcraft.[69] Through these manuals the inquisition voiced an admission – not to be confused with an acceptance – of the populace's lack of insight into theological issues. This meant that the majority of trials acknowledged that the crimes of which the people were accused had not been committed with intent. The three texts examined are *Prattica per procedere nelle cause del Sant'Officio* (circa 1625, in English *Practice to proceed in cases under the Office of the Holy Tribunal*, hereafter *Prattica*), *Sacro Arsenale ovvero Prattica dell'Officio della Santa Inquisitione* (First edition 1621, *The Holy Arsenal or Practice by the Office of the Holy Inquisition*, hereafter *Sacro Arsenale*) and finally *Instructio pro formandis processibus in causis strigum, sortilegiorum et maleficiorum* (possibly late 16th century, roughly *Instruction Concerning Witchcraft Trials, Witches and Sorcerers*, hereafter *Instructio*).[70]

My main focus has been the *Prattica*, which is believed to have been written by Cardinal Desiderio Scaglia. Scaglia had himself been an inquisitor, before advancing with the Curia. The manual was never published, although it was frequently used by the Roman inquisitors. *Sacro Arsenale* was also written by a former inquisitor, Eliseo Masini. It was published in a printed version in 1621 and has since been revised and republished several times. Both *Prattica* and *Sacro Arsenale* were written in Italian. The origins of *Instructio* are more uncertain. This small Latin pamphlet was used regularly by the inquisition as a manuscript, long before it was published in print in 1659. The manual does not state its author, and until recently researchers have presumed it to have been written by the aforementioned cardinal Scaglia.[71] The German historian Rainer Decker has recently identified Giulio Monterenzi (d. 1623) as the author of *Instructio*, and dated the text to between 1593 and 1603. After an academic career at such places as the highly esteemed university in Bologna, Monterenzi was appointed *Governatore* in Rome in 1610 and in 1618 he was installed as bishop in Faenza and ended his days as the Pope's deputy legate in Ferrara.[72]

All three manuals are rooted in the teachings of Thomas Aquinas, which assert that magicians are guilty of heresy and apostasy. *Prattica* and *Sacro Arsenale* take the form of instructions of general procedures and list various crimes against the Catholic faith. *Instructio* is first and foremost a warning against jumping to conclusions about accusations of witchcraft.[73]

Practitioners of magic and witchcraft

Chapter 8 of the *Prattica* initially defines the various witchcraft offences that an inquisitor might encounter in his work amongst illiterate villagers.[74] Cardinal Scaglia began with a broad definition of witchcraft (*sortilegio*). 'Witchcraft' was the collective term for all kinds of magical experiments and rituals, and served as an all-embracing term for the Roman Inquisition.[75]

A presentation of the concept of witchcraft was followed by a more thoroughgoing clarification of the things that would normally be regarded as signs of the practice of witchcraft. This covered a broad spectrum. In *Coeli et terrae* Sixtus V describes how unknown words and letters, the abuse of sacraments and of consecrated objects, and religious observance directed towards evil powers and the summoning of the Devil would all provide grounds to suspect witchcraft. By being able to identify such things, it should be possible for the inquisitor to commence his investigation. Scaglia made it clear that an inquisitor should not place all these signs and suspicions within the same bracket. In his preliminary investigation, the inquisitor would have to distinguish between the *qualificate* offenders and the *non qualificate* offenders, which would be the credited and non-credited indications of witchcraft. Suspicious activities that were attested not to be qualified for trial were special recitations of prayers (*orationi*), including those that used God's name or words from Holy Scripture. These could also include making the sign of the cross to protect oneself or others. These actions were *not* witchcraft, but simply an improper use of Christian ritual. Once this had been established by the inquisitor, the perpetrator would simply be punished by being given a penance.[76]

The credited (*qualificate*) indications of witchcraft involved acts that proved the practice of witchcraft. Such cases had to be prosecuted, and the accused had to be sentenced and punished. The tricky thing about witchcraft was that on the surface its rituals could appear to be pious but would on closer inspection prove to be an abuse of sacraments and holy objects such as holy water and the like.[77] Such abuse could also involve prayers to certain saints or kneeling in front of the cross. The practice of witchcraft was, however, usually recognizable through prohibited acts like the summoning of demons, the use of unknown words and letters, letters written in blood or the blatant abuse of sacraments. Such abuse could include performing a baptism outside the church or without a priest being present.[78]

It was the responsibility of the inquisitor to investigate such cases more closely with a view to exposing the source of the crime. Here Scaglia aligned himself with the distinction proposed by Nicolau Eymeric, mentioned above, in his inquisitorial manual *Directorium Inquisitorum* (1376). The *Directorium* was based on Eymeric's own experiences as an inquisitor in northern Spain. The intention of the manual had been to create a broad handbook to be used in all cases relating to the inquisition.[79] In 1578, the *Directorium* was published in a new version, revised and updated by the authoritative Spanish theologian Francisco Peña. This new edition also became equally used by the Roman inquisitors.[80]

Love magic, a violation of free will

To cardinal Scaglia, witchcraft represented both a belief and a practice. It was a belief when magicians renounced their Christian faith and instead entered a pact with the Devil. Witchcraft became a practice when it was applied to acquire power over something or someone and by that means gain love, status, wisdom or money, or even inflict injury.[81] All forms of witchcraft practised included the abuse of sacraments and an explicit or implicit pact with the Devil. If a person, often a woman, attempted to acquire love through witchcraft, in the eyes of the inquisition she would be attempting to control someone's love and affection.[82] The Catholic Church viewed these experiments as attacks on the doctrine of free will, regardless of whether or not they had been made with intent.[83]

The doctrine of the free will of man was considered to be a fundamental part of Christian teachings and its status was reinforced in the post-Tridentine Church. The doctrine of the free will was inextricably connected to the idea of sin and grace. Only when human beings were in possession of free will would they be able to sin. The doctrine of free will was given special emphasis in post-Tridentine theology. According to the Church, it was not possible to make man responsible for his actions if his will was not free. The Devil only existed because God allowed him, and leading man into corruption was the Devil's preferred activity. Witchcraft was the bait that tempted mankind into believing that it could change the nature of its existence through supernatural agency. If a person believed in the effect of love magic, it would be a sign that this person thought it possible to influence or control the will of another person. In cases concerning love magic, the main priority of the inquisitor was to discern whether or not the accused had believed it possible to control the will of another human being. In coming to his conclusion, the inquisitor would take into consideration that the accused might have acted out of ignorance. Had the accused been aware that the practice of love magic was a violation against man's free will, then no mercy would be shown; the penalty of death was mandatory.[84] Such a severe punishment was justified by the magician's explicit invocation of the Devil. Only evil itself could have an interest in making an assault on man's free will. Although, according to Catholic theology, the Devil could not force the will, he could indeed deceive the imagination and lead the chosen individual to believe that he was in fact in love.[85] Taking his cue from Thomas Aquinas' teachings on miracles, Scaglia warned that it was a common, but nonetheless false perception that witchcraft could incite love. The love that the bewitched might feel for the magician was not true and would soon disappear again.[86]

In Italy prostitutes (*meretrici*) were often accused of love magic and for that reason prosecuted by the inquisition.[87] They were believed to be particularly vicious in their use of witchcraft. This meant that the inquisition could eradicate witchcraft and immorality in one fell swoop. Cardinal Scaglia's instructions on prostitutes signalled the inquisition's negative view of such dubious women, who could be characterized as women of loose virtue. Scaglia, like his colleagues, presumably had a somewhat broader interpretation of *meretrice* than we have today. This group of loose women did not only include prostitutes but also concubines and women engaged in sexual relationships outside marriage. Such women would employ love magic to lure customers or lovers to their home, and the inquisitor had to be aware that they would summon the Devil with blessed beans and abuse sacraments and church symbols.[88] When the congregation was gathered for mass, these women of loose virtue would perform their rituals by reciting secret spells that would often include secret formulas and offensive words.[89] They would similarly abuse sacraments by reciting vulgar words and phrases especially during communion or when the priest sang *dominus vobiscum*. Abuse of church symbols could also happen outside the church. Holy water was used in their rituals and the women would utter prayers that would appear to be addressed to specific saints but would in fact be aimed at the Devil.[90] The Orbetello trials against *meretrice* goe a long way towards confirming the inquisition's view on this particular group of women. Several of the women convicted were engaging in sexual relationships outside marriage.

The *fons et origo* of witchcraft: the pact with the Devil

When magicians prayed to saints, knelt in front of images and medallions or in any way prayed to holy beings for help with their rituals, these would *appear* to be Christian acts. The inquisition, however, was in no doubt that the agency at play was the Devil. On the basis of Thomas Aquinas' teachings, cardinal Scaglia argued that every kind of witchcraft implied a relation to the Devil. Witchcraft could *only* be practised with the aid of the Devil, and he did not act out of charity. There was a price to pay, since all magicians engaged in a pact with the Devil. Like his colleagues, Scaglia distinguished between two types of diabolical pact: the explicit and the implicit pact, and as determined by Thomas Aquinas, entering into a pact with the Devil meant that the soul would be lost to an afterlife in eternal agony.[91]

Any contact with the Devil was connected to a great risk. The Devil was a deceitful trickster and he would openly delude or mislead human beings into believing that they were acting according to Catholic doctrine. To the inquisitors, illiterate villagers who dabbled in magical rituals were naive people, who had fallen into temptation. The open and explicit pact with the Devil was the more serious, since the practitioner had been conscious of temptation and was therefore knowledgeable of the pact having been made. The meaning of the pact was indisputable: magicians had traded their souls to gain the assistance of the Devil. Furthermore, magicians could pledge someone else's soul to the Devil. The essence of this violation was that the Devil was receiving payment for his assistance.[92] Scaglia noted that, even though the magicians might sell another person's soul, they would themselves be doomed. Indications of the pact having been made could be quite difficult to establish. There could be spells or abuse of sacraments.[93] The desecration of Christian symbols and sacraments were seen as particularly odious signs of the explicit pact. This could in practice involve magicians spitting or stamping on the cross. Rather than serving God, they agreed through the pact to serve the Devil in his battle against God. If a person admitted to having entered an explicit pact, the inquisitor would then have to ascertain how long this diabolical relationship had existed.[94]

Generally the majority of the inquisitorial trials involved an implicit pact with the Devil. The indications of the implicit pact were the same as the explicit. As already stated, the difference lay in the perpetrator's intent. An implicit diabolical pact meant that the person was not aware of it having been made. The practice of witchcraft, however, depended on a pact with the Devil, whether or not the magician was aware of it. This distinction between the implicit and the explicit pact provided the inquisitors with a tool to convict popular use of magical rituals within a Catholic theological perception, which stated that, in order to be effective, magical rituals required the aid of the Devil. If, therefore, a spell had an effect it was because a diabolic pact existed between the practitioner and the Devil.[95]

The witch: the Devil's handmaid

An important part of cardinal Scaglia's chapter on witchcraft concerns diabolic witchcraft (*stregoneria*[96]). Diabolic witchcraft is introduced as the most serious and most reprehensible kind of witchcraft and it is distinguished from *sortilegio* in comprising traditional demonological elements. The sole aim of diabolical witches (*le streghe*) was to cause harm, either through love or through death.[97] The damage would appear in many forms and could affect both adults and children.[98] Diabolical witches used many of the same rituals as were applied in 'milder' forms of witchcraft. Where Scaglia had previously drawn attention to the abuse of sacraments, he now also highlighted the evil intent and the harm caused.[99] These witches could use tools in their rituals; the inquisitor had to be particularly alert to signs or letters having been sliced in fruit.[100] Witches were also known to have mixed various kinds of powder into food. In addition, in his *Sacro Arsenale* Eliseo Masini warned against their use of mirrors, medallions and small bottles.[101]

The evil intent of a diabolical witch became apparent when she made small wax figures of her enemies.[102] She would pierce the figures with needles, whilst roasting them over a fire.[103] The figure would resemble the person that the witch sought to harm and should preferably have nails, hair or other personal items from the person attached to it. The ritual of piercing wax figures with needles and melting them was considered to be the most serious, seeing that the aim was so obviously destructive. The diabolical witch could also coax the victim into consuming the juice from poisonous plants or poisonous powders that could not be traced by a physician. In short, a witch of this kind was characterized by being particularly hateful, because she did not need a motive to cause harm. She would cause destruction entirely through her hatred and evil.[104] Diabolical witches had always made an explicit pact with the Devil and they worshipped him by offering salt and bread.[105] To the inquisitors these witches were, without doubt, the most dangerous group of magicians, seeing that they committed the two cardinal crimes against the Catholic faith at the same time: deliberate and wilful abuse of church sacraments and symbols, and submission to the Devil.

According to Scaglia, when questioning the suspect, the inquisitor had to devote considerable attention to determining how and when the pact with the Devil had been struck, and for how long the accused had been the Devil's subject. Diabolical witches were known to attend the witches' sabbath. The inquisitor's questioning of the suspected witch would involve an examination to expose how long she had participated in 'the Devil's game'.[106] Both Scaglia and Masini warned against those who participated in the witches' sabbath (*gioco*) but in reality the inquisitors of the late 16th and 17th centuries rarely encountered these.[107] In his examinations of the inquisition in Siena, the Italian historian Oscar Di Simplicio has ascertained that only seven of the 81 full-blown trials involved accounts of participation in a witches' sabbath.[108] These manuals were intended as guides to the inquisitors in their fieldwork, they described elements of the diabolical witch that the inquisition found necessary to communicate. Scaglia refrained from including other demonological perceptions of the witch, such as those concerning sexual acts with the Devil or metamorphosis into other shapes and life forms.[109]

In *Sacro Arsenale* Eliseo Masini expressed the same fundamental attitudes towards diabolical witchcraft as Scaglia. Many of the paragraphs seem to have been more or less copied from Scaglia's manual. Where Scaglia worked from the overall term *sortilegio* (sorcery), Masini preferred the term *stregoneria* (diabolic witchcraft). Masini's idea of *streghe* (witches) was broader and his distinction between *streghe* and other magicians less consistent. The malevolent deeds of the witch were particularly highlighted, and Masini at the same time included the idolatry aspect by warning against witches, who summoned white and black angels, knelt and lit candles.[110]

It could also be argued that the perception of witches that is expressed in the manuals primarily represented popular notions about the evil intentions of witches and about their practice of malevolent magic, which Scaglia must have known from his work as an inquisitor. Where Scaglia found it necessary to include elements taken from the learned, demonological image of the witch, referring to black sabbaths and the harm caused by hatred alone, he kept them so brief that the reader might easily believe that their inclusion was nothing but a formality. Most importantly, Scaglia defined diabolical witchcraft as the gravest form of *sortilegio* in that it was practised with the explicit and exclusive intention of causing harm.

Instructio in causis strigum

Trials of witchcraft were usually administered under the same procedural directions as trials for heresy in general. The fact that the inquisition still found it necessary to publish special guidelines concerning witch-craft trials is an acknowledgement that in theory as well as in practice the offence lay in a grey area between a secular and inquisitorial court. In the years following the reorganization of the inquisition in 1542, the secular authorities, mainly local town courts, made particularly strenu-ous efforts to maintain their jurisdiction over witchcraft. The Church, however, insisted on witchcraft being a spiritual transgression and that this required it to be submitted to a religious court of justice.[111] Historian John Tedeschi has estimated that the *Instructio* may have been kept in manuscript form until the mid-17th century rather than being printed in order to prevent the conflict with the secular authorities from esca-lating. The dispute came about because the secular authorities believed that the inquisition was too lenient in its sentencing. However, Vicenzo Lavenia has contested this in an important article from 2001, in which he documented that executions for witchcraft carried out on orders from the inquisition took place from the 1550s to the 1570s in several Italian cities, including Rome.[112]

The introduction to *Instructio* states that the intention of the guidelines is to end the many grave procedural errors being made on a daily basis by inquisitors, bishops and other ecclesiastical figures.[113] The text is probably the best example of a moderate inquisition that was highly sensitive to pro-cedures. While some scholars have had a different view, the past 25 years of research on Venice, Modena and Siena indicate that the *Instructio* confirmed already existing and moderate procedures in witchcraft trials.[114]

From the *Instructio* it appears that the most common mistake in treating accusations of witchcraft was that the inquisitors failed to gather the *corpus delicti*, the body of evidence.[115] Far too often the accused had been imprisoned and tortured early in the process, without the *corpus delicti* having been iden-tified. In other words, many people would end up imprisoned by the inqui-sition accused of witchcraft without any investigation having substantiated the case against them.

It was important that the inquisitor did not just investigate the physi-cal damage that might have been caused. The case had to be judged in its entirety: the motive, the act itself and the consequences. It was the task of the inquisitor to examine this in full, *before* he proceeded to commit the accused to inquisition custody. The problem was that many judges in witch trials regarded the question of guilt as having been settled as soon as physical dam-age could be demonstrated. The *Instructio* made clear its aversion to such a practice and stated that illness and death were rarely caused by witchcraft.[116] If the accused was suspected of having cast a magic spell on someone that resulted in illness or even death, then a doctor would always be required to conduct a thorough examination of the victim. If anything suspicious was found or if there were any grounds for doubt, the doctor would be required to get a second opinion from a colleague. The *Instructio* distanced itself from the many instances in which an illness attributed to witchcraft would have been clarified by a simple medical explanation. Cardinal Scaglia also referred in *Prattica* to the need for a doctor to be consulted if there was suspicion of witchcraft.[117]

The *Instructio's* discussion of *corpus delicti* touches on several procedural irregularities that the inquisitor might be at risk of committing. It warned against passing judgement under pressure from outside elements. Such pressure might come not only from the secular authorities but also from witnesses or relatives as well as other elements of local society.[118] Inquisitors had to be aware that, to lay people especially, witchcraft was often given as the plausible and oversimplified explanation for what was in fact a complicated and delicate problem. Trained doctors were few and far between in the 17th century, and it would often be easier to explain an illness to the local population by referring to witchcraft than by seeking a medical explanation.

The inquisitor would have to avoid deviating from official procedure. He would have to be aware of the fact that witnesses, the accused, the victim or relatives would often have contradictory views of what had happened, and he could not allow himself to be affected by this. The responsibility lay solely with the inquisitor. He was the highest authority in the case and had to secure a fair trial. He could not just prosecute a suspect purely on the basis of a witness's denunciation of an alleged witch for suspected past or future acts of witchcraft. Even the examination of the house where the accused lived had to follow a strict set of measures. When the officials of the inquisition had taken the accused into custody, they had to execute a search of the address. The inquisitor had to be aware that objects used for witchcraft were often also part of the general household.[119] These could, for example, be mirrors, threads, wax or needles.

Furthermore, the inquisitor would have to be wary of trusting testimonies from bewitched or possessed people.[120] This meant that the inquisitor should not allow victims of sorcery to point out the perpetrator themselves due to the delicacy of such a case. If the bewitched was truly bewitched then this person would be in the Devil's power and this condition would, by definition, be considered untrustworthy. Man could never trust the Devil nor put faith in his actions. A testimony from a person possessed by the Devil could therefore never be regarded as reliable. This assessment was made on the assumption that the possessed really was possessed and not the object or the perpetrator of a delusion. Before the case got as far as this, the inquisitor had to examine the relations of the implicated parties in their local community. The *Instructio* was based on a pragmatic understanding that witchcraft could have substantial influence on local society and that local disputes and quarrels had tremendous significance in determining who was suspected of witchcraft. The inquisitor had to avoid being influenced by rumours of witchcraft surrounding the accused, and such rumours could in no way be included as evidence in the case. According to the *Instructio*, rumours of this kind flourished in small communities.

Renunciation and punishment

The inquisitors always had to consider the crime from on high, as it were. Nicolau Eyemeric's distinction of 1376 between *suspected heretics* and *heretics* was the norm among the Italian inquisitors. An accused could be found guilty of being a *heretic* on the basis of a confession, a heavy burden of proof and/or of having been caught in the act. In cases of *suspected heretics*, the evidence had not been sufficient to reckon them as true heretics.[121]

Abjuration was an integral part of every sentence passed by the Roman Inquisition. The accusation, the intention and the circumstances were all factors that influenced whether or not the convicted had to abjure *de levi*, *de vehementi* or *de formali*. The mildest form of abjuration, *de levi*, meant that the convicted had to renounce his or her heresy in private, and this would often take place at the bishop's palace. The stronger abjuration, *de vehementi*, involved the convicted having to renounce in public, usually in front of the church. The strongest punishment, *de formali*, meant that the convicted had been sentenced to death. The decisive aspect of the abjuration was whether the accused was aware of the gravity of her actions. Did the convicted heretic know that she had summoned the Devil? Did she believe that it was possible to control the free will? Had the convicted heretic managed to convince the inquisitor that she had not acted with intent?[122] The death penalty was reserved solely for (a) a particularly heinous crime, (b) the heretic who obstinately refused to renounce her or his heresy, and (c) the previously convicted heretic.[123] In reality this meant that if the convicted repented, then she would instead be able to be readmitted to the Catholic Church. The group of accused that risked facing the death penalty was very small. The majority of the convicted actually wanted to be reconciled with the Church – records from Orbetello show that this meant *everyone*. Even though the Roman Inquisition seldom found the death penalty necessary, this did not mean that those convicted could escape with promises of repentance and improvement. The inquisitor required the guilty to observe a number of penances such as prayers, confessions, participation in the mass and so on. The convicted could also be ordered to wear the mark of a heretic and on holidays stand in front of the church with a candle in their hand. Finally the person could be sentenced to imprisonment.[124] Scaglia pointed out that the inquisition had the authority to sentence the guilty to be flogged, but he warned against the consequences of applying this in practice:

> Sometimes we flog them, but it is true that, if they are married or have little girls, the Roman Inquisition abstains from this punishment out of mercy, as it brings shame [to daughters and husbands], so that the daughters cannot be married, and the husband loses respect for a flogged wife.[125]

Taken as a whole, the inquisition conformed to the basic tenets of Catholicism in its aim that individuals should serve their sentence and pay their penance in order to be granted readmission into the Catholic Church. The inquisition's preference for public abjuration, which compared to the Danish punishment for witchcraft has to be considered very lenient, was motivated by a consideration that it would have a preventive effect. If convicted heretics were displayed in front of the church, then the churchgoers would be repelled by them and hopefully desist from venturing into a similar transgression. The shaming ritual would also isolate the culprit in the local community. According to *Canon Episcopi*, it was to prevent 'the plague from spreading'. For the inquisition it was more important to re-Catholicize its members than to banish them.

3
The condemnation of witchcraft in Denmark

Witchcraft in medieval Denmark

It is not possible to extract much information about witch trials in Denmark before the Reformation. Court records from the medieval period are generally sparse, and it has only been possible to trace a handful of trials, all of them conducted in the early 16th century. A few judicial texts have been preserved, and these at least make it possible to determine which authorities dealt with the offence.[126]

Before the Lutheran Reformation in 1536, the Danish Church was an institution more or less independent of the monarch, and only subjected to the Holy See. This meant that ecclesiastical law and secular law could apply to the same offence. The foundation of secular law was *Jyske Lov* (Law Code of Jutland), which by the later Middle Ages, despite its name, had gradually come to apply to the entire kingdom of Denmark. *Jyske Lov* was first passed in 1241 and was extended in the following centuries. The table of contents of the first manuscripts make it clear that a chapter had been added concerning witchcraft as early as the 13th century. The wording of this chapter is only known from an early 15th century edition.[127] It translates as follows:

> On witchcraft. If a man accuses another for having bewitched (*forgjort*)[128] something that belongs to him with witchcraft (*trolddom*), and the accused does not admit to the deed but denies it, and the accuser swears to the accusation against him, then the accused shall himself make his defence at a tribunal in the parish, against the accusers as well as the bishop.[129]

The ruling made in *Jyske Lov* is the first known legislation in Denmark on witchcraft.

Alongside this secular law code, two church laws mentioning the offence of witchcraft have been preserved.[130] In medieval Denmark, the legislation upheld by the Church was dependent on the diocese, each having their own set of laws and regulation. In the Church Laws for Skåne (Scania) and Sjælland (Zealand), regulations regarding the procedural aspect of witch trials are few and far between. Taken as a whole, Danish church laws confirm that the forms of witchcraft and magic regarded as religious offences covered a broad spectrum and that the Church was to be responsible for the conduct of any such trial. In cases involving divination and healing magic, the penalty had to be penance and abjuration, which would lead to subsequent absolution. In all probability the Church held complete jurisdiction over cases of benevolent magic, since secular authorities were unlikely to have any desire to prosecute these practices.

In cases involving harmful magic, the course of action was less simple. According to *Jyske Lov*, in addition to breaking the laws of the Church a case of witchcraft (*trolddom*) also involved a secular proceeding similar to that of a murder trial in which a suspect did not confess to the crime. It is in cases relating to maleficent magic that the crime most clearly displays its nature as both a religious and a secular concern, a *crimen mixti fori*. In these trials both the secular and clerical authorities had an interest in the prosecution. Out of consideration for the local community, the secular authorities had to allocate the responsibility for the damage caused to one or more individuals. In medieval Denmark it was common judicial procedure that damages had to be settled between the accuser and the convicted: the injured party was entitled to restitution for any damage caused. In *Jyske Lov*'s regulation on witchcraft, the accused was required to mount a defence before a tribunal against accusations of witchcraft by calling upon a number of people to bear witness that he or she had not committed the offence. The Church excommunicated the guilty. As specified in the previous chapter, Roman inquisitors were often accused of passing sentences that were too lenient in cases concerning witchcraft. There is no doubt that a similar claim could be made about Denmark before the Reformation, but the regulation on witchcraft in *Jyske Lov* implies that compensation for damages could be obtained, since this was implicit in the demand for defending oneself at a tribunal in the parish. The injured parties and their relatives would probably have found excommunication from the Church too mild a sentence when set alongside the loss of a family member or their entire livestock. Although excommunication from the Church did have social consequences, it was a purely clerical sanction and did not provide the injured with financial compensation. In cases of maleficent magic, excommunication served as a means of apportioning responsibility. When the Church had pronounced a guilty verdict, it was possible for the accuser to demand compensation or to send the convicted to the stake.[131]

In 1521, shortly before his conversion to Lutheranism in 1536, King Christian II issued his national law (*Landslov*), which contained certain regulations on witchcraft – a predominant consideration still being the damage caused. This law code presented a view of witchcraft that relied heavily on a perception widespread in early 16th century Denmark. The most evident element of this demonology in the law is the witches' sabbath, and it reflects how the idea of witches gathering in particular places at particular times of the day or year was clearly not foreign to the Danish elite. Shortly after introducing this issue in article 78, the text goes on to list specific places and times that might raise suspicions of witchcraft:

> They appear in places that are out of the way [to people], and as follows [:] night time, late in the evening [and early] morning, near running water, and other holy times [such as] Maundy Thursday and Walpurgis Night, and that they are said to spend more time on these than on other (festive) times during the year.[132]

The law did not contain the gender-specific statements seen most disturbingly in the *Malleus maleficarum*, but the behaviours described reflect those of witches found in Danish and Swedish church murals of the time and are similar to the actions of witches condemned in the *Summis desiderantes* of Innocent VIII.[133] Although only short-lived due to the king's removal in 1523, the law nevertheless supports the notion that in Denmark, as in Rome, regulations concerning witchcraft were continuously issued from the late medieval period and throughout the 17th century.

The Reformation and 'a better world'[134]

In 1536 the Danish king officially broke with Rome, and the kingdom of Denmark-Norway was converted to Lutheranism. Protestant preachers had been making their presence felt ever more frequently during the 1520s, and reform of the Church became a bone of contention in the power struggle between two political factions of the kingdom. There was even a period without a monarch and a civil war before King Christian III could finally pronounce Denmark Lutheran in 1536.[135]

The Lutheran Reformation meant a thorough reorganization of society. All property and land that had previously belonged to the Church passed into the ownership of the Crown, making the king by far the largest landowner in the kingdom. The king held indisputable power in the country, and the Church was from now on only supreme in cases involving its internal disciplinary matters. Judicial issues that had previously been subject to church law such as adultery, sodomy and witchcraft were placed under the secular courts. Cases related to marriage were the preserve of a special newly created court *Tamperretterne* (marriage courts) made up both of lay and ecclesiastical members.[136] In other words, church laws were now no longer decisive, and legally witchcraft was now defined only as maleficent magic as presented in *Jyske Lov*. The new organization and reformist programme of the new Church were inscribed in the Church Ordinance, published in

Latin in 1537 and in Danish in 1539. Bearing some resemblance in its aim
to the decrees of the Council of Trent, albeit on a smaller scale, the Church
Ordinance defined the new Evangelical Church, distancing it from the
Catholicism of the past and dismissing some archetypical Catholic practices
such as the worship of saints.[137]

The Devil's milkmaids

In 1537, following the new Ordinance and his own ordination, the first
Lutheran bishop of Zealand, Peder Palladius (d. 1560) went on pastoral
visitation around his diocese. In parallel to the post-Tridentine Catholic
Church, the new Danish church authorities had seen the need to instruct
further parishioners in the practice of their faith. For about four years Peder
Palladius travelled extensively through his Zealand diocese, and from his
hand we have a text that has become one of the most important sources for
information about the early Danish Reformation and the common people.
During his journey Palladius recorded his experiences, which he later transformed into the book *En Visitatz Bog* (*Book of Visitation*). The text was originally written in Latin around 1538–1540 and first translated into Danish at
the beginning of the 20th century as a part of a move to translate all the writings of this important theologian into Danish. The translator, Lis Jacobsen,
argued that the book had only been intended for the bishop's personal use.
Others have maintained that the book must have been written with publication in mind. The manuscript was published in a new edition in 2003 by
leading Danish Church historian Martin Schwartz Lausten. He regarded the
Book of Visitation as a guide to younger parish priests, and if we accept this
interpretation, the text acquires a similar status to cardinal Scaglia's inquisitorial manual, which was a guide for younger colleagues (The *Prattica*).

Like Scaglia's *Prattica*, the *Book of Visitation* was not aimed solely at witchcraft. The book is divided into five sections, dealing with all aspects of the
parishioners' contact with the Church, including how an Evangelical church
was to be furnished and how individual groups were to be treated by and
in the church. It also contained warnings against women in confinement,
midwives, witches (*troldfolk*) and so on. Throughout the book Palladius has
scattered comments of a more or less explicit nature, as warning against
the rejected papist religion.[138] Palladius makes use of a rhetoric that bears
notable similarities to that of cardinal Scaglia. The strategy was clearly to get
the clerical readers of the *Book of Visitation* to believe themselves to be part
of a powerful authoritative community. Just as Scaglia's colleagues within
the Roman Inquisition enjoyed strong support from the Congregation in
Rome in correctly administering their office, so the efforts of Palladius and
his colleagues received the backing both of the Crown and the Church in
their efforts to convert every parishioner to the Evangelical faith and to
instruct them in its correct practice. It is important to bear in mind that this

manuscript was written by a first generation reformer and that elements of propaganda against the dismissed papist religion were clearly in evidence. In his chapter on witchcraft, Palladius' references to witch trials bear testimony to such propaganda, and he did not tone down his dramatic effects when he described the many trials currently being conducted in Denmark and neighbouring countries:

> They have burnt a group in Malmø, in Køge and other places, and now we learn that there are a lot who have been captured in Malmø and who are to be burnt. In Jutland and the Smålands they hunt them down like wolves. Recently a number were caught on Als and in the surrounding areas, between 12 and 40 witches.[139]

The many executions mentioned here are considered by scholars to be an exaggeration, and we have no direct source material providing evidence that they did, in fact, take place. Still, when Palladius refers to the many witches imprisoned in Denmark and the Danish borderlands and on the continent, it is a way for him to point the attention towards the witch trials that he knew were taking place around Europe and to make it look as though a massive campaign had been launched. No witch nor those who consulted witches and 'cunning folk' could feel safe. Palladius made it appear as though a campaign was under way and that this was supported both by the Church and by the king. According to Palladius, the king's officials did, in fact, work as 'civil agents' to catch witches. Palladius warned the witches:

> They [the king's courtiers] do it [pretend to consult the witch for advice], to get some word from your mouth that will expose you. Then they will immediately seize you, to bring you to the gallows to be burned to glowing ashes with skin and bones, flesh and body.[140]

Although execution by fire was the standard penalty for witchcraft in Denmark, this warning has to be read more as rhetorical than literal. Palladius' intention was to make it clear that, in their mission to make sure that the populace became Lutheran, spiritual leaders were supported by the authority of the Crown as well as by the Church. The individual vicar or bishop should be aware of the fact that he was part of a powerful Lutheran fellowship between the king and the Church. The message of the *Book of Visitation* would then reach the illiterate parishioners of the kingdom. But the responsibility of prosecuting a guilty witch and having her burned on the stake also lay with the common people. Hunting witches was not just the responsibility of the highest authorities. It was also the duty of each individual: 'You should not remain silent about a witch. They [the witches] shall now receive their due punishment. They can no longer hide in this clear light of Evangelical day.'[141]

In the dark ages of Catholicism, it had been easy to hide as a witch. Every Lutheran theologian knew that the Pope himself was the Antichrist, the biggest wizard of them all.[142] In this sense Palladius was consistent with his European colleagues in weaving the condemnation of witchcraft into his condemnation of Catholicism, a strategy that, as we shall see, became even more clearly defined in the work of another famous Danish theologian. Palladius had directed his attention particularly at the *belief in* rather than at the *practice of* witchcraft, and in so doing confirmed his aim to educate the population in the new faith. The precautions needed to prevent the witches from harming one's family were simple. According to Palladius, every parishioner needed only to have faith in God, to practise a devout Christian life and to make sure that his family did the same.[143] On this point Palladius differed from Luther. According to Luther, every man was a potential victim of witchcraft, whereas Palladius could provide some reassurance, that people had some influence on whether evil would strike. He could also provide an answer to the vexed question of why people should be victims of evildoing, namely that their belief was not strong enough. Thus, in warning against consulting witches, Palladius was constructing a pedagogically strong argument for embracing the new faith.

Peder Palladius' admonitions against consulting 'cunning folk' must be seen in the same light. The rituals of such benevolent witches would mostly be a mixture of old Norse with varieties of Catholic ritual introduced by monks before the Reformation. Palladius did not contest the possible effect of these benevolent magical rituals, but the positive effect was only temporary and would be superseded by an irrefutably undesirable consequence: 'It might well be that you believe your cow will get better, but your soul will be condemned to the pits of Hell with your signing.'[144]

There is no doubt that Palladius' motive for focusing primarily on benevolent magic and cunning people was linked to his mission of eradicating the Catholic rituals that were still being used by the general population. From a theological perspective, these rituals – and they included making the sign of the cross (*signe*) and the casting out of evil (*mane*) – were felt to undermine God's power. They led man to believe that it was possible to control his own fate, but to the reformed Church these rituals would be tantamount to taking the power out of God's hands. In practice, the task confronting Palladius was to provide an explanation to a population needing to understand why praying to saints and keeping images and shrines were now considered to be idolatry. They were offered only one solution. The only way out of adversity was through fear of God and trust in him. A true Lutheran Christian would pray to God and patiently await his help.[145]

Ultimately Palladius throws light on the witches' relationship with the Devil. Here Palladius follows theological doctrine standard elsewhere in Europe when he states that the witch was the most dangerous of all creatures. She and the Devil have entered into a contract. He will teach the witch the black arts and in return she will serve his cause. 'A witch is the Devil's milkmaid; she milks him, and he milks her, and they milk each other to the deepest pits of Hell.'[146]

The witch's mere existence is dangerous, as she is the Devil's instrument on earth. Similar views were found amongst other prominent theologians of the time. The first Lutheran bishop of Ribe, Hans Tausen, writing a pastoral letter of 1542, describes the witches as 'the apostles of the Devil'.[147] Both Hans Tausen and Palladius refer to the witch as a woman. The title of Palladius' chapter on witchcraft is *Om Troldkvinder*, which literally translates as 'About Sorceresses', here referred to as witches. In the Catholic tradition, it was common knowledge that women were more superstitious than men, the notion being found in its most extreme version in the *Malleus maleficarum*, and, although Palladius only states this indirectly, we find this view reiterated by his successor at the university, Niels Hemmingsen, who will play a significant role in what follows.

Refining witchcraft trials

During the 16th century Danish lay authorities issued three procedural regulations as additions to *Jyske Lov*. In 1547, Christian III issued the Copenhagen Recess. This large collection of laws contained two regulations that would become significant for witch trials. Article 8 related to dishonest felonies in general. Alongside theft, rape and other offences, witchcraft was regarded as a dishonourable crime in the Danish system, and special legal regulations on prosecuting and sentencing applied to such offences. Article 8 instructed that no denunciation obtained from a person convicted of a dishonest crime could be included in the evidence against a suspect. This clause had a major impact on the conduct of witchcraft trials, since here it becomes apparent how the Danish medieval tradition, in which the concepts of honour and dishonour remained crucial, came into conflict with the demonological ideas of collective witchcraft and the notion that witches would report each other.[148] In practice, the regulation meant that when convicted witches named their accomplices, these testimonies were not allowed to be included as part of the evidence, because by definition they would be involved in the dark arts and thereby not eligible to give evidence. Article 8 is a continuation of the Second Copenhagen Recess of 1537, which stated that those with previous convictions or known to be dishonourable were prohibited from appearing as witnesses in criminal trials. The paucity of preserved court records makes it difficult to establish whether or not the 1537 regulation was upheld. In a letter, Christian III commanded a group of people denounced by convicted witches to be captured.[149] It can be assumed that, even though denunciation by a sentenced witch was not legally allowed as evidence, in the conduct of trials it served as strong circumstantial evidence. A large number of the trials on Jutland in the 17th century confirm this. If a suspect was denounced by other witches, the fact is often noted, and this seems to be common practice.[150] In a less explicit manner, judges would always note whether the suspect was reputed to be a witch, and if so, for how long. As we shall see, a reputation for being a witch could often be traced back to a denunciation from a convicted witch.

Article 8 meant a restriction of the prosecutor's use of evidence, since, according to Palladius, witches always gave each other away.[151] Some 25 years later, the leading Danish theologian and professor at the University of Copenhagen, Niels Hemmingsen, emphasized that the dishonest nature of witches was due to them being 'the servants of the Devil and not Christ' and 'infected and sinful'. Hemmingsen had no qualms about believing that no one could trust the testimony of the witch. Where the secular authorities had a clear perception that the witch was being dishonourable in the same way as a thief would be, theologians would argue that her dishonesty was due to her pact with the Devil. According to the Church, a sentenced witch was guilty of conspiring with the Devil. Article 8 in this sense not only protected the suspected witches on trial, it also went hand in hand with the Church's perception of witches.

The Copenhagen Recess included an additional regulation that had an immediate impact on witchcraft trials. Article 17 ordered that cross-examination under torture was only to be commenced after a guilty verdict. Once again this regulation was not exclusively aimed at witchcraft, for the law refers to the offence as 'misdeed' (*ugerning*), still it became extremely significant in the conduct of the trials. As with Article 8, this regulation in the Copenhagen Recess of 1547 benefited the accused. It meant that no witch could undergo torture before she was sentenced. Danish scholars have only briefly touched upon how to interpret the regulation regarding torture. Johansen has argued that the instruction demonstrated a strict supervision of witchcraft cases, which is partly supported by the issuing of the regulation on appeal in 1576, as discussed in the following. Still, one has to emphasize that the regulations on witchcraft in 1547 applied to misdeeds in general. Merete Birkelund has seen it as marking a way of distancing Danish practice from trials in other parts of Europe, where confessions were frequently obtained under torture.[152] Although Birkelund merely refers to 'Central-European laws', one can support this view through comparison with the use of torture and reputation according to the *Carolina*. Here, evidence (*indicier*) for being a witch was required before applying torture. If one had a reputation for being a witch this was considered sufficient evidence for initiating the torture. However, since reputations were often if not founded then enforced by a denunciation (*udlæggelse*) from a convicted witch, it meant a denunciation could only qualify as evidence and hereby lead to the painful cross-examination.[153] Article 17 of the Copenhagen Recess required a sentence for witchcraft before torture could be applied. In addition, the law countered any misuse of denunciations obtained during torture by issuing Article 8. According to legal historian Poul Johs. Jørgensen, the regulations were issued to prevent violations of testimonies among the lower courts and on higher levels, that is, the provincial courts and the King's Court, the regulations were strictly followed.[154] At least formally, the regulation drew a clear line between the accused and those convicted. In the first place, this prevented torture being used to acquire a confession and in the second made it impossible for such a confession to be used as evidence against others. The purpose of applying torture will be discussed in the following chapter.

In 1559 Christian III had died, and his son Frederick II had been crowned. The new king differed significantly from his late father. As a biographer put it, *Præstekongen* (The priest king) had died, and the young *bon vivant* had ascended the throne. The country felt that quite a different spirit was directing the country's affairs, a bold and powerful spirit that stood in starkest contrast to the hesitancy of his father.[155] In 1576 Frederick II issued the Kalundborg Recess, which served as a further tightening of procedures in trials of witchcraft. This time the changes were explicitly aimed at witchcraft and were to avoid innocent people being executed. Article 17 ordered that anyone who was found guilty at lower courts should have their case tried at the provincial court before a sentence could be executed. This regulation is thought to have been occasioned by a number of cases in which the king had been presented with evidence that local judges did not obey the articles of 1547.[156] The regulations confirm that the Danish King and his Privy Council took the procedures of witch trials very seriously.[157] Sentencing people to death should not be left to less well-versed judges at the lower courts. In addition, the lower courts used local district and town bailiffs, who were often only too well aware of local quarrels and conflicts and who were even involved in these skirmishes at times. By passing a trial on to the provincial courts, the authorities wanted to ensure that impartial judges handled these cases, and the regulation appears to have halted the number of convictions, at least for a period.

Protestant versus Protestant

In the mid-16th century, the conflict loomed between Calvinists and Lutherans south of the Danish border and would eventually exert an influence on the elite of the Danish theologians. Luther's successor in Wittenberg, Philip Melanchton, spoke of there being a symbolic sense of Christ's presence at the communion, an interpretation that appeared to bring him close to the Calvinists. While Melanchton was still alive, it had been possible to keep tensions between these groupings under control, but after his death in 1560 an open struggle broke out between supporters and opponents of Lutheranism and Calvinism.[158] The Elector of Saxony was brother-in-law to King Frederick II and at the same time a devout Lutheran.

In 1574 the Elector had had a group of leading theologians imprisoned for having extolled the Calvinist interpretation of the communion as the true doctrine.[159] In the Calvinist interpretation of the communion, the wine and the bread were only symbols of the blood and body of Christ. For Luther – and according to the Augsburg Confession – the blood and body of Christ were present in fact. During their interrogations the theologians incarcerated in Saxony had referred to the teachings of one of Europe's most highly esteemed theologians, Niels Hemmingsen. According to the estranged theologians, this leading theologian and professor of theology at the University of Copenhagen shared their belief. The news astounded the Elector. Did the Danish King really support a crypto-Calvinist at the finest institution of learning in the kingdom? The Elector called for action from Frederick II. The Danish King had no desire for religious instability inside the kingdom, and in this sense the 'humanistic' currents from Philipism were challenged by the demands from the Lutheran Elector. As a consequence, Hemmingsen was commanded to withdraw offensive paragraphs from his works. In the end this proved not to be enough to convince the Elector, and in 1579 Frederick II gave in to the demands of his brother-in-law and suspended Hemmingsen from his professorship.

I have presented this event in a European context for two reasons. Firstly, it is important to understand Niels Hemmingsen's status not only on the domestic Danish stage but also in Europe. The communion case poses a good example of Hemmingsen's high position among Protestant theologians in 16th century Europe. The simple reference to his name by a group of incarcerated theologians and the consequences brought about by that reflects his standing as a theological lodestar. At the same time it reflects how sensitive leaders at the time were to religious and political instability. Secondly, when it comes to discussing Danish witchcraft, Niels Hemmingsen was a key figure, even after his suspension. His views on witchcraft, as they were communicated in his treatises, were not revolutionary. In fact, the language used by Hemmingsen about witchcraft more or less echoed the general Protestant demonological discourse on witchcraft.[160] The interpretation of communion came to matter to Danish witchcraft discourse because Hemmingsen's suspension meant the removal of the most influential representative of Philipism in Denmark, and thereby paved the way for a move in a different theological direction, to a Lutheran orthodox era in the first half of the 17th century.

The dreadful profanity

Niels Hemmingsen was extremely productive and published several treatises on theology and on how to live as a true Christian. Even after his suspension from the university he continued to enjoy a high standing and was referred to as 'Teacher to the entire Danish kingdom' (*Universalis Daniae praeceptor*). Many of his writings were translated into Danish in the 16th and 17th centuries.

Niels Hemmingsen was the only Danish theologian in the 16th century to publish a treatise entirely devoted to discussing witchcraft (*trolddom*). The Danish edition is known by the title *En undervisning af den hellige skrift, hvad man dømme skal om den store og gruelige gudsbespottelse som sker med trolddom, signelse, og manelse og anden sådan Guds hellige navn og ords vanbrug* (hereafter *En Undervisning*), which can be translated as *A teaching in Holy Scripture. What one is to think about the great and terrible profanity that takes place in witchcraft [trolddom], making the sign of the cross, conjuring and other forms of abuse of God's holy word and name.*[161] This volume is an edition of approximately 80 pages, which was originally published as three small Latin treatises. The year of publication of the text was intensively debated by Danish scholars in the 1980s and the beginning of the 1990s, but in recent years, scholars have settled on the years 1570–1574. The Danish edition of *En Undervisning* was translated by the clergyman Rasmus Reravius.[162] The very fact that the treatise was published in Danish makes it interesting in this context. By means of the Danish edition, Reravius was making sure that the teachings of Hemmingsen reached secular authorities, and, like Peder Palladius' *Book of Visitation*, the text can be perceived as a step forward in the Church's campaign of enlightenment as to what constituted sin, witchcraft – and the papist religion.[163]

One way of reading the Danish manuscript *En Undervisning* is to see it as a text whose primary intention was to influence secular authorities to condemn witchcraft on the basis of theological teachings. It has been brought to light that Hemmingsen made himself an advocate of severe punishments of all kinds of witchcraft, both of the healing and the malevolent kind.[164] Danish historian Karsten Sejr Jensen has argued that Hemmingsen's interest was first and foremost in healing and benevolent magic, as well as prophecies at the expense of the malevolent magic.[165] This opinion is a central point in his dissertation, but it is probably too narrow a view of Hemmingsen. It is more likely that, as has also been argued, Danish theologians might have focused specifically on benevolent witchcraft, given that the judicial framework already prohibited malevolent magic.[166]

The emphasis on benevolent magic in *En Undervisning* has to be understood within the context of religious reform. Catholic rituals were still widely accepted among the common people, and translating the Latin treatise into Danish became a way of reminding secular authorities of the gap in the existing legislation, whereby only malevolent magic was prohibited. Like Peder Palladius, Hemmingsen felt himself to be an authority of the Church and therefore obliged to instruct the secular authorities in their obligations towards God.[167]

Hemmingsen emphasizes that the Devil's attempts to eclipse Christianity have once again become so frequent that it is necessary to get people to understand the seriousness of resorting to witchcraft.[168] Like Peder Palladius, Hemmingsen's primary message is that the practitioners of malevolent witchcraft (*trolddom*) represented only half the depraved story. The other half was made up of those who knew about them and made use of their rituals, in other words the clients. They, too, were sinful:

> The number of signs of the cross made and of incantations used, especially in the villages, when cattle fall ill, is quite countless. And they are used not only by heathens who know nothing of God, or by the impious, who set themselves up against God, for then it would not merit so great a complaint, but such blessings, spoken and written, are now used for illnesses suffered by man and beast, time and again, and are defended most of all by those who ought to be Christians and members of the Church [...][169]

What Hemmingsen was doing in *En Undervisning* was essentially to follow the path laid down by Luther and others, in that he insisted that witches had renounced God and submitted to the Devil. In this they were offending against the First Commandment.[170] As his motive for publishing the treatise, Hemmingsen advances the need to clarify whether witches have any place whatsoever in the Christian community. He puts forward five reasons why such people should be condemned.[171]

For the second generation of reformers, these five reasons for condemning witchcraft provide incontrovertible evidence that magical rituals constituted a religious offence in which the transgressor was guilty of a number of mortal sins. In his discussion there is no mention of the possible harm they might cause to people or livestock. The acts and beliefs of witches confirm, first and foremost, that they mock God. This brings out two crucial key concepts regarding witchcraft for Hemmingsen: heresy and idolatry. Such people are to be condemned, because they 'in their wickedness more greatly revere this false belief and idolatry than God's commandments and precepts', a disdain that has serious consequences for their relation to God, since they are condemned to everlasting perdition. They also cause damage to others, according to Hemmingsen, but this is not through their actions but by 'their evil example'.[172] It is not only their own souls that are infected with heresy; they also inspire others to commit sin, with the result that the evil will spread, with yet more souls being lost. Hemmingsen makes use here of the same rhetoric that was used by the Catholic Church in condemning the great heresies of the Middle Ages and which was also used in the pre-Reformation condemnation of witchcraft and magic, namely to compare practitioners of such arts with an infectious disease.[173]

As we have seen in the previous chapter, Catholic theologians stressed that practices involving magic and witchcraft were heresy and apostasy. For Luther the essential thing had been the heresy and the idolatry committed by these practitioners. Although resembling a traditional Christian condemnation of witchcraft and magic, there was a difference of emphasis in Hemmingsen's next two arguments, however, which reflects further on his position. He condemns witchcraft, but places it more explicitly in the context of religious education.

Witches used letters and words in their rituals, assigning the attribute 'holy' to them, which for Hemmingsen means that the words are assigned supernatural powers. In so doing, they purloin due honour from God.[174] Once a person has dared to venture out into the sinful life such practitioners lead, their evil ways have a cumulative effect: 'Wherefore, anyone using this wickedness and false belief has forsaken and denied the faith and has fallen from God's grace, and shown himself to be the servant of the Devil and not of Christ.'[175] These assertions are, for Hemmingsen, indisputable and form the basis for condemning such people. This leads Hemmingsen to pose five questions that the treatise seeks to answer:

1. Who are the originators of witchcraft?
2. Are they a force in themselves?
3. Why does God permit anyone to practise devilish arts?
4. What passages in Holy Scripture forbid witchcraft?
5. How great a sin are such practices?

In answering Question 1, Hemmingsen is in line with both his Protestant and Catholic colleagues. Witchcraft always originates from the Devil. The fact that Hemmingsen found it necessary to state what by this time was so integral to the theologians' comprehension of magic and witchcraft can only be explained by the lack of understanding displayed by the secular authorities in relation to benevolent magic. Danish lay people, like the illiterate population in other parts of Europe, found it hard to understand how the Devil could be behind benevolent magic. Hemmingsen argued that God made use of divine acts and miracles to get people to understand the true faith, and the only tools he used were his Holy Word, the sacraments and the Holy Spirit.[176] But, Hemmingsen warned, the Devil would always try to tempt man to commit wicked acts. The Devil has his own sacraments, and these he would tempt man to receive.[177] Diabolical sacraments were many and involved objects reminiscent of Catholic practices – images, signs, figures, combined with traditional witchcraft remedies such as salt, earth, water, paper or thread. The religion of the Devil was a false religion, the wrong belief, and for Hemmingsen witchcraft was an abuse of God's word – it was false opinion and heresy.[178]

In answering Question 2, Hemmingsen again deals with the problem of the ritual use of words and letters. Hemmingsen is back once more with the objects of witchcraft and magic to which a special force or power was assigned by the Catholic Church. Many people continued to believe that signs, figures, images and readings possessed a power in themselves, but they were mistaken.[179] It was only the Devil that imbued them with such a power. Despite the fact that Hemmingsen himself does not draw attention to it, he is here expressing the theological dogmas systematized by Thomas Aquinas. Only when the magician had entered into a pact with the Devil would magical words and letters be imbued with this power.[180] Hemmingsen's focus on images, signs, figures and readings is interesting, because, like the warnings of Catholic inquisitors, it dealt with church rituals as practised by the populace. The Catholic Church's attempt to eradicate such use of rituals was based on the fact that it belonged to the category of unauthorized use of religion, to the 'abuse of the sacraments and sacramental objects (*cose sacramentali*)'.[181] Hemmingsen had a different agenda. For him, the use of Catholic rituals was unequivocally linked to witchcraft and magic. The argument is underpinned by Hemmingsen's distinction between such arts as practised by pagans, exemplified by Chaldeans and Arcadeans, and the same arts as practised by Christians.[182] Pagans could be excused, since they did not know Christ. They were simple and ignorant. But Christians who practised such arts had made a deliberate choice, and in doing so they had renounced Christ. Christian witches and magicians were to be viewed as 'twice as bad and wicked', because they had deliberately committed a sin. For Hemmingsen, then, witchcraft was a deliberate act. If their rituals were effective, the power at work derived from the Devil. But, as we know, the Devil gives us nothing for free. If the Word of the Lord were taken in vain, the abuse would lead to perdition. If, however, offenders acknowledged the sin they had committed and did penance, there was hope for them.[183] The alternative was dire, indeed, for 'anyone who does otherwise try God, in whom he will find a strict judge on the Day of Judgment, unless he does penance in time and reforms'.[184] In accordance with the Protestant view, God was not a mild, forgiving father but a zealous and punitive judge: 'As Elias said to Aschab: God is jealous, therefore he does not allow the tiniest part of his honour to go to the Devil.'[185] That God nevertheless countenanced witchcraft was because it was a way of testing people's faith. Hemmingsen asked rhetorically why God allowed this mockery of his name. His answer was simple and commonly finds an echo among Protestant theologians: the Devil had been sent to tempt people to sin, and only those who managed to resist could entertain any hope of salvation. Here all were subject to Lucifer's temptations, and responsibility for committing sin is placed with the individual. For God allowed the Devil to insinuate himself into all the crevices of evil where man had sinned. So if man is afflicted by witchcraft or other misfortunes, he himself is solely responsible.[186] There is no mistaking the moralizing tone in this section, as Hemmingsen starts to attack healing rituals by anticipating the injustice some people must feel when their neighbour escapes illness. Hemmingsen warns against giving in to the temptation to use such (Catholic) rituals. Good health was a gift from God, but if you did not have it, you must not resort to witchcraft or magic. Instead, parishioners were to believe, to submit to God's will and practise their faith correctly.

Basically, then, Hemmingsen saw witchcraft and magic as being a breach of the First and Second Commandments: that is, they were idolatry and sacrilege. With reference to certain biblical passages about committing idolatry, most obviously the First and Second Commandments, Hemmingsen argued that this consisted in such people having chosen the Devil's 'false religion' and the sacrilege lay in the acts they carried out through witchcraft.[187] Hemmingsen made it clear that, since witchcraft had to be considered as idolatry, the many condemnations of idolatry in the Bible were therefore also to be regarded as condemnations of witchcraft.[188]

Hemmingsen used the terms 'idolatry', 'heresy', 'apostasy', 'Catholicism' and 'sacrilege' to denote witchcraft, a choice which, as mentioned earlier, was in line with Protestant witchcraft discourse in the mid-16th century. His condemnation of those who committed these sins follows the same path. In common with 16th century demonology, Hemmingsen stresses that women are particularly disposed to resort to the practice of witchcraft and sorcery. The book of Exodus emphasized the female nature of the witch because, according to Hemmingsen, women in all countries had always been more inclined to sin, and this also applied to Denmark.[189]

The many references to Catholic practice must be seen in the light of Hemmingsen's express wish to stamp out Catholicism. This should not be interpreted, however, as meaning that Hemmingsen simply used the condemnation of witchcraft and magic to conceal his true agenda, namely to defame Catholicism. Catholicism, witchcraft and heresy are hard to tell apart in Hemmingsen's treatise. They are interwoven into a single texture and this must be because Hemmingsen sees them as being inseparable, as the warp and the weft, so to speak, of ungodliness. The underlying desire of Protestants was to return the Church to its original, pure status, which had God's Word at its heart. The many rituals that Catholics regarded as necessary for practising their faith were equated by the reformers with witchcraft. Any causal effect whereby the practitioner expected a result to take place after conducting the ritual was regarded by the Protestant theologians as tantamount to witchcraft.

The Danish translation of Niels Hemmingsen's *En Undervisning* turned the text into a more applicable tool for making the secular authorities aware of the absence of the legislation necessary to prohibit benevolent magic. To avoid God casting his wrath upon society, the king had to expand the laws to include benevolent magic and the diabolical prophecies. According to Hemmingsen, witch trials had to be led by skilled and knowledgeable judges in compliance with Christian teachings. On the basis of *En Undervisning* it can be concluded that Hemmingsen believed that secular judges should handle all forms of magical offence, but in his *Admonitio* Hemmingsen alters his view to allow for other treatments. Here Hemmingsen argues that practitioners of benevolent magic should first be reported to their vicar. Only if the guilty person failed to improve should the cases be brought to the secular authorities.

Witchcraft in an era of Lutheran orthodoxy

Half a century would pass before Niels Hemmingsen's instructions on extending the legislation on witchcraft would be implemented. With the Recess of Kalundborg in 1576, the intention of the secular authorities had been to secure a fair legal process for the complex offence that witchcraft was considered to be. When Protestant theologians urged the prohibition of all forms of magic, they did so, like their Catholic colleagues, by arguing that even benevolent magic came from the Devil. A king had to understand the divine responsibility that had been entrusted to him. He was king by the grace and favour of God, and it was his duty to punish sinners to ensure that God did not subject the entire nation to his wrath. Niels Hemmingsen had explicitly shown how witches were serious in provoking the wrath of God in that they were, in the words of Revelation 21:8, in the company of 'the fearful, and unbelieving, and the abominable, and murderers, and whoremongers, and sorcerers, and idolaters, and all liars, [who] shall have their part in the lake which burneth with fire and brimstone: which is the second death'. They should be abominated like the Devil himself. According to Exodus 22:18 a witch should not be suffered to live, and, to the Lutheran theologians, secular legislation had so far been inadequate in this respect.

Following Hemmingsen's removal as professor at the Faculty of Theology, new currents appeared. In 1596 Christian IV had installed Christian Friis to Borreby (1556–1616) as chancellor (1596–1616). After this the picture changed significantly, and the era in Danish Church history known as Lutheran orthodoxy gradually began to take shape. Church and state were working together with a joint agenda of the centralization of power and of uniformity in administration of the kingdom. In legislation this can be detected in the publication of several laws on public morality and an increasing focus on a strict Christian discipline among the populace. All subjects of the Crown had to be truly subordinate to the Lutheran faith, which meant that all parishioners needed to think, believe and practise the true faith in every aspect of life.

Not only Danish theologians but also members of the Privy Council (*Rigsrådet*) in the early 17th century exalted the Lutheran interpretation of Christianity to the exclusion of any other faith. In this lay a confrontation with all other kinds of Protestantism. The dominance of Lutheranism in the first quarter of the century has traditionally been attributed to Hans Poulsen Resen (1561–1638). Resen had become professor of theology at the University of Copenhagen in 1591, and in 1615 he was appointed bishop of Zealand.[190] In other words it was Resen who was the leading theologian in

Denmark in the years of the great witch-hunts (1617–1622), and according to him all kinds of magic sprang from a pact with the Devil.

With the approach of the jubilee in 1617, the theologians' efforts to elevate and purify the Lutheran faith by expunging impure elements intensified still further. King Christian IV had taken over the throne in 1588. As monarch, he was a complex figure. On the one hand, he is known for the military misfortunes of the Thirty Years War, which almost drove the country into bankruptcy; on the other hand, he provided Copenhagen with some of its finest Renaissance buildings. The king was also not only deeply religious but also superstitious and particularly sensitive to the threat posed by witches. The religious efforts led by Hans Poulsen Resen found support with the king and Privy Council during the first decades of the 17th century.[191] On the centenary of Luther's publication of the theses in Wittenberg, the king and Privy Council published three ordinances, all of them aimed at tightening the general morality of the people. One of them was 'On witches and their accomplices' (hereafter the Witchcraft Regulation).[192]

This legislation marked a turning point in the official view on witchcraft seen through the eyes of the state, for in it the Church and its spiritual considerations finally became visible. In his Visitation Book, Peder Palladius had already drawn attention to the need for the entire kingdom to come together in the fight against the Devil's milkmaids, the witches. In 1617 this was finally written into the Danish law books with the Witchcraft Regulation. The king announced that the responsibility for eradicating this diabolical threat to society fell on all subjects of the Crown:

And in order that our earnest wish and ordinance better be complied with for the honour of God, we herewith issue the gravest command and instruction to all our officers of state and aristocracy, and to bishops, deans and clergymen, mayors, councillors, bailiffs and others who work to the calling and good of the public, that each according to his ability as soon as he becomes cognizant of someone, to whom this ordinance refers, reports, accuses and permits them to be punished, insofar as they do not wish themselves to come before the court as accomplices to these persons and acquiescent to them.[193]

If the officials of the kingdom failed to obey this command, they would be punished as privy to the act. Like the earlier laws, the Witchcraft Regulation contained procedural directions on the handling of witchcraft cases; and, for the first time since the Protestant Reformation, witchcraft was an offence explicitly defined by law.

Besides being the first post-Reformation law to define witchcraft as an offence, the Witchcraft Regulation was also the first in a Danish context to condemn those who consulted cunning folk and made use of their cures. The Witchcraft Regulation presented a judicial definition of witchcraft, which also included benevolent magic such as healing and divination. In the Witchcraft Regulation, healing, blessings and conjuration are described as secret arts (*hemmelige kunster*) and punishment for such magic was banishment for life and the confiscation of all property. This direction can still be considered mild in the light of Hans Poulsen Resen's conviction that any form of witchcraft originated from a pact with the Devil. The failure of Lutheran Orthodox theologians to implement more severe punishments for the practice of benevolent witchcraft is probably due to the Privy Council's scepticism towards this attitude.[194] For the practitioners of malevolent magic known as 'true witches' (*rette troldfolk*), there was no mercy. They were to be sentenced to be burned at the stake.[195]

Throughout the 16th and 17th centuries the Danish Reformed Church attempted to teach the people to adhere to the Lutheran faith, which meant abandoning healing rituals, blessings and conjurations. Several sections in the Witchcraft Regulation indicate that it was vital that everyone in society understood that the eradication of witches was the duty of each and every member of society. As will be discussed later in this book, trials for witchcraft show that the condemnation of benevolent magic was as incomprehensible to ordinary run-of-the-mill people in Denmark as it was in other parts of Europe. Added to this is the fact that the Witchcraft Regulation did not distinguish between those cunning folk who practised healing, fortune-telling and counter-magic. In the Witchcraft Regulation they were merged into one and seen to represent the thin end of the wedge, so to speak, *at verre alle trolfolkis første alfabet* (the first alphabet of every witch). Benevolent magic was the beginning of what was considerably worse – malevolent magic and a pact with the Devil. This *prospect* of the connection to the Devil was the dominant argument in pursuing performers of the secret arts. The authorities were clearly intent on getting the populace to engage in rooting out all kinds of magic. By defining cunning folk as potentially harmful, the authorities were, as we shall see later in the analysis of the trials, only identifying a belief already shared by the common people. By emphasizing the pact with the Devil that lurked behind their activities, the Witchcraft Regulation explicitly presented cunning folk as a threat to the wellbeing and stability of every village. If healing, blessings and conjurations were seen as the first small steps towards a life of witchcraft, then it was a matter of time before the practitioner became 'true witches [...] who have tied themselves to the Devil' (*rette troldfolk [...] som med dieflvelen sig bebundit hafver*).

In *En Undervisning* Hemmingsen had written that no man could support both God and the Devil. This was confirmed in the Witchcraft Regulation in its prohibition of the rituals not only of cunning folk but even of their accomplices (*medvidere*).[196] By defining any such participation as an offence, every individual was from now on duty-bound to denounce those practising magical rituals of any kind. A similar development can be detected in the

Roman Inquisition when it sent out edicts ordering villagers to denounce any neighbours suspected of practising magic or of consulting magicians.

It is interesting that the 'secret arts' were defined as the first step on witchcraft's descent into the abyss. Was this a definition grounded on theological or secular foundations? I argue that the prohibition indirectly responded to both a theological and a popular notion. Theologians regarded all kinds of magic as the work of the Devil. To the illiterate villager, cunning folk were regarded as those with knowledge of the power to heal, and that power could equally be used to harm. Nevertheless, the populace saw a difference between magical healers and practitioners of the dark arts. With the introduction of the Witchcraft Regulation, the core of witchcraft as a judicial offence had become the pact with the Devil. Danish historian Jens Chr. V. Johansen has pointed out that in practice, in the years following the publication of the Witchcraft Regulation, the pact with the Devil was not central to evidence. In fact the diabolical pact was only rarely mentioned in these trials. The verdicts passed by the lower courts prove that the judges continued to focus their attention on the harm caused by the witch, and the provincial court judges generally followed this lead. Johansen rightly points out that the pact with the Devil was by and large impossible to prove without the use of torture, and, as we have seen, torture was not allowed until after the accused had been found guilty. If the provincial judges had considered that proof of a diabolical pact was decisive to being able to sentence an accused, the consequence would have been that the great majority of cases would have been dismissed. Despite the regulation criminalizing benevolent magic, surviving court records show no sign of people being prosecuted solely on the grounds of alleged use of benevolent magic.[197] The reason for this reluctance was probably a combination of general lack of understanding and general reluctance to persecute 'cunning folk'.

The Witchcraft Regulation contained a distinctly theological form of argumentation, and the fact that its directions on benevolent magic were not complied with in practice is a sign of the cultural gap between those members of the populace who were accused of witchcraft and the lawmakers. Even though jurisdiction over witchcraft as a judicial offence had been placed with secular judges throughout the Reformation, the Danish Lutheran Church and religion in general had an ever-increasing influence on legislation in the 17th century. A little more than a decade later a comprehensive ordinance on church discipline was sent out with the title *Ordinance on the Office of the Church and Authority against the Impenitent* (1629) (*Forordning om Kirkens Embede og Myndighed mod Ubodfærdige*), and in fact church discipline seems to have been the main activity of the church authorities in the decades following 1617. Secular courts handled the judicial offence of witchcraft, and the Church, at least in practice, concentrated on educating and reforming the populace. The prosecution of magic and witchcraft was left with the secular courts, and, judging from surviving documentation of bishops who had encountered popular magic and witchcraft, it can be concluded that the Church refrained from encouraging and participating in trials. Instead the Church concentrated on admonition and education.[198]

The regulations issued in 1617 were repeated in Christian IV's Recess of 1643 together with other regulations on moral life, and it was not until 1683 that the law on witchcraft was altered. The Church continued its efforts to reform the population within the framework of the Lutheran faith. The evidence leaves an unmistakeable sense that the law on witchcraft was crucial to the shaping of public morals in this way, and that this explains the explosion in the number of trials in the years 1617–1622.[199]

In 1683 *Danske Lov* (The Law of Denmark) was published.[200] This included updated regulations on witchcraft, even though prosecution of the offence was practically a thing of the past. The last witch was burnt at the stake in 1693, and the last trials conducted in 1696–1698. The kingdom had come under absolute monarchy in 1660, and *Danske Lov* was the king's legal masterpiece – a huge complex of regulations involving moral as well as criminal offences. The law contained five instructions regarding witchcraft, most interesting among them the distinction between (diabolic) witches, who had explicitly abjured their Christian baptism, and those who had merely harmed other people with intent.

Even though the *Danske Lov* is constructed according to the principles of Mosaic Law, the regulations on witchcraft moved away from the very theological definition of the offence. *Danske Lov* in some way came close to the actual practice of the courts in the sense that the law distinguished between witchcraft with or without a diabolical pact. On the one hand *Danske Lov* formulated a concrete definition of witchcraft, but on the other it expressed an awareness that ordinary women with a traditional knowledge of herbs were rarely the malicious devil worshippers that they had been made out to be in the Witchcraft Regulation.

4

Comparing procedures against witchcraft in the Roman Inquisition and the Danish secular courts

Differences between the views of witchcraft held by Danish Lutherans and those of Italian Catholics did not lie in the condemnation of witchcraft. Both confessions/churches referred to witchcraft as combining two of the gravest sins: heresy and apostasy to the Devil. Niels Hemmingsen would have agreed with the Roman Inquisition that heresy was a terrible sin, but to him and his Evangelical colleagues, the concepts of heresy and witchcraft were associated with Catholicism and Calvinism. The harsh condemnation of witchcraft found in both Protestant and Catholic theology was based on the idea of the diabolical pact. The key difference in attitude lay in the proper jurisdiction in witchcraft trials and on the appropriate penalty.

Identifying witchcraft

The legal and theological frameworks of Danish and Roman inquisitorial courts were moderately clear: it was not a question of whether to prosecute witchcraft and magic or not. Instead, the challenge was how to recognize and identify the offence, and how to punish its practitioners. What forms of rituals and behaviour were to be condemned? To the Roman Inquisition, the legal grounds for condemnation were synonymous with the theological; this had been made clear in *Coeli et terrae* of Sixtus V (1585), which condemned *all* kinds of magic performed outside the Church. The bull's focus was on magicians rather than diabolical witches. The inquisitorial manuals guided inquisitors on how to recognize signs of magical offences and how to divine its purposes. The inquisitors had to be especially cautious of abuse of the sacraments and sacramental objects, which because of their sacred nature, had always attracted magicians.

To the Roman inquisitors, witchcraft and magic could involve a kind of idolatry, since, subject as he was to the Devil, the offender had broken the first commandment *non habebis deos alienos coram me* ('Thou shalt not have other gods before me'). The magician would continue to worship and practice *latria*, the rituals intended for God, or *dulia*, those addressed to the saints. In the hands or on the lips of a magician, these actions became idolatry since the magician was, in fact, addressing the Devil and demons. The aspect of idolatry was more evident in the writings of Niels Hemmingsen, who insisted on calling witchcraft (*trolddom*) idolatry and in this way launched his attacks directly at Catholicism and its worship of the saints.

To sum up the concept of witchcraft for the Roman Inquisition, the key notion was the understanding of magic and witchcraft as a form of heresy and apostasy. Magicians could be tried as heretics, as had been established by Alexander IV in the 1250s.[201] Classifying witchcraft and magic as heresy justified why the offences had to be prosecuted by inquisitors and not by lay judges. If no inquisitors were present, bishops had to preside over the trials. In other words, when defined as heresy by the inquisitors, the offence became classified by its religious nature. Danish theologians of the Post-Reformation also comprehended witchcraft as a religious offence – as heresy apostasy, idolatry. However, the secular courts, which were conducting the trials, continued to perceive witchcraft as a way of harming others. Following the Reformation, the king and the Privy Council limited the influence of the Danish Church. The Kings Christian III and Frederick II were hesitant in persecuting witches, and it was not until the reign of Christian IV (1588–1648) that stricter legislation was introduced.

The bull of Sixtus V had confirmed a broad definition of magic and witchcraft within the Roman Inquisition. The Danish Regulation of 1617 was not sent out until thirty years later, but it was based on a similarly broad perception. In the Roman Church there had been some doubts as to whether to proceed against astrology and divination. Earlier in the 16th century, astrology in particular had been widely used within the Curia. In Denmark, the Lutheran Church had fought for a long time for legislation to include a broad concept of witchcraft that would also condemn divination and beneficial magic. Therefore, the two regulations resembled each other in introducing a broad and well-defined conceptual framework for the offence of witchcraft.

Accusations and denunciations

There were significant differences in the procedures that governed the course of the trials in Roman inquisitorial and Danish lay courts. In an inquisitorial trial, the majority of cases began with a denunciation, the so-called *sponte comparente*, or 'voluntary testimony'.[202] A denunciation usually came from a neighbour, local priest or confessor turning up at the inquisition's office with information directed at a particular person. It was up to the inquisitor to decide whether or not to proceed with the investigation, and it was only he who decided whether to initiate a trial.[203] In standard cases counselling from the local tribunal was considered sufficient. More complicated trials were held in close communication with the Holy Office in Rome.[204] Consequently cases could be very time-consuming, often going on for months and sometimes years. A sentence from the inquisition was final and not open to appeal. It was fundamental to inquisitorial procedure that the inquisition initiated the trial, investigated the charge and passed the sentence. In this sense the inquisition had to agree with the denunciator that an offence had been committed, before formal charges were pressed.

There is a judicial difference in that the denunciations delivered to the Roman inquisitor were merely reports on whatever heretical behaviour people had observed in a local society. In Denmark allegations from lay-men could ultimately lead to a formal accusation (and charge). The Danish procedures followed legal practices that could be traced back to the early medieval period and which had a significant accusatorial feature. A trial was conducted between two parties of which one acted as accuser and needed to present evidence against the accused party. The trial resembled a kind of negotiation in which the person with the strongest case won the right to claim compensation. The charges were official when the accuser laid his hand on the head of the suspect and declared that the person was a witch. Sometimes more than one person accused a suspect. A hearing of a number of witnesses against the suspect followed this and, where they existed, of the defence witnesses. Still, a trial included elements of inquisitorial practice since the judge or the jury (*nævningene*) could initiate interrogations and further investigation, as well as decide who had the better case. In trials for witchcraft, the judge sentenced not on the basis of the suspect's beliefs but according to the evidence and the trustworthiness of the witnesses.[205] It was customary also to question the local vicar of the parish. As mentioned in the previous chapter, the Kalundborg Recess, article no. 17 (1576) pre-scribed that a trial had to be brought to the provincial court if there was a conviction, and here the procedures of formally accusing the suspect had to be repeated. Even when the lower court had sentenced a suspect, it was perfectly possible that nobody appeared at the provincial court to make a formal accusation.[206] This was the case in the trial of Anne Lundtz, a woman convicted of witchcraft by the town court in Skagen on the northern tip of Jutland. Numerous witnesses had testified to her use of malevolent magic, but when the trial was brought to the provincial court in Viborg, no one turned up to accuse her formally. The judges therefore dismissed the case.[207]

Slander trials concerning witchcraft were not common in Denmark, which is interesting in the light of the high number of slander trials in general during the 16th and 17th centuries.[208] The slanderers were not sen-tenced to the harsh penalties known from other parts of Europe, where they 'rather than the alleged witches came off worst'.[209] According to the Danish medieval laws (*Landskabslovene*) a convicted slanderer was fined 3 *mark* and subsequently pronounced a liar. Thereby the slanderer was deprived of his honour. If he was unable to pay the fine he was sentenced to *kagen*, which meant he was to be whipped publicly while tied to a post referred to as a *kagen*. This punishment was, as it was by the Roman inquisitors, regarded as defaming *per se*.[210] In 1683 Danske Lov repeated the penalty of 3 *mark* and added an additional fine for verbal slander. A slander distributing libels faced a harsher punishment of defamation of honour, losing one's property and ultimately imprisonment for life (*livstid i jern*).[211] In his mapping of the Danish trials, Johansen has recorded only few slander trials at provincial level in Jutland and a survey of the lower level cases from Falster does not change this picture.[212]

In all witchcraft cases the losing party had to pay the costs of the trial. This meant that it was important to be pretty certain of a case before bringing accusations of witchcraft to court. Without doubt, this prevented a number of possible accusations from going further. At the provincial courts, the question of guilt was no longer in the hands of local judges, and this might explain why about half of those people sentenced by the lower courts were acquitted by the provincial courts.

In the Danish system, the injured party determined whether a crime had been committed. The primary purpose of the Danish trial of witchcraft was to settle the question of guilt, in order to make it possible for the injured party to claim compensation. Throughout the 17th century, Danish court trials remained a way of settling disputes between individual parties. During the 18th century trials gradually altered to become a means of settling disputes between the state and the individual, but by then witch trials had become obsolete.[213]

It is possible to detect different consequences for the defendant depending on whether they were tried under the Roman Inquisition or under Danish law. In the former, the inquisitor alone decided whether to press charges, as he was the sole judge of whether or not a crime had been committed. In Denmark, it was the injured party who formally indicted a suspect, and the judge's role was essentially that of mediator who settled the question of guilt. The role of the lay judge was to resolve a conflict between the parties, not to question the beliefs of those implicated. The question of belief was reserved for clergymen, and they did not play a part in the Danish trials until after a guilty verdict.

Procedures of torture and the question of evidence

The use of torture was an important component both of Roman inquisitorial and of Danish lay witchcraft trials. In both court systems, the purpose of employing torture was to ensure that defendants admitted to all their errors. However, the point at which painful interrogation was employed differed significantly. The witchcraft trials of the Roman Inquisition always proceeded with torture *before* sentencing the suspect. The Danish trials did not instigate torture until *after* sentencing had taken place.[214]

In an inquisitorial witchcraft trial, torture was usually instigated as the final interrogation. Subsequently, suspects would be asked to confirm the statements they had given during torture. These examinations are always referred to in detail in the protocols, often making the testimonies harrowing reading. A conspicuous example is in the case against Faustina di Leusta, a 28-year-old woman denounced for love magic in 1649. The protocol describes how, when she was suspended by a rope that bound her hands behind her back, she wept, repeatedly begging for mercy and calling upon St. Filippo Neri and the Virgin Mary.[215] The protocols of Orbetello indicate that the inquisition here employed torture as standard procedure in all full-blown trials.[216] All those convicted in Orbetello had undergone torture before their sentence. In addition, the protocols show that the defendant was not placed in the torture chamber before a thorough investigation, including the questioning of several witnesses, had provided the inquisition with sufficient evidence that an illicit deed had been committed. Many of the Orbetello denunciations never evolved into full-blown trials. They remained denunciations often with testimonies from 1–5 witnesses attached. Usually, at least 5–7 witnesses were questioned before a suspect was arrested and the defendant herself would be examined at least twice before the interrogation under torture. The purpose of torture was not to make the defendants confess their errors, but to make them confess *all* of them.

The use of confession was, in fact, a feature of the evidence needed in an inquisitorial trial. Since heresy was considered a crime of the intellect, admitting to the offence was considered the only definite evidence.[217] Torture was thought of as the most efficient way of obtaining a confession. By confessing, the accused demonstrated the will to be reconciled with God. Here the inquisitor played a dual role of judge and confessor. On one hand, in his role as protector of the faith, he had to proceed against an offence, namely heresy. On the other hand, he had to save the soul of the suspect. Only by confessing, could the suspect obtain the possibility of absolution.

When applying torture, the inquisitors followed a set of strict rules. Inquisitorial manuals contained regulations on methods, duration, and on which type of people would have to endure torture. The customary method was the *la corda* (the rope), where those accused had their hands tied behind their backs with a rope from which they were then suspended. Torture was never intended to leave the accused with permanent injuries, although some of the accused from Orbetello did later complain about shoulder-pain.[218] Furthermore, the defendant had to be in a certain state of health before torture could be applied. A case from Orbetello demonstrates how the inquisitor was having doubts about whether to proceed with the torture of a pregnant woman. He summoned a physician, who examined the woman and found no reason not to implement torture, since the 'rope' would not cause damage to her unborn child.[219]

In Danish witchcraft trials, torture was standard procedure subsequent to a conviction.[220] According to the Copenhagen Articles of 1547, torture was never to be applied until after the verdict was pronounced. The customary method seems to have been the rack, in which the witch was tied to a ladder and stretched, or instruments such as screws on legs.[221] Protocols rarely contain descriptions of torture, although a dozen or so trials contain the witches' confessions given under torture. In these trial records, information about the torture used is limited to the initial sentence in the witch's confession, which usually opens with the words 'on the rack [*pinebænken*] she confessed to the following deeds'.[222]

Although the article on torture in the Copenhagen Recess was a general regulation, it corresponded to the view on witchcraft as an offence against God, along with the idea of witches as collaborating with other witches. This made the purpose of torture twofold.[223] First, it was for the sake of the witch's soul, and second, to obtain information for future trials. By confessing, the witch demonstrated the will to be reconciled with God. Initially the interrogators would demand her to reveal when, where and in the company of whom, she had abjured her faith. During the torture, a clergyman would repeatedly pray for the suspect. The second part of a confession concerned the malevolent deeds of which the witch had been found guilty. In both parts of the confession, the abjuration of the faith as well as the description of the practice of witchcraft, the witch put forward the names and villages of her fellow witches. However, it is important to underline that according to the regulation of 1547 no denunciations given during torture could lead to a trial, as opposed to the *Carolina*. This must have prevented a number of witchcraft allegations from making it to court.[224]

During the time between torture and execution, the witch was often confronted several times with her previous statements.[225] This frequently led to her accusations being withdrawn. In 1612, Maren Jensdatter from Aalborg in Denmark was accused of carrying a 'child' of wax under her armpit for the purpose of bewitching another local woman. During the trial Maren accused yet another woman from Aalborg called Apeloni Ibsdatter.[226] However, Maren withdrew her accusations before she was pushed into the flames. But, unfortunately for Apeloni, the seeds of suspicion had been sown, and she was convicted of witchcraft five years later.[227]

In Denmark, torture was not always limited to a single occasion. In the trials he conducted, the notorious witch-hunter Jørgen Arenfeldt of Rugaard held the suspected witches imprisoned in the dungeons of his castle. This gave him rich opportunity to interrogate the suspects by any means he found necessary, including torture. Sometimes torture would take place even when the convicted witch had been tied to the ladder and was waiting to be pushed into the flames.[228] At this point, it was common for the vicar to question the witch one last time, making sure that she had confessed to all her diabolical deeds. Only by confessing to all her sins would God spare her from an afterlife in eternal agony. These torture procedures reflect a significant focus on the afterlife in Protestant Denmark compared to Catholic practice. The Danish judges put a high value on statements given immediately prior to execution. This was based on the idea that people would not dare to lie when they were so close to meeting their Maker. Likewise, denunciations made on a deathbed were regarded as more reliable.

The Copenhagen Articles also supported a theological view of witches as dishonest and unreliable. A similar theological understanding lay behind inquisitorial procedures. The inquisitorial notion of confession as the only definite proof and torture as a way of obtaining such evidence is interesting from a comparative perspective, since confession in the Danish trials played only a minor part in assembling evidence. Danish lay judges relied on a principle of causality, which made them emphasize 'the threat of evil', by which they meant that the witch had threatened a person with evil, whereupon some form of accident had befallen them. Usually these threats were directed against the person's health, family or livestock. In order to be taken into consideration, the 'threat of evil' had to be found by the judges to have been realized before it could be included as substantial evidence. This is reflected in many trials, among them that of Chresten Lauridtzen of the village of Jerslev. In 1634, the local court had sentenced him for performing malevolent magic, and the case was then brought to the provincial court in Viborg. Here he was accused of having threatened a woman, saying she would become a cripple. In addition to these accusations, Chresten had been reputed to be a witch ever since the death of a local villager eight or nine years before the trial. The provincial judges nevertheless dismissed the case. They emphasized how the woman who had allegedly been bewitched was in good health, married and had given birth to two children since the reported threat to turn her into a cripple.[229] In this sense, the Danish judges, although without employing the actual concept *corpus delicti*, dismissed the case with reference to guidelines similar to those prescribed by the Roman Inquisition.

Presumably a large number of people confessed under torture in Denmark, but confession did not alter their fate in this life.[230] As in the inquisitorial system, confession was important only for the sake of the soul.[231] In early modern Denmark, a convicted witch was always sentenced to be burnt at the stake. Confessions made under torture could not change this sentence. However, by confessing, the defendant had demonstrated the will to repent, and it was now up to God to mete out the proper sentence in the hereafter.

Judgement and sentence

Although all kinds of magical experiments were condemned in the bull of Sixtus V, some were considered graver than others. Throughout a trial under the inquisition, the defendant's intentions carried significant weight. This was also reflected when it came to passing judgement and sentence. All of the defendants in the Orbetello trials were convicted of heresy, though all were placed in the milder category 'suspected of heresy' (*sospetta/o di heresia*). The worst offender was labelled 'seriously suspected of heresy' (*gravemente sospetta di heresia*).[232] According to the *Instructio*, the verdict was to be based on a thorough investigation of the *corpus delicti*. The gravest offence was that which combined an explicit diabolical pact with an explicit desire to harm, as opposed to those who entered into an implicit pact with no intentions to do other than to heal.

In the medieval articles of the Law of Jutland in Denmark, witchcraft had legally been defined by its physical consequences, which meant that concern focused on the damage caused. The distinction introduced by the authorities in 1617 between the 'secret arts' and 'true witches' signified a shift marked by an increased emphasis on the underlying intention of the suspect, which had become essential in determining the verdict. In the Witchcraft Regulation of 1617, the Church's ideas of witchcraft were given renewed expression and adopted by a secular system that reintroduced the religious aspect of witchcraft and prohibited all kinds of magic, be it healing, divination, counter-magic or destructive.

The Witchcraft Regulation of 1617 had included an extended set of penalties. Until then, those convicted of witchcraft were sentenced to the death penalty, which meant ending their lives at the stake.[233] Tied to a ladder, the convicted witch was offered absolution by a vicar before being pushed into the flames. It was not until the late 17th century that witches were executed by hanging prior to being placed on the fire. After 1617 practitioners of the 'secret arts' were exiled and forced to leave their property behind. Special penalties were passed on nobles, who were executed by the sword instead of being sent to the stake. Surviving records of witchcraft trials in Denmark provide evidence of only one noble woman having been convicted. This was the noble woman Christenze Kruckow, who was beheaded in 1621 in Copenhagen.[234] Even though Danish administration had introduced new penalties, an overwhelming majority continued to be sentenced to death by burning.

The Roman Inquisition made use of several types of penalties throughout the post-Tridentine era, and the death penalty was not commonly applied to practitioners of magic and witchcraft.[235] In Orbetello, the most severe penalty used by the inquisition was public whipping and exile. The flogging took place in the streets of the town to the sound of trumpets. Penalties also included imprisonment, fines and galley duty, although none of the people of Orbetello who were sentenced for magical offences were sent to the galleys. Every sentence included 'salutary penances' (*penitenze salutari*), consisting of the recitation of prayers, regular communion and confessions, attendance at mass and the like. The inquisitor drew on his manuals in devising the sentence, but combinations were numerous. In Orbetello, the gravest case was brought against Mensola di Tiracoscia, referred to by witnesses as the only true witch (*strega*). She was sentenced to five years' imprisonment and sent to Rome, where the judges had to reassess her.[236] In another case, the priest Stefano Tommei was accused of various kinds of magic and witchcraft. His penalty consisted of a fine of 500 *scudi* and arbitrary imprisonment in Rome.[237]

The narrow definition of witchcraft as either benevolent or malevolent meant that the Danish judges followed two standard alternatives when it came to sentencing: either execution or exile. With the Roman Inquisition, the wide variety of combinations of error and circumstance and the emphasis on the *corpus delicti* made punishments equally varied. By 1617, both legal systems were operating against a range of magical offences. However, for the Roman Inquisition the offence alone did not automatically determine the sentence. This explains why no standard punishment for love magic existed. It always depended on the person, the rituals and the *corpus delicti*.

When comparing the two legal systems, it is important to emphasize the evident differences in the sentences. The lightest sentence in the Danish system more or less matched the harshest sentence pronounced by the Roman Inquisition in Orbetello. Inquisitors dealt with witchcraft as a sin that needed repentance and absolution and as an offence that sometimes required corporal punishment, which would then be exacted by the secular authorities. The harshness of the Danish secular judicial system derives from a particular combination of theological and secular concerns that surfaces in Danish witchcraft trials. Here Mosaic Law and Lutheran ideas were woven together, a tendency that was reinforced during the 17th century. The key to Lutheranism was the interpersonal relationship with God. God alone was able to forgive man. This part of Lutheranism rejected the Catholic idea of penance as a way of atoning for sin. In Denmark witchcraft was prohibited by secular law, and as a consequence corporal punishments were applied. Still, in the secular legislation the interpersonal relationship with God was combined with Mosaic Law, which held a still greater influence on Danish administration at the beginning of the 17th century. The king was installed by the grace of God, and Mosaic Law required the king to punish his subjects. Otherwise, God would vent his anger on the entire kingdom, and this would result in war, famine or plague. In other words, the Danish Lutheran king was obliged to punish sinners, while he was never able to grant forgiveness of sins. Forgiveness could not be obtained in this life; sinners had to wait until the after-life, since God alone could forgive. In this way the prosecution of witches became an act carried out on behalf of society to demonstrate to God that the lay authorities would not tolerate such transgressors under any circumstances. The intention of the authorities was not to re-socialize the individual sinner but to protect society from divine vengeance.

While the Regulation of 1617 pushed the secular Danish legal system into wholesale execution of witches to protect the state from divine retribution, the Roman Inquisition avoided such confusion between secular and spiritual spheres. The rare use of the death penalty by the inquisition also demonstrated the Catholic idea of penance. Practitioners of witchcraft and magic were not to be eliminated; the intention was to eliminate their practices. In order to be made to regret their errors, performers of magic and witchcraft had to realize that their behaviour was sinful. If they did so, they were able to return to the Church. Even in the gravest cases, in which the convicted witch had been whipped, the inquisition had to act carefully. As in the Danish legal system, the inquisitors considered whipping deeply defamatory to the individual.[238] Hence, the whip was only used when errors were particularly grave. Even then, the inquisition had to be cautious, since the convicted witch needed to have the opportunity to return to the Catholic Church.

A *crimen mixti fori*

After the middle of the 16th century, the crime of witchcraft had become more carefully defined in the legal system of the Roman Inquisition as well as in the secular system in Denmark. The Catholic Church continued to hold a strong position in the Italian peninsula, and the Roman Inquisition had tribunals in most of the Italian territories by the mid-16th century. The Roman Inquisition viewed witchcraft as heresy and apostasy, and since these were crimes against the faith, this meant that no one but the Holy Office was competent to conduct the trials. This definition of witchcraft as an offence against the faith rendered the physical and secular aspect a reflection of the diabolical pact. In the Danish legal system, the Lutheran Reformation had placed the jurisdiction of witchcraft with lay judges.

In the Danish legal system an accusing party was needed and a person had to feel injured otherwise a trial could not be initiated. This created an inconsistency since benevolent magic was usually not regarded an offence among villagers. Thus, the Danish legal system made it difficult if not impossible to enforce the Witchcraft Regulation, but it signalled the Danish authorities' will and intention to prosecute benevolent magic. Statistics show a dramatic increase in the number of trials after 1617. The question is how much should be attributed to the Witchcraft Regulation. Some have argued that the number of trials had already been increasing and have emphasized that the Regulation was only escalating an increase that was already in progress. The hypothesis is intriguing, although it is not yet possible to find reliable evidence for it, since no relevant sources survive from the years 1612–1617.[239] The influence of orthodox theologians like Hans Poulsen Resen and his election to bishop of Zealand in 1615 do, however, indicate the tendency to intensify the witch-hunt in Denmark. Further studies of theological writings in particular are likely to shed further light on this aspect of Danish witchcraft prosecution.

Part II
The Prosecuted

5
The local studies

Jutland

The Kingdom of Denmark-Norway did not go through the same religious conflicts as the German states south of the border. Kings of the 16th century sought internal stability and consensus, a line followed by Christian IV in the 17th century. The possessions and estates of the Church had been assigned to the Crown, making the king by far the wealthiest and greatest landowner in the kingdom. The new Protestant or, in the term used by reformers, Evangelical Church, was no longer a legislative authority except in religious matters against its own. Many of the leading reformers had studied in Wittenberg, and for most of the 16th century Philipist Protestantism was the dominant form among theologians. This changed from the end of the century with the suspension of Niels Hemmingsen, professor at the university and a famous theologian.[240] The removal of Hemmingsen in 1579 made way for the more strict Lutheran Orthodoxy that came to dominate the 17th century, theologically as well as in legislation.

During the 16th and 17th centuries Denmark was involved in several wars with Sweden as well as in the Thirty Years War, and with the sacking of towns, heavy taxation and a rise in poverty as consequences. Jutland was generally hit harder by these misfortunes than the other parts of the kingdom. The Emperor's War (1625–1629), the part of the Thirty Years War in which the Danish King Christian IV was engaged, caused particularly severe damage in Jutland. Towns were plundered, civilians killed and lay offices, including the provincial court in Viborg, were put out of service. The devastation carried out by the Emperor's troops extended right up to the northern trading centre of Aalborg.[241]

Lay administration divided Denmark into about 200 manors and a number of counties (*len*).[242] Each manor held its own manor court, which was a permanent court led by the bailiff for the purpose of settling local disputes.[243] Towns had their own town court (*bytinget*), where the town bailiff held the position as judge. If a dispute was not settled by the lower courts, it was brought to the appellate court, the provincial court. In towns, the highest local authority was the Magistrate (*Magistraten*) consisting of mayors and councillors, usually grand merchants. The Magistrate represented the town to the rest of the world and looked after the town's interests, including overseeing the collection of taxes and charges and the determination of prices on the local market. Judicially the Magistrate was represented in the council court, which mostly settled economic disputes between the people of the town. The jurisdiction between the courts was not clearly defined, and cases were sometimes submitted to the council courts only to be referred to the town courts. Market towns (*købstæder*) could be allotted special privileges by the king, which would raise the status of the council court to provincial court. As a consequence the people of these towns did not need to travel to Viborg to appeal and settle their legal disputes.[244] The highest judicial body was the High Court (*Kongens Retterting*, after 1661 *Højesteret*). Usually cases for witchcraft were settled by the provincial courts, but a trial could go all the way to the High Court, on the request of the accused, the accuser or even the king himself.

The market towns at that time were largely self-governing, but they were still liable to a number of demands from the Crown. Every town had to pay taxes, provide lodging and carriages and horses for the king's men, and was obliged to arrange the transport of goods and mail. In addition, the towns' military obligation to the country came in the form of demands for ships and men. The king's highest authority in local areas was the vassal (*lensmanden*).

Orbetello and the presidios

The presidios was established in 1557 by the Spanish King Philip II following the abdication of his father, the Hapsburg emperor Charles V (1500–1558), in 1556. Philip II had inherited Charles V's possessions in Spain, The Netherlands and Italy. The presidios consisted of the towns Orbetello, Talamone and Porto Ercole on Argentario, Porto Longone[245] in Elba, and Piombino.[246] The Spanish Crown conducted secular and military administration corresponding to the Spanish *vicerè*. The presidios was not a state in the modern sense.[247] Rather, it was a group of military units with Orbetello as its headquarters.

On many occasions in the 16th century, the region formed the battleground in a complex series of events and diplomatic negotiations between the Grand Duchy of Florence and various allies on the one side, and Siena and her allies on the other. In 1555 Cosimo di Medici had captured Siena with the support of the Habsburgs, and the emperor, Philip II, formally gave the town to Florence as fief. Following this series of events, Philip II created the garrison state of *Stato dei Presìdi* in 1557.[248] The area held the status of garrison state up until 1707.[249] Spanish interests in Orbetello were mainely militarily strategic. Orbetello and the garrisons played a vital part in the political ambition to maintain Spanish control of the Italian peninsula. The Spanish territories in Italy included Milan in the north and the Kingdom of Naples along with Sicily in the south. In addition to this came satellite states such as Ferrara, Mantua and Parma. This was the result of a Spanish strategy that looked to create Spanish domination of the Italian peninsula. Between the Spanish territories lay the Florentine *Granducato* (Grand Duchy) and the Papal State. The presidios strengthened the Spanish grip on the peninsula, due to the fact that the garrison towns were placed along the road between north and south, so they could function as independent facilitators to maintain Spanish rule.[250]

In the Hispano-Franco confrontation during the final years of the Thirty Years War, Orbetello and the presidios became a battleground once again. The dispute led to a French siege of Orbetello and the occupation of Porto Longone in May 1646. In the court records there are numerous references to the French siege, and generally the inhabitants of Orbetello used the siege as a chronological point of reference.[251]

Single women and a garrison of Spanish soldiers

The vicars of Roman inquisitor generals stood in contrast to the Danish lay courts, which were permanent judicial institutions. In 1612–1613 a series of cases had been tried against people from the area, and they had led to three convictions.[252] In late 1648 a vicar was sent to Orbetello by the Franciscan tribunal of Siena, although he did not initiate prosecutions until the winter of 1649.[253] Edicts of faith were issued by the Roman Inquisition at intervals, and they ordered the parishioners to vouchsafe whatever knowledge or suspicions they had of heresies.[254] The Roman inquisitor in Orbetello, a Franciscan friar Francesco Pedrosa, initiated his work in the town by decreeing such an edict of faith in the autumn of 1648. In the edict, he ordered every parishioner to report any heresy, witchcraft and other acts against the Catholic Church, underlining the need for a clear conscience and the importance of individual salvation. The response must have overwhelmed the inquisitor.[255] In the years 1649–1650 more than 100 denunciations of witchcraft and magical practices were submitted, only few of which developed into formal trials. The number of denunciations is in stark contrast to the number of convicted. Fewer than twenty ended with a sentence.[256] During the following decade the number of denunciations of witchcraft steadily decreased, and the last case leading to a conviction was in 1656. Sporadic denunciations of witchcraft continued to be submitted over the following decade, but the inquisitor no longer prosecuted them. It is difficult to establish specific numbers of Spanish soldiers in Orbetello, but the presence of the military meant that soldiers were an integral part of everyday life. An account of the reports that were submitted to the inquisition shows that many accusations of blasphemy were directed against the soldiers. From the inquisitorial protocols it is clear that soldiers often engaged in sexual relationships with women from the town.[257]

Historical work on Orbetello has primarily focussed on the Etruscans and the area's military significance in the 16th and 17th centuries. The quadricentennial anniversary of the death of Philip II in 1978 caused a rush of research conferences, of which a few were in Italy, one of them about Orbetello. The result was a volume that included various predominantly political aspects of the history of the presidios.[258] In the present comparative study, it is the people of Orbetello, especially its women, who play the leading roles. Little information is to be found on the history and daily life of the people of the Maremma area.[259] On several occasions in the inquisitorial records, the inhabitants are referred to either by themselves or by witnesses as poor. [260] The surrounding fields had yet to be recultivated.[261] The inquisitorial protocols only occasionally mention people employed in farming and these were invariably shepherds. Ivano Tognarini confirms that there was a crisis in the years 1646–1650. He notes that several of the garrison towns in this period were heavily affected by naval battles and sieges, and that the crisis culminated in the French siege.[262] Following this, the Spanish imposed increased control of the garrisons and fortresses, but it is not clear to what extent the resources provided benefited the local population as well. One of the conclusions from the conference in 1979 about the presidios was that the Spanish presence in the area did not reduce poverty among the local population, but that it did provide internal stability for the area.[263] Another challenge in the region came from the swamps and the Tuscan heat. These offered the perfect conditions for mosquitoes, and malaria was a problem for the soldiers and possibly also for the local population.

Introducing two trials: from gossip to accusation

As discussed in the previous chapters, it is possible to isolate a number of differences in the legal procedures framing witchcraft cases in early modern Italy and Denmark. The previous chapters dealt with the legal setting, focusing on how the courts justified prosecutions and identified the offence. The second part of this book focuses on the people on trial. In northern Jutland as well as in Orbetello these generally belonged to the common people. Before investigating the cases further it is my intention to introduce two cases as they were conducted in the two courts, with the aim to give the reader an idea of the main features of a trial for witchcraft in the two courts, but also to, hopefully, illuminate the differences. The Italian denunciations and the Danish accusations illustrate how the court records offer rich information about the social relations existing between suspect and witnesses. The inquisitorial records generally contain significantly more information about the parties involved, especially about the suspect, than the Danish court records. It was standard procedure for the inquisitor to question those interrogated about their age, birthplace, current place of abode, marital status and time of last confession and communion. In the Danish cases, by contrast, information about age and marital status usually has to be drawn from testimonies; and religious practice is rarely ever investigated.

Virginia di Leandro, Orbetello

On 14 August 1649 inquisitor Pedrosa in Orbetello was approached by a woman referred to as *donna* Mariana. Her intention was to denounce a certain Virginia di Leandro, fellow inhabitant of Orbetello.[264] According to Mariana, a few weeks earlier she had been standing in the street gossiping in the company of some women including Virginia di Leandro. The women were talking about the execution of two sentences passed on two local women by the Roman Inquisition. These women had been flogged in the streets to the sound of trumpets for having practised love magic. Not surprisingly, the talk amongst Mariana and the group of women had fallen to this kind of magic. At some point during this conversation Virginia had exclaimed in an arrogant manner that she would gladly offer herself to the Devil, if this would only help her to get a husband. This was the statement that had motivated donna Mariana to denounce Virginia to the inquisitor.

Following this initial denunciation, the court records state that several people denounced Virginia for this blasphemous statement. More accusations of various kinds soon followed. A woman named Alviria di Fortunio claimed that Virginia had always been very interested in the activities of the two convicted women. According to Alviria, the women had performed love magic on behalf of Virginia on numerous occasions. Furthermore, Alviria suspected that Virginia had healed a number of people with magical rituals.

Suspicion had now been raised, and so the inquisitor systematically summoned witnesses. At the same time, additional denunciations continued to be reported. Several spoke of Virginia's magical healing rituals, some of which would work on animals and others on humans. She knew the rituals to secure the harvest and she could recover lost or stolen objects. When Virginia had to recover a lost object, she would take its owner's hand and kneel before St. Anthony (*Sant'Antonio*). In her other hand she would hold a lighted wax candle. Virginia would then ask the client to say the Ave Maria or the Lord's Prayer, after which she would mutter some unknown words.

It soon appeared that Virginia was well known as a practitioner of love magic in Orbetello, and the inquisitor apparently found the case against her to be significant enough to warrant her arrest. Five days passed from her being taken into the inquisition's custody until her first interrogation took place. In those five days, the inquisitor received a further six denunciations against her. The case against Virginia di Leandro reflects how the inquisitor followed a standard procedure for interrogation, which can be detected in the other cases in Orbetello. In this first questioning the inquisitor had only a few questions. It emerged that Virginia was a widow; she was 31 years old and living at the time with a man named Carlo. She had not confessed nor received the sacrament for two years, because her confessor had refused to receive her on grounds of the relationship with Carlo. Virginia assured the inquisitor that Carlo's intentions were genuine and that he would eventually marry her.

The following day Virginia was questioned once more. This time the inquisitor probed further into the relationship with Carlo. Virginia maintained that there was no sin in the relationship and she was finally sent out to speak to her defence lawyer. This conversation apparently made her realize the sinful nature of living with a man outside marriage. Judging from the records, this seems to have been the aim of the inquisitor's questioning of the relationship with Carlo. He now once again turned his attention to Virginia's practice of witchcraft (*sortilegio*).

The next interrogation was conducted in the torture chamber. Permission for proceeding with this painful cross-examination had been obtained from the Tribunal in Siena. During this agonizing interrogation, the inquisitor's questioning repeatedly returned to Virginia's perception of the Devil and to the part he played in acts of witchcraft, particularly in love magic. At first Virginia denied everything, but having been raised up in the ceiling by the rope her confession started to change. Led on by the questions of the inquisitor, she gradually admitted to have been tempted by the Devil, admitting that she now understood how deep a sin resorting to witchcraft was. Her cohabitation with Carlo was also brought up, and Virginia was once again confronted with the sinfulness of living with a man outside marriage. Towards the end of this interrogation Virginia clearly saw no way out. She admitted to having been under the Devil's spell when she had claimed it was acceptable for women and men to live together without being formally married. Although Virginia was undoubtedly marked by her torments, she maintained that she was nothing like the two women previously convicted of love magic.

After the cross-examination under torture, Virginia had to either confirm or retract her confession. The inquisitor focussed on her relationship with Carlo and on Virginia having performed love magic to make him offer marriage. She confirmed the confessions she had made under torture, but refused to admit that she had ever sold her soul to the Devil. She then swore her allegiance to the Church and renounced the Devil and his works.

The inquisition passed its sentence on 14 November 1649. Like the two women she had insisted she bore no relation to, Virginia di Leandro was to be flogged in the streets of Orbetello to the sound of trumpets. Then she was to be banished forever from Orbetello and the surrounding areas. If she did not abide by this, the inquisition would once again have to punish her. Before the execution of the sentence Virginia would have to abjure her heretical acts. After this she would be regarded as reconciled with the Catholic Church.

Sidsel Christens, Hostrup

On 19 July 1617 the provincial court in Viborg confirmed the guilty verdict on Sidsel Christens from the village of Hostrup.[265] The conflict that eventually led to Mikkel Christensen taking Sidsel to court and accusing her of being a witch could be traced back to at least 1610, possibly further. Back then Sidsel had been denounced (*udlagt*) as a witch by a convicted witch, whose name had not been revealed to the court now sitting. At the time Sidsel's husband had tried to clear her name and to do so he had attempted to find character witnesses from among his fellow parishioners (*sognevidner*) to vouch for her good name and reputation. Mikkel Christensen had upset this plan, since, if the confession of the aforementioned witch was to be believed, Sidsel was to blame for the death of some of his cattle. This allegation had caused Sidsel to threaten Mikkel, saying that he would suffer from 'shame and misfortune'. After this he had lost even more of his cattle.

A few years later Mikkel had once again suspected Sidsel of witchcraft, this time for bewitching (*forgøre*) his horse. Ivar Marqvardsen, a burgher from the nearby town of Varde, testified that when he had asked Mikkel Christensen to drive him to the market in Ribe, Mikkel had refused, saying that his horse had fallen ill and was lying in the stable unable to move. Ivar told the court that, after showing to him the poor horse, Mikkel had left the house to go and see Sidsel, accompanied by two other men. What the men had said to Sidsel, Ivar could only speculate, but shortly afterwards the horse was once again well. The two men accompanying Mikkel also testified in court and shed additional light on what had happened. When they had called on Sidsel, while standing in the door Mikkel had, publicly accused (*sigtet*) her of bewitching his horse, whereupon the horse had immediately started eating again.

The skirmishes between Mikkel and Sidsel also involved Mikkel's wife, Anne Mikkels. In dramatic tones she testified that she had been struck by fever and that she had been terribly ill for seven weeks. During her illness she had not hesitated to complain to 'God and people'; in other words her illness had been a rather public affair. Anne blamed Sidsel for her illness, and on the same night that she had fell ill, three of her cows and bulls had come running home from the field, their tongues hanging and their mouths foaming as if they had gone mad. Anne had then tethered the cattle and at that very night she had been struck with her terrible illness.

The court records contain additional accounts of Sidsel having bewitched cattle. A man named Niels Hansen also had had a dispute with Sidsel. This incident is undated, but apparently Sidsel had been evicted from her house, and her master, Frederik Munk, had sold some of her furniture and livestock to Niels Hansen, one of his other peasants. Not surprisingly, Sidsel had been far from happy at this turn of events and had threatened Niels, saying that nothing good would come to him from the possessions of hers he had bought from their master. After this Niels had suffered many misfortunes, including much pain and misery, the death of a cow and some sheep. Niels believed these deaths to have been caused by Sidsel's witchcraft.

From the testimonies against Sidsel it appears that in the local society she was rumoured to be a witch. According to local gossip, Sidsel had taken the life of her own husband, although this was not part of the formal accusation against her. Niels Hansen described that three years before the trial he had witnessed a quarrel between Sidsel and her husband, which had ended with him hitting her. This had caused Sidsel to hit her husband back, saying that he would 'sink into shame' if he was ever to hit her again. Eight days later he had died, and the witness was convinced this was due to witchcraft. The reason for Sidsel and her husband quarrelling had been because he had become angry, since a convicted witch had once again denounced her for witchcraft. Mikkel Christensen's testimony also stresses Sidsel's dubious reputation. He testified how he had gone to church one Sunday and asked all the parishioners present that day what testimonial they would give her and what her reputation was. They had all unanimously replied that Sidsel had been accused of witchcraft several times, that she was reputed to be a witch, and that those whom she threatened with evil did indeed experience misfortune. Mikkel Christensen also presented the confessions of two convicted witches, which further contributed to her bad reputation. Both of them accused Sidsel of also being a witch.

Sidsel Christens herself was present in court that day in Viborg, but, in contrast to the inquisitorial court, her testimony had little bearing on the outcome of the case. She claimed to be innocent of performing acts of witchcraft (*trolddomskunster*), but, as the court makes clear, she could not prove her innocence. Here the court was referring to the fact that Sidsel presented no witnesses in her defence. In other words nobody in the village would stand up for her and declare that she was honest and 'of upright character'.

When the provincial judges in Viborg pronounced their sentence, they offered a short explanatory text in regards to the verdict. The judges emphasized that Sidsel had been threatening people with evil and misfortune, and that these things had come to pass. The judges also stressed that she was publicly accused of being a witch and that two convicted witches had denounced her as a witch. Finally no one would stand up in her defence in court and assert that she was a good and honest Christian woman; on the contrary, the court stated, it was her own fellow parishioners who had found her guilty at the manor court in Skast. Since Sidsel Christens was convicted of being a true witch, who caused harm to livestock and humans and since her 'evil ways and evil deeds' were considered proven, the provincial judges in Viborg sentenced her to be burned alive at the stake.

6
Constructing an accusation of witchcraft for the court

The two trials presented in chapter 5 each represent significant differences in the construction and content of allegations of witchcraft in the two courts. In chapter 7 various kinds of allegation of witchcraft will be examined more closely. To pave the way, this chapter introduces the main categories that the allegations fell into.

The categorization of the allegations of witchcraft has been less challenging to Danish scholars than to their Italian colleagues. Danish historian Jens Chr. V. Johansen used *maleficium* as the word to describe the malevolent magic and 'blessings (*signen*) and conjuring (*manen*)' about the healing kind. In her studies on the trials in eastern Jutland, Merete Birkelund used the terms 'witchcraft' (*trolddom*) and white magic (*hvid magi*).[266] With the Witchcraft Regulation of 1617, Danish law introduced the two terms 'secret arts' and 'the true witches' to describe witchcraft. Danish legislation in this sense left less room for variation, since magical offences belonged to either one or the other category.

The inquisition's theologically based condemnation of witchcraft has led scholars to attempt various forms of classification for witchcraft. In his examination of the witch cases of the Siena Tribunal, the Italian historian Oscar di Simplicio has applied *il quadro generale* (the general frame) consisting of (1) love magic (*magia amatoria*), (2) divination (*magia divinatoria*), (3) healing magic (*magia terapeutica*) and (4) invocations of the Devil (*invocazione del demonio*).[267] The category he calls 'healing magic' is identical with the category applied in this study. The analysis of the Orbetello cases suggests, however, that common people saw divination as way of acquiring knowledge magic, rather than realizing its theological implications. Di Simplicio's typology cannot be applied in this comparative study, since his categories work from the theological concepts of the inquisition, rather than attempting to focus on popular perceptions. In his categories Di Simplicio does not take the difference between the inquisitor and the people on trial into account. Instead, his four categories all express 'actions against the Christian faith' (*fatti contrari alle fede Cristiana*).[268] His categories are in line with the conclusions drawn by Tedeschi, who found that the inquisition regarded witchcraft as heresy and therefore 'a sin of the intellect', rather than physical actions with real consequences.[269] However, the judges and populace alike disregarded the physical outcome of magic, although for very different reasons. The people on trial did not question the material or physical outcome of magical rituals. A ritual might not result in the desired effect, because magical rituals could fail. This was not uncommon, and if so, the ritual simply had to be repeated or the setting changed. The absence of an effect did not mean that the magical rituals were ineffective. The inclusion of the popular perception of magical rituals means that placing invocations of the Devil as a separate category of magical offences is superfluous. To the inquisitor, obedience to the Devil was a religious offence, and it was the worst imaginable offence against the Christian faith. To early modern lay people the worst conceivable offence was the explicit intention to harm and harm being done. According to theologians, malevolent rituals included employing evil powers, provided by the Devil or demons, although the popular perception of the source of evil was less explicit as will be discussed further in chapter 8.

In the attempt to achieve an understanding of popular perceptions of witchcraft, a distinction between black and white magic, indicating evil and good, has often been applied. However, this has proven to be inadequate, certainly in studying the Roman inquisitorial cases.[270] Instead, denunciations regarding magical rituals submitted to the inquisitorial court in Orbetello can be divided into four categories, which will be elaborated below. The provincial court in Viborg was faced with only one kind of accusation, namely malevolent magic conducted by true witches. The cases do, however, reflect how a reputation for being a witch sometimes also included a reputation for performing various kinds of benevolent magic, that is, secret arts. Nevertheless, an accusation for benevolent magic usually occurred during the trial and was never a part of the initial accusation against a suspect. I have divided allegations that ended as accusations before the two courts into the following four categories: (1) healing magic, (2) love magic, (3) counter-magic and (4) malevolent magic.

(1) Healing magic included magical rituals aimed at curing what were regarded as natural diseases, in other words those not necessarily caused by witchcraft. Such rituals were denounced neither in northern Jutland nor Orbetello as a separate offence. The category is nevertheless important to include, since such magical rituals were subject to legal and theological prohibition, and since many performers of magical rituals offered services within all four categories.

(2) Rituals concerning one's love life were far the most common in Orbetello. Divination was usually practised for acquiring knowledge of one's future love life, but also for finding lost or stolen objects, and rituals of love magic were applied to manipulate or control the desired person. The cases

that came before the provincial court in Viborg also involved allegations of people attempting to gain something such as stealing someone's luck or good health, however this never involved love. The harm induced by the witch was often described as the witch stealing from her victim. For instance, to harm a cow's ability to produce milk was described as stealing one's 'fortune in milk' (*mælkelykke*), which meant ruining the cow's ability to produce milk.[271] In this sense, the accusations in the Danish cases were always referred to as malevolent and labelled *trolddom*. In Orbetello, practices of love magic were referred to as *sortilegio*.

(3) Both the inquisitor in Orbetello and the provincial judges in Viborg were confronted with cases of counter-magic. Such allegations included various rituals performed in order to lift a malevolent spell. The symptoms of bewitchment were usually sudden, coming in the form of an inexplicable illness to humans or livestock, and, especially in the Danish cases, the accuser was always able to link the illness to a threat of evil uttered by the suspected witch. In both courts, allegations of counter-magic only appeared if the suspect had already been accused of practising other and explicitly malevolent kinds of magic.

(4) At the most severe end of the spectrum were the malevolent spells referred to by witnesses and accused in Italian cases as *fattura* and in the Danish cases as *forgøre(-lse)*. The courts and the populace did not disagree about these offences. It was obvious to everyone that malevolent witchcraft should be punished.

Love magic: an Italian specialty?

The many denunciations of love magic in Orbetello confirm the general picture of the Italian inquisitorial trials. Meeting the requirements of the inquisitorial manuals and the theological doctrines, the Roman inquisitors found it crucial to prosecute love magic. The court records of Orbetello also reflect a reality in which the common people and not the inquisitors initiated these cases. When denunciations of people who had used magical rituals to acquire romantic bliss were received, common people adhered, at least on the surface, to the inquisitor's prohibition against magical rituals. The purpose of denouncing practitioners of love magic was more complicated, however. The inhabitants of Orbetello had an ambiguous attitude towards the practice of this kind of magical ritual. To the inquisitor, love magic was a violation of the doctrine of free will. To ordinary people, what determined the nature of the magic was the intention behind the magical ritual, that is, whether it should be regarded as good or evil.[272] It may appear as a paradox that magical rituals to obtain love and marriage were so frequently practised and at the same time frowned upon. Marriages that were reputed to have been possible only due to love magic were the talk of the town. This is reflected in the references made by witnesses to marriages reported to have come about because of magical rituals. The majority of those accused of love magic were women who belonged to the lower orders of society. This may also have contributed significantly to the negative attitude towards love magic. On this matter Orbetello can be compared to Venice and Modena half a century earlier. Here the most experienced practitioners of love magic were full-time prostitutes or simply women engaging in sexual relationships outside marriage.[273] In Orbetello, the women accused of love magic would distribute their magical rituals, and the majority of those consulting them were single women of lowly estate. To contemporaries there was nothing sophisticated or praiseworthy about using magical rituals to get a man to offer marriage. To the women of Orbetello it seems to have been regarded as a last resort, when every 'traditional' option had been tried. In addition, the women who offered such magical services were often labelled wicked women,[274] which would only have enhanced the negative aspect of love magic.

Most of those denounced for magical practices in Orbetello had attended mass, had confessed and taken communion and generally thought of themselves as good Christians; they declared as much on numerous occasions. Nevertheless, their magical activities clearly went against the directions of the Church. Many performers of love magic apparently believed that this was not sinful *per se*; or rather they only considered some kinds of love magic grave. The people on trial express a perception of sin as something that could be mitigated through the use of prayers, images of saints, medallions and other objects related to the Church and to the divine. Still, the rituals practised in Orbetello all contained additional elements that could not be related directly to the Church. Some examples were rituals using charms and prayers attributed to the stars, forbidden words, urine or other bodily fluids. The Danish trials do not hold much evidence of ritualized magic. When rituals were described in detail, they were similar to the Italian ones in being a combination of Christian symbols and practices with no direct links to the Church.[275] In Orbetello, the general perception of love magic as something likely to cause harm and to be sinful is repeatedly expressed by witnesses. To the people in the court records, it was the physical outcome of a magical ritual combined with the intention behind it that determined whether or not the ritual was regarded as maleficent. If love magic was so widely practised, it must be assumed that it was not considered unduly or exclusively harmful. The common opinion would have been that love magic was to some extent harmful, but as long as the ritual did not inflict *visible* signs of damage, common people could argue that it had a *beneficial* consequence at least for one of the parties involved. For someone to be given the opportunity to marry the one they loved was, at least from the individual's own perspective, both positive and beneficial.

However, envy between women most likely played a part as well. Mary O'Neil has argued that in Modena love magic was looked down upon by the man in the street, in that it could be used to break with the social hierarchy of local society.[276] A similar view existed among the inhabitants of Orbetello. The trial records do not contain clear examples of love magic being used by women to marry into wealthy families. Still, from the court records it can be difficult to establish the social status of the men being pursued, since it is not always revealed.[277] The argument of envy must, therefore, be supported through the evidence of the status of women performing love magic. Many of these women belonged to the lowest social layers of society, and to them marriage was preferred whatever the social status of a potential husband might be. Although the women of Orbetello used terms like 'affection' and 'love' to justify their use of love magic, marriage was practically the only way that a woman of lower rank could achieve any kind of social status, even when her husband, too, was poor.

The denunciations found in Orbetello allow us to assert that the populace did not automatically condemn the practice of magical rituals in order to obtain marriage or love, since neither visible or physical harm was inflicted on people or livestock. The significance of the absence of physical damage overrides, then, concerns regarding the sinful nature of love magic. In other words, it seems that the people of Orbetello were pragmatic and more concerned with coping economically in their daily life. The other side of this coin was the idea that when a woman did, in fact, acquire a husband through love magic, there would be one husband fewer for those women who adopted an honest approach. Like other resources in life, love and a husband were limited goods.

The practice of love magic was mostly aimed at getting a certain person to propose marriage. Sometimes ill will became a dominant feature in the ritual, and love magic was practised for the purpose of eliminating a rival. In these incidents love magic moved from magic for personal gain to become malevolent magic. When this took place, the people of Orbetello referred to the magical ritual as a *fattura*. In these cases, the desired person was already spoken for and could only be made available to marry anew by getting rid of the spouse. The one purpose of a *fattura* was to cause harm, which also made it an effective means of revenge. The *fattura* could be used to affect the victim's love life by making men impotent and women infertile. The protocols of Orbetello only contain few examples of this.

The Danish trials do not contain many accusations of love magic, which makes it difficult to determine how the offence was regarded. However, the idea that one could gain something (or somebody) by means of magic appears commonly and the term 'gain fortune in' is found in a number of variations, such as milk fortune, butter fortune and beer-brewing fortune. Henningsen lists an example where a mayor was reputed to have the luck of seven men, which as a natural consequence led to the belief that seven men would be walking around with no luck. When one person had too much luck or too much fortune, it meant that there were others who would have less.[278]

As already mentioned, the Danish cases were characterized by accusations of malevolent magic, and this element was evident in all the cases. Cases for love magic in Denmark were characterized by the elimination of a rival or the loss of fertility. There were only a few cases of impotence caused by witchcraft in Orbetello, one of them being against Madalena di Maura. She had allegedly made her married lover impotent in revenge for him not taking responsibility for their two illegitimate children. In Denmark too, only a few cases dealt with impotence.[279]

Reputed to be a witch

To focus on the intention behind the use of magic is to see an emerging pattern of the motives behind the allegations in northern Jutland and Orbetello. Three factors were predominant. Ordinary people estimated the gravity of the offence from the *intention*, the *physical act/ritual* and from the *outcome*. A fourth factor that contributed to a denunciation/accusation was a *reputation* for being a witch. The significance of the reputation was evident in Orbetello as well as in northern Jutland.

Oscar Di Simplicio introduces the term *maturazione dei dubbi*, which translates more or less as 'maturation of suspicion', about the process that took place when a reputation for being a witch was under construction.[280] This expression refers to the gradual establishment of such a reputation to the point where to those around them conditions and episodes are increasingly seen as indications of witchcraft. Di Simplicio points to the existence of numerous examples of growing reputations for being a witch in the inquisitorial protocols. This can also be detected in the Orbetello cases. The personality of a suspect and the future course of events were crucial to whether or not the reputation would catch on. If the person was well liked and was not further involved in the misfortunes of others, then a reputation would be starved of nourishment, before it could take hold among the co-villagers. For less popular individuals, it would usually only take a few suspicious episodes before the reputation for being a witch had became established. If the suspect had already been imprisoned once, it would serve as a strong indication of the reputation being true. The majority of the people denounced in Orbetello did not have a consolidated reputation for being a witch, meaning that their reputation did not go back for years. Instead, they had a recently formed reputation. It was the repeated course of actions that would distinguish a potential reputation from a well-established one.

The chronology of the Orbetello cases clearly shows how the most serious cases took place in the first 18 months after the inquisitor's arrival and the issuing of the edict of faith. Only these court records contain cases of people with a solid reputation for practising witchcraft. After the first 18 months it seems that the most professional sorceresses had been prosecuted and from then on cases were only against those who had practised magical rituals once or a few times. It could be argued that the decision as to whether or not a case should be pursued rested with the inquisitor alone, but there are strong indications that the inquisitor did not need to track down possible suspects himself, since the inhabitants of the town themselves were only too ready to denounce their neighbours. The cases in Orbetello were almost all initiated by a *sponte comparente* testimony. The people of Orbetello apparently had no compunction in complying with the inquisition's demands of informing against every practitioner of magical rituals, and not surprisingly those most notorious were first in line. All extensive trials were characterized by a large number of denunciations. This has to be seen as a reflection of how well established the suspect's reputation was for being a witch. The denunciations of Orbetello indicate that it was not only people suffering from solid reputations of witchcraft who were at risk of being denounced to the inquisitor. People with a recently established or poor reputation were equally at risk.[281]

Reputation played a key role in witchcraft cases in Orbetello as well as northern Jutland. The Danish cases would always record whether a suspect had a reputation and often also details about when and why that reputation may have originated. When details were put forward they revealed how a reputation could normally be traced back to an accusation made by a convicted witch. Typically, such allegations were made several years before, in one case more than 40 years before the case, and they tended to accumulate if new incidents occurred, compare Di Simplicio's *maturazione dei dubbi*. The Danish judges always noted in the sentence if and for how long the person on trial had been reputed to be a witch even though the reputation, according to the Recess of 1547, was not enough to sentence a person. The picture from Orbetello is a little different in that people on trial and witnesses rarely specified the age of the reputation, but simply stated that it was *pubblica voce e fama* (publicly known) that the suspect knew about witchcraft. The examination of a reputation for being a witch and its origin suggests that greater value was attributed to such a reputation by the Danish judges than by the Roman inquisitor in Orbetello – and this despite the fact that the reputation could not be formally included in the evidence in the Danish cases. To the inquisitor in Orbetello, the reputation remained the factor that initiated a case, while it appears that it was the testimony of the suspect that played the decisive role in the outcome of the case. The denunciations revealed the suspect's reputation, but the vital factor was the suspect's plea to the accusations. In the Italian cases the reputation was primarily significant to witnesses, in the sense that it was used as a sort of endorsement for making the denunciation in the first place. It is, however, remarkable that the inquisitor would at no point decide to investigate the origins of the reputation. The judicial treatment of the reputation for being a witch obviously differed from inquisitorial court to lay court, but among ordinary people in both Italy and Denmark a person's reputation was an essential element in the motive for initiating a case.

One witch reveals the other

In Danish cases the suspects commonly stated that they had been reputed to be witches ever since they had been denounced (*udlagt*) by a convicted witch. As mentioned in chapter 4, it was standard procedure in Danish trials to have the witch cross-examined under torture after a guilty verdict. When so interrogated, she often revealed the names of others, who she would claim had participated in particular events. As a consequence, the majority of the suspects before the provincial judges in Viborg could give details as to when and why they had acquired their reputation. Sometimes these testimonies included accusations that led to the initiation of a trial, although according to the Kalundborg Recess, denunciations could not stand as evidence alone. Judicially they were merely circumstantial. Denunciations were not legally institutionalized in the same way in the Roman Inquisition. It can be argued that the procedures of the cases before the inquisition excluded denunciation as decisive evidence, seeing that the inquisitor could not pass a sentence on a person without first having investigated the case and having found compelling evidence. It was always exclusively the decision of the inquisitor whether a person should be investigated and convicted. This would have been the main reason why none of the suspects in Orbetello was charged and convicted purely on the basis of a denunciation.[282] Suspects, the accused and the convicted of Orbetello would, however, frequently denounce each other, yet, the inquisitor's investigation and the definition of witchcraft as a heresy ensured that the cases were far from decided in advance.

In Danish research the term 'chain of denunciations' (*udlæggelseskæde*) is well known.[283] A similar term can be applied to the interconnected cases in Orbetello, which will be discussed below. Chains of denunciations were characterized by individuals accusing others in their own village or the neighbouring village of being co-conspirators. The Danish denunciations usually included information about when and where the malevolent deed had been committed or the threats had been pronounced. This was also the case in Orbetello, where those denounced knew each other and had exchanged magical rituals. The aim of the following section is to compare the nature of the denunciations made in Orbetello to two groups of accused in northern Jutland.

A tense atmosphere must have prevailed among the practitioners of magic in Orbetello in 1649. Judging by the edict issued by the inquisitor on his arrival, the group of women, notorious for their regular practice of magical rituals, must have been aware that they were at risk of being accused. The content of these cases will be dealt with in the following chapters and for now the string of denunciations is merely presented. Pollonia di Gallo was one of the first to be denounced, and her case proves the special scenario that must have been played out in the town after the arrival of the inquisitor.[284] The women in the chain of denunciations in Orbetello denounced each other as shown below (Table 6.1). The first denunciation of Pollonia di Gallo was received on 20 March 1649, which was almost a month before she was arrested. A few days later one of the key witnesses in the case, Faustina di Leusta, appeared voluntarily before the inquisitor. Her denunciation concerned Pollonia di Gallo and two other women, namely Mensola di Tiracoscia and Lucida di Canino.[285] A further five days later, 28 March, the same Lucida di Canino appeared before inquisitor Pedrosa to inform on Pollonia.[286] Faustina di Leusta, Mensola di Tiracoscia and Lucida di Canino were eventually sentenced by the inquisition. Pollonia di Gallo was one of the main characters in the chain of denunciations in Orbetello in 1649–1650. Pollonia was placed before the inquisitor for the first time on 17 April 1649.[287] During the course of her trial, she was interrogated four times and she managed to denounce five women, all of whom were subsequently sentenced.[288]

Table 6.1 Linked cases in Orbetello 1649–1650

Name	Year	Denounced by	Denounces	Sentence
Mensola di Tiracoscia	1649	• Pollonia di Gallo • Lucida di Canino • Faustina di Leusta • Agata di Camillo • Lucia di Tiracoscia	• Pollonia di Gallo • Lucida di Canino • Lucia di Tiracoscia	Convicted
Pollonia di Gallo	1649	• Mensola di Tiracoscia • Lucida di Canino • Faustina di Leusta • Agata di Camillo • Lucia di Tiracoscia	• Mensola di Tiracoscia • Lucida di Canino • Faustina di Leusta • Agata di Camillo • Lucia di Tiracoscia	Convicted
Lucida di Canino	1649	• Mensola di Tiracoscia • Pollonia di Gallo • Faustina di Leusta • Agata di Camillo • Lucia di Tiracoscia	• Mensola di Tiracoscia • Pollonia di Gallo • Faustina di Leusta • Agata di Camillo • Lucia di Tiracoscia	Convicted
Faustina di Leusta	1649	• Pollonia di Gallo • Lucida di Canino	• Mensola di Tiracoscia • Pollonia di Gallo • Lucida di Canino	Convicted
Agata di Camillo	1649 1650	• Pollonia di Gallo • Lucida di Canino	• Mensola di Tiracoscia • Pollonia di Gallo • Lucida di Canino	Convicted
Lucia di Tiracoscia	1650	• Mensola di Tiracoscia • Pollonia di Gallo • Lucida di Canino	• Mensola di Tiracoscia • Pollonia di Gallo • Lucida di Canino	Convicted

Witchcraft societies in northern Jutland

Although Danish legislation determined that denunciations (*udlæggelser*) could not serve as evidence, they were common in Danish witch trials, and they were often incorporated in the judges' explanation of the sentence. Unlike in Italian cases, Danish denunciations were often delivered under torture. Sometimes the convicted witch would denounce members of her own family, most often a daughter or a mother, or another person whom she knew socially. However, most commonly, the witch would give up names of those already reputed to be witches or in other ways unpopular in local society. In this sense the denunciations could easily accumulate, as is supported by the frequent withdrawals of denunciations immediately before execution.[289]

In northern Jutland denunciations usually took place between people in a limited local area, who would denounce each other for malevolent witchcraft, and so create a chain of denunciations. These testimonies were usually standardized descriptions of how the witch in the company of other witches had been out with their 'boys'[290] to cast evil on people, and the judges would then question the witch about the names of the other witches present. Examples of this are legion; one is found south-east of Aalborg in the area of Storvorde-Sejlflod (see Table 6.2), where Johanne Pedersdatter from Sejlflod was convicted of witchcraft in 1620.[291] Before she was executed, Johanne denounced two other women from the neighbouring villages, Storvorde and Romdrup, both between two and five kilometres distant.[292] The woman from Storvorde, Else Jacobsdatter, then denounced Else Lauritzdatter, who lived in Sejlflod.[293] Else Jacobsdatter and Else Lauritzdatter were both convicted of being 'true witches'.[294] Johanne Pedersdatter had also denounced Anne Jensdatter from Romdrup, but the provincial judges acquitted Anne. They did not believe that there was enough evidence to

Table 6.2   The denunciations from Storvorde-Sejlflod, 1620–1637

Name	Year	Denounced by	Denounces	Sentence
Johanne Pedersdatter	1620		• Anne Jensdatter • Else Jacobsdatter	Convicted
Else Jacobsdatter	1620	• Johanne Pedersdatter	• Else Lauritzdatter • Kerstin Thamisdatter	Convicted
Else Lauritzdatter	1620	• Else Jacobsdatter		Convicted
Anne Jensdatter	1620	• Johanne Pedersdatter		Acquitted
Kerstin Thamisdatter	1634 1637	• Else Jacobsdatter		Acquitted

support a conviction. Fourteen years later, in 1634, yet another woman from Storvorde, Kerstin Thamisdatter, was accused of witchcraft. The accusation against her concerned some spoiled milk. The case against Kerstin ended in acquittal at the provincial court. Before this Kerstin had disclosed that she had been denounced by Else Jacobsdatter back in the 1620s, and that ever since she had borne a reputation for being a witch.

Aalborg forms the basis of an exceptional series of cases conducted at the provincial court in Viborg (see Table 6.3). These were extraordinary firstly because those involved were accused of practising explicit diabolic witchcraft in the house of one of the accused, and the trials bear elements of ritualized witchcraft uncommon for a Danish context, but also because the cases culminated with the execution of the noble woman, Christenze Kruckow.[295] These interlinked trials and denunciations illustrate just how easily a fire could spread from just a few sparks.

These cases against a total of nine people from Aalborg took their course over several years. The chain of events started with the accusation of Maren Nielsdatter Knepis in 1612 and continued for nine years until the King's Supreme Court (*Kongens Retterting*) confirmed the sentence on Christenze Kruckow. The accusations were serious, as the group was accused for having practised witchcraft collectively and of a particularly malevolent nature. To this purpose one of the women, Metter Pedersdatter, had 'borne' a wax child, which was later 'delivered' by Maren Nielsdatter Knepis.[296]

Despite the long period of time, the accusations against all of the suspects related to collective witchcraft with the explicit intention of harm, and all of the suspicions could be led back to one particular St. Lucia night in 1611.[297] There is, however, an interesting difference between the three cases from 1612 and the cases from 1620. In 1612 Maren Nielsdatter Knepis and Mette Pedersdatter confessed to having been in the same society of witches, and they claimed that Apelone Ibsdatter was also a member of their group. Even though none of the three had had a reputation for being a witch before the accusation, all of them ended up being convicted both at the town court and the provincial court.[298] When the case was brought to court once again, it was as an accusation against Jens Andersen and his wife in 1620. Apelone Ibsdatter had denounced them both. The provincial court in Viborg deemed the denunciations groundless and a later denunciation of Jens Andersen's wife was withdrawn.[299] The remaining four cases were directly related to the first cases from 1612. From Figure 6.3 it appears that four women were denounced by at least one of the accused from 1612. Further accusations were added from 1612 to 1620, and not until 1619 did Christenze Kruckow come under suspicion for having participated in that episode of nocturnal witchcraft back in 1612. Suddenly it occurred to some of those accused of attending the 'birth' of the wax child in 1612 that Christenze had also been present.

As regards to the reputation for being a witch, several people testified that Maren Knepis was known to bicker and quarrel with others, but neither she

Table 6.3 Denunciations amongst the witches of Aalborg, 1612–1620

Name	Year	Denounced by	Denounces	Sentence
Maren Nielsdatter Knepis	1612		• Mette Pedersdatter • Apelone Ibsdatter • Maren Pedersdatter	Convicted
Mette Pedersdatter	1612	• Maren Nielsdatter Knepis	• Apelone Ibsdatter • Maren Pedersdatter	Convicted
Apelone Ibsdatter	1612	• Maren Nielsdatter Knepis (withdrawn) • Mette Pedersdatter	• Jens Andersen and wife • Dorete Jensdatter • Ellen Nielsdatter • Christenze Kruckow	Convicted
Jens Andersen and wife	1620	• Apelone Ibsdatter		Acquitted
Maren Pedersdatter	1620	• Maren Nielsdatter Knepis • Merete Pedersdatter • Apelone Ibsdatter	• Mette Pedersdatter • Apelone Ibsdatter • Jens Andersen's wife (withdrawn) • Dorete Jensdatter • Ellen Nielsdatter • Christenze Kruckow	Convicted
Dorete Jensdatter	1620	• Apelone Ibsdatter (withdrawn) • Maren Pedersdatter	• Maren Jensdatter Knepis	Convicted
Ellen Nielsdatter	1620	• Apelone Ibsdatter (withdrawn) • Maren Pedersdatter	• Maren Nielldatter Knepis • Apelone Ibsdatter • Dorete Jensdatter • Christenze Kruckow	Convicted
Christenze Kruckow	1620-1621	• Apelone Ibsdatter • Maren Pedersdatter • Ellen Nielsdatter		Convicted

nor Mette Pedersdatter was reputed to be a witch before their trials.[300] In all four cases from 1620 the accused stated that ever since the executions of Maren Knepis and Mette Pedersdatter they had had the reputation for being witches. In other words, their poor reputations were induced by the denunciations of the two convicted witches.

The testimonies that eventually led to the formal accusation in 1620 related to the participation of all four people in the evil night-time deeds at Maren Knepis' house in 1612. Christenze Kruckow had once previously been accused of witchcraft on Funen – in 1592 – but back then she had avoided a conviction. In 1612 there had been no mention of Christenze, but by 1619 several witnesses were claiming that she was in fact the leader of the group, which had gathered with evil intentions that St. Lucia night in 1611. In addition, the fact that the person now accusing Christenze of having put a spell on his wife to make her mad (*vanvittig*), was none other than the clergyman, David Jensen Klyne, only made matters worse for Christenze. The years had apparently not erased suspicions that a society of witches had existed in 1612, and now the renewed accusations only fuelled the flames.

Aalborg and Orbetello, then, each saw a group of interrelated cases of women who were accused and convicted of witchcraft. However, whereas the cases in Aalborg originated from one central episode, which was the birth of the wax child on St. Lucia night in 1611, the Italian denunciations were the consequence of the inquisitor's arrival and the edict of faith.[301] When the trials against Pollonia di Gallo et al. commenced, it quickly surfaced that several of the accused commonly practised several kinds of witchcraft. Lucida di Canino and Pollonia di Gallo in particular had shared their diabolical experiments to a great extent. The magical activities of Lucida and Pollonia will be explored further in the following chapters. A similar pattern can be detected in Aalborg. The accusations of a group of witches here showed how the reputation of being a witch accumulated in the years following the executions in 1612.

In Italy, as in Denmark, to be denounced or have the reputation for being a witch must be viewed as related to the concept of honour.[302] As will be discussed in chapter 9, a good reputation was crucial when defending oneself in court. The link is implied by the Copenhagen Recess, which prescribed that the testimonies of dishonourable (*uediske*) persons could not be relied on in court. In Denmark denunciations (*udlæggelser*) from a convicted witch could be included or even lead to the opening of a case, but a formal accuser was needed to bring the proceedings further and to formally charge the suspect. The protocols show that in these cases usually no one appeared formally to accuse the suspect and therefore the denunciation was dismissed. When this dismissal took place, the suspect could consider her name cleared, an outcome which had a bearing on any possible future accusation.[303] The case of Sidsel Christens is a good example of the negative consequences and the strain that often followed a denunciation. Sidsel was denounced for the first time seven years before being sentenced. This denunciation had led to the fight between Sidsel and her husband, and the husband's attempt to clear her name. This is evident from the account of Sidsel's husband going on the offensive and trying to take a parish witness (*sognevidne*) to testify to her good name. The man who later conducted the trials against her, a co-villager Mikkel Christensen, disallowed the attempt. When Mikkel himself eventually charged Sidsel with witchcraft, he could present two denunciations from convicted witches, stating that it was common knowledge that Sidsel was reputed to be a witch supported this. To legally restore one's honour, a person could also initiate a case of defamation. In these trials, the court could legally declare a rumour or a denunciation invalid, and the person's honour would legally be restored.[304]

7
From allegation to formal accusation

The signs of witchcraft

The Danish and the Italian trials alike usually began by someone feeling offended by the suspected person. It is the aim of this chapter to explore more thoroughly the content of the allegations of witchcraft that were submitted to the courts, then to identify the kind of behaviour associated with them. Focus in this chapter will, therefore, be especially on the initial phase of an inquisitorial trial, the denunciation, and on the allegations found in testimonies in the Danish trials. The intention is a close reading of the narratives surrounding the suspect, in order to establish what eventually led to a formal accusation. The narratives in denunciations and accusations tell us about the limits of socially acceptable behaviour and what kinds of behaviour contributed to raising suspicions. Common to both Italian and Danish cases is that perceptions of witchcraft were closely linked to norms and transgressions of social and moral behaviour.

The denunciations in the Orbetello trials reflect a society in which the practice of magical rituals and witchcraft was widespread and at the same time ambiguous; and a population not hesitating to report each other to an outside authority.[305] If people had not themselves performed such rituals, they would know of a friend or neighbour who had. Sometimes people would testify about rumours of events brought about by magical rituals, most commonly marriage, illness or death. According to their testimonies many spectators were exposed to the practice of forbidden rituals, usually as part of a gathering, in which individuals had performed witchcraft in front of the rest of the group. Others had witnessed episodes almost by accident, in which people had been behaving in strange ways, typically at night. Covert and secretive behaviour would always provoke suspicion. For instance, a witness who saw through her window Virginia di Leandro leaving her house at night, had automatically assumed that Virginia was on her way to practise witchcraft. Walking about outside in the darkness at a time when street-lighting was more or less non-existent aroused suspicion.

Similar preconceptions are to be found in Danish cases; for instance if someone were to walk around the house of another person without an obvious
reason, or if they were to enter a house and then leave again uttering no
form of greeting.[306]

Love magic: *Magia ad amorem, maleficium ad amorem*

It was distinctive of the Orbetello cases that the majority of those practising
love magic or consulting love magicians did so with marriage in mind. These
marriage seekers were often already involved in a sexual relationship with
the chosen person. All of them were women, and they were typically motivated by the lover having given a promise of marriage that he had yet to
fulfil or, even worse, by the lover having simply withdrawn his promise.[307]
Even in 17th century Orbetello, marriage was used as bait to get a woman to
engage in a sexual relationship. Virginia di Leandro had shared her bed with
her lover, Carlo di Luca Antonio, for several years without the two having
been officially married. Carlo had promised to make Virginia an honourable
woman, but his proposal remained unfulfilled, and Virginia had resorted to
dealing with this herself by means of magic.

The protocols include a number of similar episodes. One other example
is found in the trial of the priest Stefano Tommei. From the testimony of
a witness the inquisitor learned how the niece of the accused, Lelia, had
participated in witchcraft.[308] It is tempting to present this story as a classic
tale of honour blighted. Young, apparently in love and believing that he
would marry her, Lelia had agreed to a sexual relationship with friar (*frate*)
Bernardino.[309] Bernardino had afterwards let her down by withdrawing the
promise. Lelia explained to the inquisitor that she had been very much in
love with Bernardino and that he had truly promised to marry her. When
he chose to break his promise, Lelia had been mortified at the disgrace she
had inflicted on her family. She had then resorted to witchcraft, which
would both make the *frate* marry her and restore the good reputation of
her family. Lelia had complained to her neighbour Girolama di Agnolieri,
and this woman had offered her advice. Girolama referred Lelia to the girl's
own uncle, the priest Stefano Tommei, who according to Girolama, knew
of a certain magical ritual that would get Bernardino to keep his promise.
Lelia had then called on Stefano, and together they had practised a magical
ritual, in which among other things Stefano had read aloud from a secret
book, the Book of St. Daniel (*libro di S. Daniello*). During this Lelia, however,
had felt uneasy about the arrangement, and when the Devil's name had
first appeared in the ritual, she had backed out of it. Afterwards, she told
the inquisitor, she had stolen the book and burnt it, much to the frustration
of Stefano.

As stated in the previous chapter, the few trials that involve allegations of
love magic in the Danish records are characterised by a different destructive

quality. The cases might more suitably belong in the category of malevolent witchcraft, seeing that the witch had often stolen the potency from a man or eliminated an opponent.[310] A single trial from Vendsyssel contains an allegation relating to the suspect wanting to obtain fortune in love (*kær-lighedslykke*). Jahan Jensdatter was rumoured to be a witch, and in 1621 she was accused of being a 'true witch'.[311] The accusations against her were of the traditional kind: that is, no talk of magical rituals but with plenty of spoken threats with the Devil. Jahan had been accused of threatening others with evil, after which evil had occurred. A witness stated that after a quarrel with Jahan, her cows had become infertile. It was entirely reasonable that the witness believed Jahan to be behind this, since Jahan was rumoured to be a witch, and her kind were known to take revenge on their enemies. In terms of the accusation of love magic, Jahan was believed to have offered *kærlighedslykke* to a man in exchange for money. At the manor court Jahan was convicted of being a true witch, and it was put about that she had a solid reputation for being a witch. In her second trial at the provincial court in Viborg, no one stepped forward to publicly accuse Jahan in front of the judges. Jahan herself denied being a witch, although she confessed to being able to bless (*signe*). Consequently she was sentenced by the provincial court to lose her possessions and to be banished from the country.

Unrequited love: the trial of Francesca di Rosata

In Orbetello, when love magic was not directly aimed at attaining marital status, the cases concerned people seeking to win the favour of the opposite sex. Generally the trials from Orbetello reflect a population who had pretty relaxed attitudes towards the Church's pronouncements on sexual abstinence outside marriage. This is reflected in the trial of Francesca di Rosata, who was accused of having practised love magic in order to prevent her lover losing interest in her. The trial, with its intricacies, is a unique case in the court records of Orbetello. In addition to the case against Francesca, the protocols also include two short cases against Francesca's lover, Pasquale Pesci, as well as a collection of denunciations of Francesca's husband, Francesco Bocchino. In trials like these, the protocols offer fascinating examples of a love triangle, as it was played out in a small Italian garrison town around 1650.[312]

Francesca told the inquisitor that she had had an affair with the young Pasquale Pesci for some time. Pasquale was her husband's assistant, and during her trial she revealed the lengths to which she had gone to maintain her relationships both with her lover and with her husband. Nothing suggested that Francesca wanted to get out of her *sancto matrimonio* with Francesco Bocchino, but she desperately wanted the young Pasquale to continue courting her. All her efforts came to nought and she ended up coming before inquisitor Pedrosa. Angela, a maid in the service of Francesca and her husband, was the first to report Francesca to the inquisitor. Angela had awakened late one night and had, probably through her window, seen Francesca perform an incantation and a special ritual. As part of the ritual Francesca had urinated into a kind of bowl (*pignatello*), and then carried this out onto the field. On that particular night Angela had spied on her, and she had followed Francesca to the field. When she reached it, Francesca had looked up at the sky and recited a prayer (*oratione*) to the stars, while holding the bowl of urine in her hands.

Francesca's magical activities of that night did not end there. Afterwards Angela had seen Francesca pull a piece of magnetic rock from a box. The two women must have spoken together about the incident, because according to Angela, Francesca had later stated that the magnet was to be used *ad effetto che li volesse bene* (to make someone want to love her).[313] Francesca wanted Pasquale to maintain his desire for her, so that he would continue their affair. She had explained to Angela that the magnetic rock was also meant to influence Francesco, so that he would not act violently towards her any more. Angela's knowledge of the powers of magnets seemed superficial, and she could neither explain where Francesca had got the magnet nor say whether it had been consecrated. Especially the consecration was of significance for the inquisitor to determine, since, if this was the case, it would imply explicit abuse of the sacrament. Angela could, however, add that Francesca mixed bits of crushed or powdered magnetic rock in her husband's soup, before it was served to him. The effect of the magnet thus came about through ingestion.

During her initial interrogation Francesca spoke of the magnetic rock herself. It would have come as no surprise to the inquisitor that her purpose was to keep Pasquale in her power. Rituals of love magic involving magnets were common and also described by Desiderio Scaglia in his *Prattica*.[314] It was the magnet's ability to attract objects that the magician believed could be transferred onto a human object. The magnet would be used to attract the opposite sex, often with the intention of marriage. In the case against Francesca, it was used both to secure the favour of the lover and to appease the husband's jealousy.

Francesca explained to the inquisitor that her husband was angry with her because of her relationship with her lover. The love triangle was apparently common knowledge amongst the dwellers of the town, and from the court records it is clear that it attracted the attention of the local community. Francesca had complained to a neighbour of the violence of her husband's reaction to her relationship with Pasquale, and apparently the spurned husband had not limited his temperamental outbursts to the home. A few days after Francesca had been taken into inquisitorial custody, a denunciation was delivered to inquisitor Pedrosa regarding a dramatic reaction evinced by Francesca's husband, Francesco Bocchino. According to the witness, a woman named Angela di Mugnarolo, a group of women had witnessed Francesco's rage. Angela di Mugnarolo had been to church to attend mass with the other women when a young girl, referred to as *la Tosa*, came running towards them, screaming. Behind her on horseback and at a gallop came Francesco Bocchino, shouting and brandishing a clutch of sticks. Angela clearly found the incident dramatic, and she explained that the young girl had come into the church screaming that Francesco Bocchino was going to kill her.

What happened after this is not clear, as Angela di Mugnarolo and the group of women failed to get an explanation for Francesco Bocchino's behaviour towards this girl. Angela di Mugnarolo seemed to be distraught, but the case was not pursued further, and Francesco does not appear anywhere else in the inquisitorial protocols of Orbetello. As far as can be seen from the rest of the Orbetello records, Francesco Bocchino had only passing contact with the inquisition, and that was through the charges brought against his wife.[315]

The intricacies of this case did not end there, however. Francesca's lover, Pasquale Pesci, was twice summoned before the inquisitor. The first time was shortly after Francesca had been taken into custody, and a rumour apparently circulated in the town that Pasquale intended to free her from gaol. Having been informed by a friar that the inquisitor had learned of Pasquale's plans, a woman by the name of Francesca di Paola approached the inquisitor demanding that Pasquale's mother and cousin be incarcerated. Why it was the two women and not Pasquale himself who were to be arrested, the protocol does not reveal. Francesca di Paola had approached the inquisitor to put the rumour to rest. According to her there was no truth in the story. The inquisitor called on Pasquale's mother, Barbara Pesci, who swore that she knew nothing of her son's planned escapade. She did, however, state that she suspected Pasquale of having brought food to the incarcerated Francesca. When Pasquale himself was questioned, he confirmed the delivery of food but justified it by saying that he had only done so, because he felt compelled to help Francesca while she was in prison.

The flow of rumours did not have any judicial consequences for Pasquale. He was never formally charged, and the case appears to have been closed. Yet a couple of months later it resumes, when Pasquale was once again reported to the inquisitor. This time it was for having spoken to Francesca di Rosata, still languishing in prison.[316] The informant was one of Orbetello's prominent citizens, Carentione Carentioni, who had been riding by one day and seen Pasquale lying on the ground by the door to the prison. Under the door was a tiny hole, through which Pasquale was speaking to Francesca. Carentione Carentioni had asked Pasquale if he was not familiar with the severe penalties for talking to a prisoner of the inquisition. According to inquisitor Pedrosa, the penalty was excommunication and a fine of 10 *scudi*. Pasquale had denied any knowledge of such a penalty. When the inquisitor questioned Francesca on the matter, she admitted that this was not the first time that she had spoken to Pasquale during the time that she had been incarcerated. Back on the stand, Pasquale now acknowledged having spoken to Francesca on several occasions. He stated that he was aware of the excommunication, but not the fine. Once again Pasquale excused his actions by stating that he had only Francesca's well-being in mind and then added that he would pay the fine immediately.

Subsequent developments in the relationships between Francesca and her two men are unclear. As so often occurs in these accounts, we are not privy to the end of the story. Once an inquisitor had determined that no crime against faith had taken place, the notary stopped writing. The inquisitor's task had now been completed. And at the point at which the notary closes his book, there, too, must the historian conclude, their glimpse into the lives of these three people curtailed. Francesco Bocchino is not heard of again. The information on him may have led to a case through a secular court, but that makes no appearance in the inquisitorial protocols. On the reverse of the trial papers relating to Pasquale Pesci, the word *morto* (deceased) has been written. This was common practice in trials where the suspect died, but it is not possible to determine precisely when this information was noted. In the case of Pasquale it must have taken place after the case was closed, as the inquisitor's protocol tells us that only a couple of months passed before Pasquale was denounced to the inquisitor again, this time for blasphemous statements. That case did not lead to a conviction either.[317]

The trials against Francesca and her two men provide a unique insight into the workings of social relations in Orbetello, indicating, as they do, which actions were deemed to be commonly accepted. They make it clear on a number of occasions that the love life of the town dwellers did not belong to what we today would call the private sphere. While sexual relationships outside the *sancto matrimonio* may not have been officially sanctioned, it appears that they were common knowledge and that it would have been impossible to keep them secret.[318] The witnesses in the trials of Francesca and Pasquale all knew of their affair, and this was only confirmed by the description of the husband's violent behaviour in the church. These townspeople appear to have had a deep involvement in each other's daily lives, which to our eyes verges on prurience, and the constant generation of rumour was significant and played a decisive role in determining the cases that ended up on the desk of the inquisitor. This related not only to cases of witchcraft but also to cases of blasphemy and, as shown above, it could play a direct part in maintaining law and order, as witnessed by responses to Pasquale's plans to free his lover from incarceration.

Inappropriate love: the trial of Agata di Camillo

Agata di Camillo was one of the first to be accused after the arrival of the inquisitor. She was described by the inquisition as *meretrice*, meaning a prostitute or a woman of loose living, probably due to her sexual relationship with a priest named Stefano Benedetto.[319] It was Stefano's two sisters, Caterina and Solina di Benedetto, who denounced Agata for witchcraft (*sortilegio*[320]). One of the sisters had initially gone to see inquisitor Pedrosa to tell him that she knew of two wicked women, who had already been arrested by the inquisition.[321] In addition to this, the inquisitor had then been given the information about Agata di Camillo. It appears from the case that Stefano, the priest, had passed away a few months before the denunciations against Agata, and much to the grief of his sisters. In their testimonies the sisters described his death as unexpected, yet witnesses confirmed that Stefano had at times been in bed ill with fever. The sisters told the inquisitor that Agata had often been with their brother at night, and they suspected her of being involved in his death. According to the sisters, Agata had substantial knowledge of magical rituals, and this was confirmed by a couple of witnesses. Amongst them was the nephew of Stefano, Desiderio, who had explained that on several occasions he had seen Agata practise a kind of witchcraft where she invoked the stars, in fact, she even invoked the Devil. To put it simply, the sisters believed Agata to have applied love magic to maintain her lover's interest. Both were certain that Stefano had wanted to end the relationship with Agata. When Stefano then increasingly became the victim of fevers, they suspected Agata of having inflicted the illness in revenge. One of the sisters, Caterina, assured the inquisitor that this could be confirmed by another woman in town who had been accused of witchcraft, Pollonia di Gallo.

In her testimony the other sister, Solina, explained that Agata supposedly had bewitched Stefano with fever with the assistance of a certain Mensola di Tiracoscia. Why the assistance of Mensola di Tiracoscia should be of significance, will soon be revealed. Accusations of fatal witchcraft were a serious matter and by no means everyday fare for the inquisitor in Orbetello. A third witness in the case, the young boy Desiderio, confirmed the relationship between Agata and Stefano. He had frequently heard Agata shout at Stefano. On one occasion she was even thought to have threatened to set the Devil onto him.

These denunciations spent a considerable time on the inquisitor's desk before anything further happened in the case. The case was not resumed until nine months later. Agata was then put before the inquisitor, but she maintained her innocence, even under torture. Even though the allegations against her were serious, the accusation of having caused the death of her lover using witchcraft was dismissed. The reason for this was that Agata maintained her innocence throughout the trial and that Stefano's two sisters held a deep grudge against her. This had been confirmed by a witness. Although a woman accused of witchcraft, Pollonia di Gallo, had testified against Agata, her statement was discredited by their mutual enmity.[322] Maintaining her innocence and the mutual disputes between the parties involved resulted in the inquisitor only convicting Agata of using a forbidden prayer. She received the symbolic penalty of having to stand outside the church during mass, dressed in the robe of a heretic and holding a candle in her hand.[323]

Wicked women: opening the case of Pollonia di Gallo

Half a dozen trials from Orbetello stand out from the others both in size and substance. The longest of the trials fills approximately 500 pages and lasted more than seven years.[324] The inquisitor described these women as *meretrici*. Witnesses referred to the worst as *donne dalla mala vita*,[325] a derogatory term in popular use that described women considered to be of loose and dishonourable living. That these women had low moral and social status is confirmed by their names repeatedly appearing in a number of trials. The records make it clear that the most notorious practitioners of magic and witchcraft in Orbetello were Lucida di Canino and Pollonia di Gallo, as well as the old Mensola di Tiracoscia and her sister Deva. Mensola di Tiracoscia was the only person in the court records to be listed as *strega* (witch).[326]

Pollonia di Gallo has been briefly introduced in the above, when she denounced Agata di Camillo. The denunciation of Pollonia that set the ball in motion was received on 20 March 1649.[327] The 25-year-old Nicola di Felitio, who accused Pollonia of performing love magic on her behalf, delivered it. The aim had been to get Nicola's lover to keep his promise of marriage. The women had performed various rituals with the help of witchcraft remedies such as salt, nails and wax candles, and Pollonia had recited special prayers in certain ways, including the Lord's Prayer together with the name of the Devil.[328] The inquisitor's investigation quickly revealed that this case involved a woman who had a remarkably bad reputation and who had been practising numerous kinds of magic and witchcraft, especially love magic, both for the benefit of herself and others. Pollonia also passed her rituals on to her clients so they could practise them when she was unable to be present. In August 1649, following a trial that lasted nearly five months, the inquisitor sentenced Pollonia to be flogged through the streets of the town to the sound of fanfares and thereafter to be banished from Orbetello.[329]

In addition to witchcraft, her neighbours also suspected her of stealing money, a crime that did not come under the jurisdiction of the inquisition but which, as an allegation of dishonesty, could cast doubt on the person's character. Inquisitor Pedrosa therefore brought in several witnesses to determine the course of these events, including whether or not personal grudges played a part in the allegations.[330] To the inquisitor, the lifestyle of an individual was a reflection of how good a Christian he or she was. Pollonia was a *meretrice*, a woman of ill repute, possibly even a prostitute, though this is not clear. If in addition to this she was proven to be a thief, she could be regarded as even more dishonest. This gave the stolen money an indirect influence on the outcome of the trial in the sense that several of the witnesses could testify to both witchcraft and theft. According to one of the witnesses, Catherina di Leonardo, Pollonia had attempted to deflect guilt from herself by accusing a certain Francesca di Niccolò Semplice of the theft. Francesca was subsequently summoned for questioning. Francesca denied any knowledge of the theft and, not surprisingly, went on the offensive by telling the inquisitor that on a number of occasions she had seen Pollonia practise witchcraft. Another witness, Catherina di Giuliano, was able to recount in detail how this Francesca di Niccolo Semplice had approached Pollonia at Catherina's one evening. According to Catherina, the intention was to get Pollonia to apply love magic with the aim of conjuring from the young Pietro di Biago Salazzaro a proposal of marriage for Francesca, which that young man seemed reluctant to make of his own volition.

Inquisitor Pedrosa lacked neither witnesses nor allegations against Pollonia di Gallo.[331] Francesca di Niccolo Semplice was far from the only person who had sought help from Pollonia. Her area of expertise seems to have been the performance of 'magical first-aid' for the love lives of women, either by practising such love magic with the client or by passing on the ritual for the client to practise on her own. Marriage was often the aim, but sometimes love magic had been applied solely to sustain a lover's interest.

People in Orbetello must have had faith in the effect of Pollonia's rituals, since several witnesses referred to marriages said to have been brought about through Pollonia's witchcraft. If Pollonia's rituals for love magic produced results, however, their benefits seem to have been reserved chiefly for her clients. She continued to make use of the forbidden rituals herself, and they did not seem to produce the desired effect. Her own lover was called Pietro, and, from the accounts in the trials, it does not seem he had any intention of making Pollonia an honourable woman. One witness, Faustina di Leusta, explained how she had met Pollonia one day and been told that Pollonia was on her way 'in the name of the Devil [to] buy Pietro's heart'.[332] Faustina had even observed how Pollonia had attempted to 'bind' (*stringere*) Pietro to her, again in the name of the Devil. She had then gone on to make an incantation (*incantesimo*[333]), which is best translated as 'Earth, Mother Earth, let Pietro's heart be consumed by you [...] so that he cannot walk about, neither drink nor eat, if he does not come to find me.'[334]

The core of the incantation was that Pietro would not find peace, in fact, not even feel well, until he was with Pollonia. It was, in other words, all about controlling the lover's behaviour and conduct. In the case of Pollonia she also wanted her lover to 'come to her' – an ambiguous expression, which quite literally could mean getting a person, who was away, to come home, or it could have a figurative meaning of capturing an emotional attachment; the woman simply seeking to attract the desire and attention of a certain man. Pollonia's attempt to obtain her loved one is an example of the latter.

Pietro was referred to as Pollonia's *amico*, and he was still in Orbetello, since a witness stated that he had passed beneath the window as Pollonia was reciting one of her secret incantations.

Evidence that the method could be used to get a person to return home appears in the allegations against Rosa di Longone, who was accused in November 1649.[335] A witness stated that Rosa knew of a certain prayer that could help get people back. The witness, Elisabetta di Jacobos, stated that her lover, a Spanish soldier, had promised to marry her. His company had now left Orbetello, and Elisabetta had been plunged into despair until Rosa di Longone had offered her help. To get the soldier back, both of them had to practise a magical ritual, where they knelt before an image of St. Anthony and said prayers to the saint and to the Holy Spirit. It is worth noting that it was roughly the same ritual that was used to help clients recover stolen or lost objects. The ritual obviously included a magical power that was effective on humans and animals as well as on material objects.

The testimonies against Pollonia included only one account of divination. This ritual also had parallels with other witchcraft rituals. When Pollonia had foretold to young Meca her marital future,[336] the ritual had included holding a bowl of urine, which is identical to the ritual applied by Francesca di Rosata to retain her young lover's interest. Pollonia could also offer help with marital disputes. A woman, donna Anna, had come to Pollonia, because she heard that Pollonia was familiar with rituals that could make peace between a couple. Yet again the ritual had involved a prayer to St. Anthony. Anna had not been present herself but had been assured that it would mollify her husband. When she had learned of the inquisition's edict and had listened to regular admonitions from the priest on how any knowledge of witchcraft should be passed on to the inquisitor, she had reported what she knew about Pollonia.

The denunciations in Orbetello accumulate: the case of Lucida di Canino

Another woman of Orbetello, Lucida di Canino, also had marital problems brewing at home. According to the testimony made by Lucida herself to the inquisitor, her husband Miliano had often beaten her, and this had motivated her to seek advice from Pollonia di Gallo. In her denunciation Lucida said nothing of her own knowledge of forbidden rituals. In parallel to the trials of Pollonia, a trial was instigated against Lucida, and she herself was arrested only a couple of days later.[337] To judge from the two trials, she and Pollonia had made frequent exchange of magical rituals.

Discretion was an important virtue for the inquisitor. There were pressing reasons to avoid having a suspect apprehended during daylight hours, such an event would only draw excessive attention to the case.[338] This case from Orbetello confirms how important discretion was held to be by inquisitors.

By the same token, hearings of witnesses took place only with a limited group of people, and, to judge from the protocols of Orbetello, it appears that only the inquisitor, a notary and a witness were present. Such procedures meant that Lucida did not officially know that Pollonia was being investigated, when she made her report about her, since Pollonia had yet to be taken into custody. However, while official procedures may have hushed things up, everyday gossip of the town certainly did not. Gossip ran fast, and Orbetello was no exception to this. When the accusation was made against Pollonia di Gallo, the majority of the inhabitants of Orbetello had not yet experienced the severity that could accompany an inquisitorial trial: that is, the flogging in the streets, exile and so on.

Lucida di Canino must have been familiar with the inquisition's edict, and for one witch to inform on another, would seem to be skating on very thin ice. It is possible that Lucida reacted to an announcement from the inquisitor offering milder treatment of offenders who confessed of their own free will. Still, the reason for Lucida di Canino appearing before inquisitor Pedrosa remains unclear. She refrained from admitting to practising any sorts of rituals herself, and according to her own statement, the motive behind contacting inquisitor Pedrosa was not officially a complaint about Pollonia, because 'I [Lucida] want what is best for everyone'.[339] In line with the majority of the witnesses, her justification for her denunciation was that it was out of respect for the Holy Virgin Mary and Jesus and to ease her own conscience.

If Lucida thought that she could mitigate the sinful nature of her own actions by complying with the inquisitor's admonitions and reporting on Pollonia, her strategy seems to have been doomed from the beginning.[340] A few days earlier a third woman, Faustina di Leusta, had denounced both Pollonia di Gallo and Lucida di Canino for witchcraft. Faustina had frequently observed Pollonia performing magical rituals, and in her confession Pollonia herself had not tried to conceal the fact that Lucida had often participated in the practice of such rituals. The interrelations between the accused meant that the inquisitor must have been able to use their separate accounts to amass a considerable amount of knowledge even before the cases came to court. In the case of Lucida di Canino, this meant that the inquisitor knew all about her actions and her reputation long before she appeared before him to denounce Pollonia di Gallo.

Denouncing for revenge: Faustina di Leusta

Faustina di Leusta's testimony ended up incriminating Pollonia. Yet in early May 1649 Faustina herself was denounced for love magic, and the inquisitor initiated a trial against her. Surprisingly, she had not been denounced by either Pollonia or Lucida.[341] After the inquisitor had heard a dozen or so witnesses, the case was suspended for more than six months, only to be resumed in February 1650. It was not until then that Faustina was taken into custody, and she was then confronted with the allegations against her. She swore that she was innocent of the accusations of witchcraft, but she once again confirmed her knowledge of Pollonia's practice of witchcraft. Pollonia di Gallo had previously been lodging with Faustina and her husband, but the latter had chased Pollonia out. Why he should have done so is uncertain, but it seems that the eviction happened after he learned that Pollonia was practising witchcraft. This event had been the end of the friendship between Faustina and Pollonia. In a later interrogation, Faustina stated that Lucida's denunciation of her must also be based on a personal grudge. The inquisitor subsequently rejected this denunciation. Furthermore, several witnesses had taken Faustina's part in the contretemps with Lucida and with Pollonia, both of whom were described as *donne di mala fama*, while Faustina came from a good and honest family.[342]

The trial of Faustina is significant in that it reflects such apparently personal grudges between Faustina and her denouncers. Throughout the trial she maintained her innocence, even during torture, and inquisitor Pedrosa did not sentence her as a *donna dalla mala vita* as he had Lucida and Pollonia.[343] As was standard in inquisitorial procedures, Faustina did not escape punishment altogether. As in the trial against Agata di Camillo, where allegations were also rooted in personal grudges, the inquisitor found Faustina guilty of having recited an illicit prayer (*oratione*), and she herself admitted to having uttered a blasphemous phrase in anger. Her penalty consisted of standing in front of the church on feast-days, and she was warned that if she ever again used magical rituals or the like, she would be flogged in public and then banished from the town.

The gravest accusations of witchcraft

The first witness in the case against Lucida di Canino had been Emilia di Baldo.[344] She is listed as a witness summoned by the court, which meant that, unlike most of the witnesses, she did not appear spontaneously. That the inquisitor chose to call Emilia reflects his systematic approach to the investigation. Emilia had been mentioned in Lucida's testimony against Pollonia,[345] which probably prompted inquisitor Pedrosa to conduct another interrogation. Emilia's testimony would soon prove to be merely the tip of the iceberg. Once the investigation on Lucida had got under way, the skeletons virtually tumbled out of the cupboard. Taken as a whole, these new accusations proved that suspicions of Lucida's witchcraft were just as solid as those surrounding Pollonia. A large number of denunciators and summoned witnesses confirmed that Lucida was indeed one of the town's *donne dalla mala vita*, and the rumours about her were rife.[346] As in the trial of Pollonia di Gallo, all of the witnesses were familiar with Lucida's bad reputation. A number of witnesses had been present when Lucida had practised magical rituals, and others had been instructed by her on how to practise the rituals themselves. Denunciators who did not have any first-hand knowledge instead recounted that Lucida had brought about several of the marriages in the town through witchcraft.

Like Pollonia di Gallo, Lucida di Canino was sentenced to be flogged on the streets of Orbetello and subsequently banished from the town.[347] The large number of denunciations, summoned witnesses, interrogations and severe punishments made the trial one of the gravest in Orbetello during the period under examination, and the execution of these sentences was also the talk of the town that day in August, when Virginia di Leandro uttered her offensive statements leading to the initial denunciation of Lucida.[348] Her practice of love magic in particular included incantations and abuse of prayers, names of saints, of the Holy Trinity and the invocation of the stars. Still, at no point did Lucida di Canino confess to having had the intention of physically harming anyone or anything through her witchcraft. She also denied ever having sold her soul to the Devil. As in the trial of Virginia di Leandro, the witnesses clearly distanced themselves from Lucida, because on several occasions she made arrogant and blasphemous statements about the Church and its representatives. Two witnesses testified that Lucida had boasted that she would 'pull out the hairs of the inquisitor's beard, one by one' and that she would make the *mal segno della Croce*, probably an inverted sign of the cross, towards him.[349] Another witness named Laudatia had said that people in the town had expected Lucida to be arrested by the inquisition. One evening, they had talked about Faustina's arrest and Laudatia had warned Lucida to watch her words, as she was next in line. Lucida's prompt reply had been that she had no fear of the inquisitor.[350]

Accusations of witchcraft at the provincial court in Viborg

When comparing allegations of witchcraft under the Roman Inquisition with those brought at the provincial court in Viborg, it is striking how few of the latter deal with love magic and marital problems. And where they do so, they have a different quality from the cases in Orbetello. In a trial from 1627, Kiersten Nielsdatter from Hyllebjerg near Års was accused of having used witchcraft to get back at her former son-in-law.[351] The case appears to have a wealth of convoluted entanglements, but Kiersten's son-in-law had apparently accused Kiersten's daughter, his wife, of fornication, and the marriage seems to have been annulled. Kiersten had afterwards been quarrelling with the son-in-law over the daughter's belongings. To this the son-in-law had declared that he had not experienced any luck or happiness since marrying Kiersten's daughter. This he believed was caused by Kiersten's witchcraft. Kiersten Nielsdatter was also accused of having bewitched the man with whom her daughter was said to have fornicated.

Kiersten Nielsdatter clearly had a reputation for bringing bad luck to those associating with her, especially those with whom she was on unfriendly terms. The trial treated in chapter 5 against Sidsel Christens contains some similar characteristics. When Sidsel was accused of witchcraft in 1617, it was clearly the culmination of a negative campaign against her, which had been accumulating for several years. Enmity had evidently been growing between her and her accuser, Mikkel Christensen, as is confirmed by several details in the court records. As early as in 1610 Mikkel Christensen had prevented Sidsel's husband from presenting witnesses swearing on her good name and reputation, since she was denounced for witchcraft. In 1613 Mikkel had charged her in public of bewitching his horse and three years later of bewitching his son. No one present in court had watched Sidsel perform witchcraft, and none of the testimonies included information on magical rituals. Instead, to the people testifying against Sidsel, it was the threat of evil and the unforeseen illness was what made them show up in court. As part of his preparation for the case, Mikkel Christensen had collected evidence against her. By presenting witnesses who defamed Sidsel and confirmed her reputation for being a witch, Mikkel strengthened his own case, before formally charging her with bewitching his horses, his son and his wife. It is difficult to tell what was the final straw, since many of the allegations against Sidsel were regarding incidents that had taken place three or four years before the trial. Sidsel herself was present in court and she was given the opportunity of defending herself, which she could not, since no one would stand up in court and speak for her.

This part of a Danish case was crucial to the defendant. It provided an opportunity to counter the allegations by providing evidence that she was a good Christian and an honest and honourable person. This could only be achieved by having others speak on her behalf. Her own word was worth nothing; what mattered was the testimonial she was given by the villagers. I will return to this part of the trial in chapter 9. Sidsel's reaction to the accusations made against her was common in the Danish trials. Most defendants claimed their innocence, but to those who were objects of dislike, and who also had the reputation of being witches, it was difficult to counteract a large number of allegations of uttered threats and accidents.

The prospect of there being no one willing to stand up and act as defence witness often made a suspect attempt to avoid formal accusation by fleeing or by bribing her way out of the trial. In a case conducted in Viborg in 1620 against Maren Lauridsdatter from Øster Hassing situated north of the Limfjord, Maren was charged with casting evil on several people in the parish.[352] Several of the allegations against her revolved around disputes over milk, Maren having been asking for milk and the request having been declined. One person, Anders Jensen, testified that Maren had cast the Devil on his family, and he was also the only one to testify that Maren had threatened with evil. He claimed that that same year he had got into a quarrel with Maren, in which he had called her a witch. To this Maren had verbally struck back telling him 'that he would pay [for calling her a witch]'. After this, the Devil, referred to as 'evil itself', had come to him for three nights in a row. The man to formally charge Maren was called Jens Lauridsen, and he was accusing her of casting evil spells on his wife, his proof being the statements of an evil spirit that had spoken through his wife's mouth, claiming Maren was guilty. In the weeks leading up to the initial trial before the manor court in Kær, it seems as if the atmosphere around Maren became increasingly tense. From the records it is evident that Maren was aware that her fellow parishioners suspected her of witchcraft. Six men testified in court that Maren had offered them money if they would set her free, and she had assured them that they would never see her again. Three weeks earlier she had managed to flee the parish, and a group of men had been sent out to track her down. Two of them testified in court that they had found her in the churchyard in a nearby village. When the men confronted Maren, she had told them that she had only fled because she was so terrified that she might be charged with having bewitched a certain woman. She had now offered the two men money if only they would let her go free. In addition, one of the two men who captured Maren testified that she had told him about a secret stone in the dyke surrounding the church in Øster Hassig. The stone had a black spot on it, and if he were to take it out, he would be blessed with so much luck that he would never need any more for as long as he lived. This act of desperation merely aggravated the case against Maren. From the legal testimonies of the trial, it is clear that, unlike Sidsel, Maren was not known for posing threats of the Devil. On the contrary, a number of her deeds supported the suspicions against her. Maren's desperation was obvious, and like her fellow villagers, she knew all too well what the writing on the wall was telling her. Before the trial even started, therefore, she tried to escape, and, when she did not succeed, she tried to commit suicide by stabbing herself with a knife. These efforts only strengthened the case of her accusers, because it seemed to confirm that she was admitting to her deeds. Ultimately she must have known what a poor recommendation the vicar of the parish would give her in court. When called, he confirmed that for many years Maren had been reputed to be a witch. Maren herself declined ever having bewitched people or livestock. She did, however, admit to having practised rituals for healing. In the case against Maren Lauridsdatter it is clear that the provincial judges in Viborg followed common practice, in that they did not find evidence that Maren had threatened with evil or that evil had occurred. Her sentence was restricted to the relatively mild penalty of exile and the abandonment of her property and with the judges emphasizing that her incantation was a disgrace to God.[353]

In the trial against Sidsel Christens, there was no doubting the enmity between Sidsel and her accuser, whereas in the trial against Maren Lauridsdatter the impression is that she was more of a general burden to local society. Common to the two was the absence of defence, which meant they lacked support from fellow villagers. The judges at the provincial court in Viborg were, however, sometimes presented with cases in which defendants put up their own active defence. These cases often ended in acquittals. In a series of cases raised by Niels Munk, a captain residing at a small manor called Rosborg not far from Viborg, one of the defendants, Anders Christensen, led an active defence for himself and his wife. In this case, too, the motive for accusations of witchcraft had been illness among livestock and humans. The case against Anders Christensen was initiated in the manor court of Fjends in the winter of 1639, but initially only a few witnesses were heard. Then the case was apparently put aside for four months, before it was resumed in June 1639 and the manor court convicted Anders Christensen on 3 of September. The appeal was soon brought to the provincial court, which passed their sentence only eight days later. The provincial judges overruled the verdict of the manor court, and Anders Christensen was acquitted. The conflict between the two men appears to have been about Anders Christensen's farm, from which Niels Munk had attempted to evict him. During the spring of 1639 Niels Munk's children and wife suffered from illness, and Niels Munk had been convinced that the illness was due to witchcraft cast on his household by local witches.[354] In the summer of 1639 Niels Munk managed to have three people convicted of bewitching his family. All three of them denounced Anders Christensen under torture, claiming him to be the leader of their witches' society. The three convicted witches had subsequently confirmed their allegations shortly before they were executed. From the testimonies of the witnesses, the enmity between Niels Munk and Anders Christensen is evident, and Niels Munk must have found considerable satisfaction in the allegations against Anders Christensen. Two people testified that they had heard Niels Munk accuse Anders Christensen of destroying his crop of rye with witchcraft, and that Anders had threatened Niels Munk, calling him a thief and that he would make sure that Niels Munk would leave Rosborg within three years as a poor and crippled man. Other parishioners confirmed that some of Niels Munk's cattle had died in a suspicious way during the winter. Although Anders Christensen was not directly held responsible, Niels Munk seem to have linked this to the evil deeds performed by Anders Christensen and his society of witches. Unlike Sidsel Christens and Maren Lauridsdatter, Anders Christensen went on the offensive in responding to the accusations and presented several witnesses on his own behalf. He was eventually acquitted by the judges at the Supreme Court (*Kongens Retterting*) in 1640.

Encountering evil

Anders Christensen and his wife faced two charges: of bewitching Niels Munk's household by causing harm to his animals; and of sending evil spirits into his children. In this sense the trial fits the general picture of the accusations before the provincial court of northern Jutland; they were always motivated by the infliction of some form of damage, which was attributed to the witch. The term applied by the witnesses as well as the defendants was *forgøre*, which means 'to cause something or someone irreversible damage'. In this sense it corresponds to the Italian word *fattura*, a 'bewitchment'. The great majority of Danish accusations of witchcraft applied the word *forgøre*, and the testimonies involved only rarely dealt with the practice of magical rituals, nocturnal gathering and the worship of the Devil. Regardless of the content of the accusations, the people in Denmark referred to witches as *troldfolk*. In Orbetello, diabolic witchcraft, in Italian *stregoneria*, was considered the most dangerous practice of magical rituals. As for Orbetello, it has not been possible to find trials containing systematic worship of the Devil. The court records of the provincial court of Viborg cover a geographically larger area, and here it is possible to document clusters of interconnected trials with traces of collective witchcraft, although it is important to point out that this was not a common occurrence. What is significant in these trials is that tales of nocturnal assembly are mostly obtained after the verdict and under torture. One exception can be found in Aalborg, where a series of cases was conducted in the period 1612–1621 against a total of nine people. Together with a collection of trials from south of Aarhus, these trials are probably the closest we get to diabolic witches in the Danish records.[355] Even so, the accusations against these suspects did not include orgies with the Devil. Furthermore, the Devil did not appear as the leader of the witches. Instead he was a kind of servant, on whom the witches could vent their frustration. This will be discussed more thoroughly when exploring the appearances of the Devil in chapter 8.

This section addresses some of the denunciations concerning malevolent magic (*fattura*) which were received by the inquisitor in Orbetello. The aim is to demonstrate how, when it did occur, malevolent magic resembled the Danish representations.[356] Numerous cases from northern Jutland show how Danish cases were all based on one accusation (or more) of inflicted injury. For instance, when the case against Johanne Pedersdatter from Sejlflod was raised in 1620, one of the allegations against her was that a woman who had visited her subsequently fell ill. A man who the same Johanne had promised would burn up in hell, indeed, did fall ill and died.[357] In a connected case, the accused, Else Jacobsdatter, had quarrelled with a weaver over some clothes, and Else had been angry and only reluctantly paid her bill. According to the weaver, Else had earlier threatened him, saying that evil would befall him, and he had never felt well after this. Another witness accused Else of having taken the lives of her livestock using witchcraft. Else had inquired about the woman's animals, and that same night several of the creatures had died.[358] North of the Limfjord at the manor court in Hornum, Siede Chrestensdatter had been charged with witchcraft in 1617. A number of people testified to Siede's witchcraft, amongst them Anders Brun, who accused Siede of having spoiled his milking. When he had confronted Siede with his suspicion, an argument between them had broken out, and Siede had, like Else Jacobsdatter, threatened him, saying evil would come upon him. His milking subsequently came good again, but shortly afterwards, one of his horses died and more followed. Anders Brun reasoned that it was Siede who had bewitched the horses.[359]

In Orbetello accounts of malevolent witchcraft applied the term *fattura*. Like denunciations of other varieties of magic, the allegations involved bringing about accidents or illness. Sometimes the denunciations were based on gossip about persons performing evil deeds, and such stories often went back fifteen years. An example of this was report of a young girl Giovanna, who had suddenly died after encountering a woman suspected of witchcraft, Madalena di Maura.[360] The girl had smelt some flowers that Madalena had held in her hand and after this she had fallen ill and died. Despite the serious nature of the accusation, it does not seem to have made a significant impression on the inquisitor, as he did not investigate the matter further.

This account of the girl in Orbetello who died after smelling a flower, was part of a collection of denunciations against Madalena di Maura. However, the central allegation in these testimonies was rooted in a love triangle, which was played out between Madalena, her lover and his wife. The denunciator was the wife, the middle-aged Giovanna Buonanno, who claimed that her husband had been bewitched by Madalena. The story behind this was that Giovanna's husband, Stefano Buonanno, had arrived in Orbetello from Mallorca some years before. His wife had recently followed, and soon after her arrival she had become aware of the fact that Stefano had taken a mistress, Madalena di Maura.[361] Giovanna Buonanno stated that when she had come to Órbetello, she had quickly been able to determine that the husband had been bewitched. The symptom was her husband's impotence. Still, Giovanna had not figured this out entirely on her own. Two women had called on Giovanna, and they had told her that her marital miseries had been caused by a certain Madalena di Maura. Madalena had practised witchcraft on numerous occasions to retain Stefano. When she had not succeeded, Madalena had taken her revenge by stealing his manhood. According to the women, it was commonly known in the neighbourhood that Madalena di Maura knew how to perform such acts of witchcraft, and she was said to have made a former lover impotent due to jealousy and by the same means, namely witchcraft.

The rumour concerning Madalena di Maura having stolen the manhood of Stefano Buonanno also surfaces in other trials.[362] In the case against Mensola di Tiracoscia it was submitted that people had gossiped about Mensola having participated in Madalena's witchcraft rituals.[363] In the trial against Lucida di Canino, a witness confirmed that Madalena had complained about Stefano having left her to return to his lawful wife. Madalena had therefore taken her revenge by removing his potency. Another witness stated how Madalena was frustrated over Stefano's lack of interest, possibly towards their two illegitimate children. Madalena allegedly admitted here that she had taken her revenge by making Stefano impotent.

When Stefano Buonanno himself appeared in the stand, he acknowledged that he had had a sexual relationship with Madalena, but he maintained that he had never wanted to cause any harm to his wife. He repented and now knew that he had acted immorally, but that he had been under the irresistible sway of his feelings. What happened afterwards in the case is unclear, but Madalena was never convicted. The inquisitor did not charge her, and the case advanced no further than the initial denunciations and testimonies. Madalena herself was never questioned. She did, however, get to have her own say in another inquisitorial protocol, as she accused Mensola di Tiracoscia of having offered to practise witchcraft to free up Stefano to marry Madalena.

Accusations of causing impotence also occurred in Danish trials, but they were not common. The accusations against Anne Jespersdatter from Gjøl share striking similarities to those against Madalena di Maura.[364] At the trial it was confirmed that the unmarried Anne had a reputation of being a witch, and several men claimed that she had bewitched them.[365] One of the accusations was that Anne had spirited away the potency of her ex-lover. He and Anne had a child together, but he was now married to someone else. A year after the marriage had taken place, he had lost his potency and had concluded that it must have been Anne trying to get back at him by means of witchcraft. When the case was brought before the judge, Anne had not been able to defend herself, but she had blamed the current wife of the accuser. Anne claimed the wife did not want any more children, so she had stolen his manhood.

The trials from the provincial court in Viborg provide numerous cases where the element of revenge is evident in the allegations. Anne Jespersdatter, mentioned above, was accused of having applied witchcraft out of revenge. The allegation of witchcraft itself also often included the element of revenge. Quarrels could easily generate evil blood between two parties, and if the one had a reputation as a witch, it was not hard for the other to suspect his misfortunes or illnesses to be caused by witchcraft. The misfortunes attributed to witches were almost always related to the household, that is, humans or livestock, and only rarely related to the weather or harvest.[366] Enmity clearly existed between Sidsel Christens and her accuser, Mikkel Christensen. In the aforementioned case against Anders Christensen, enmity had grown over issues of property, and this ultimately caused Niels Munk to blame Anders and his wife for the illnesses that had struck Niels Munk's wife and children. A similar incident took place in Aalborg in the years 1618–1619, when the clergyman, David Klyne and his wife had had a long-term dispute with their neighbour, Christenze Kruckow, over a rain gutter. When the wife of the clergyman lost her sanity, Christenze was blamed for causing this through witchcraft.[367]

One true witch in Orbetello: Mensola di Tiracoscia

One trial in Orbetello stands out from the rest, and that is the one against Mensola di Tiracoscia. The protocols from 1648–1650 include several references to this older woman and her magical activities. The trials against Pollonia di Gallo and Lucida di Canino in particular contained testimonies and denunciations in which these three women are mentioned at the same time. When a witness mentioned these three, they were always presented explicitly or implicitly within a sort of hierarchy, which spoke of a clear difference between them. Lucida di Canino and Pollonia di Gallo may have been *donne di mala vita*, but Mensola was undoubtedly worse. She was a *strega*, a true witch.[368]

Like Lucida di Canino and Pollonia di Gallo, Mensola practised magical rituals within all four categories, so in this sense she covered the entire spectrum of magical purposes. The great majority of the allegations against her regarded love magic, often with a malevolent purpose. A witness told the inquisitor how her husband had been bewitched four years earlier, and that she had then called upon Mensola to perform counter-magic. In another case, against the aforementioned Agata di Camillo, Stefano's infatuation with Agata was far from welcomed by his family, and his sisters regarded his feelings as being caused by witchcraft.[369] During the case it appeared that Mensola had offered to perform counter-magic in exchange for money to release Stefano from his affair with Agata.

As for love magic with a malevolent aim, Mensola had not been hesitant in helping her clients to remove their opponents from the running. Below, three episodes will be examined, each of which led to a denunciation of Mensola. These have been chosen amongst the more than thirty voluntary testimonies which were delivered to the inquisitor, in order to clarify the difference between Mensola's repertoire of magical rituals and that of other Orbetello suspects.

The first to report Mensola to the inquisitor was the 29-year-old Isabella Vega, who had personally made use of Mensola's skills. Isabella had lived for some time with a captain from Naples named Francesco Antonio Cuccino, but she was worried about the fact that he had yet to propose to her. She had discovered that the reason for this was that he was already married to another woman in Naples. Isabella had heard of Mensola di Tiracoscia, and she had thus called upon her. According to Isabella, Mensola did indeed have advice to offer. The plan was to get rid of the captain's Neapolitan wife, so that he could then marry Isabella. To aid her, Mensola made use of a ritual where amongst other objects she needed some lace from the Neapolitan wife. She also needed some blood from Isabella's little finger.

The blood would be used to write letters on plant leaves, which the captain would then have to eat. In this sense Isabella would literally enter the captain's physical body.[370]

After a couple of days Mensola came to see Isabella again. This time she needed something belonging to the captain, and Isabella therefore gave her a pair of his trousers. Mensola had also asked for money to buy flour. When Isabella had questioned what the flour might be used for, Mensola had explained that it was to be mixed with wax, possibly from a church candle, and then Mensola would make a small doll that would look like the captain's wife. The wax figure then had to be placed in the fire, and when it melted, the effect would be transferred to the captain's wife. In this way her rival would be eliminated, and Isabella would then be able to marry him.

However, Isabella had to call on Mensola again, since the spell had not worked; the wife was apparently still alive. Mensola assured Isabella that she had actually been to Naples and that she had seen the captain's wife. The subsequent events are unclear; unfortunately, damp has damaged the protocol. Yet Isabella had told the inquisitor that what had happened between the captain and her had taken place a few years earlier. The inquisitor had not shown any particular interest in Isabella's present marital situation; his focus remained on Mensola di Tiracoscia and her alleged deeds.

In one of the denunciations that followed, Caterina di Giovanni Pesci had turned to the inquisitor to report on Mensola di Tiracoscia's practice of counter-magic. The episode had concerned Caterina's daughter, who lived with her husband in Porto Ercole, a small port on Argentario. Domenica, the daughter, was described by her mother as melancholic, and her condition caused serious problems in the marriage to her husband Pietro. According to the mother, Domenica refused to see her husband, and Mensola had on her own initiative called on the mother to tell her that many people in the town had noticed that Domenica appeared to be very sad. Mensola offered to help, as she was certain that Caterina's daughter had been bewitched. Caterina had discussed Domenica's condition with her son-in-law and told him of Mensola's alleged powers. The two of them then called upon Mensola.

When Mensola saw Domenica, she confirmed that the condition could be treated, but that the mother had to participate in the cure herself. Together they placed several objects under Domenica's head, while she was sleeping. This included small rocks and a ring. When the ritual had been completed, Caterina claimed that her daughter had calmed and regained her good spirits. Mensola had returned a couple of days later to perform another ritual on Domenica, and when she had taken her leave of Caterina, she had reminded her that she now had to have faith in God.

After Mensola was convicted in 1649, the denunciations kept coming in. One of them came from Angela di Menuta, whose testimony is recorded in the spring of 1651. Here the inquisitor's role as confessor is evident.

Although Mensola was already sentenced by the inquisition, Angela di Menuta must have felt a desire to ease her conscience by recounting some serious events that had taken place three years earlier.[371] This concerned Angela's neighbour Carlo, who had engaged in a relationship with a married woman named Domenica. Domenica's husband, Mauro, was rejected and betrayed by his wife's infidelity and so he treated her badly and forced her to stay in their house. Desperate at not being able to see his mistress any more, Carlo had now asked Angela di Menuta if she could provide him with contact who could help him get rid of Mauro. Angela had refused, but a few days later she had learned that Carlo and Domenica had allied themselves with Mensola, who would make sure that the husband departed this life.

According to the plan, Mensola would have to leave Orbetello under cover of night for Domenica and Mauro's home in Porto Ercole. Even though water separated Porto Ercole and Orbetello, the journey required no boat. Mensola would transform herself into a fly to cross the sea. During this nocturnal visit Mensola was to kill Mauro, but she had afterwards told Domenica that she had failed to do so. Although she had managed to crawl up Mauro's back in the shape of a fly, she had not been able to complete her mission.

The failed attempt to kill Mauro had left Domenica openly impatient. Mensola still knew how to correct the mistake, however. After a couple of days she had asked Domenica to cut a nail and some hair from Mauro. Together with some bread that Mauro would otherwise eat, it all had to be handed over to Mensola. The things would then be placed in a small box that would be used in the ritual to bewitch the despised Mauro. Domenica was to place the box with its bewitchment (*malia*) under the threshold of the entrance to the house. This would surely kill the husband. At the same time Mensola had also summoned three devils from hell, who would appear as *tre bellissimi giovani*, three beautiful young men. Whether these devils were to help Mensola in her diabolic arts, or whether they were to ensure that Domenica remained patient is, like the outcome of the case, unclear. However, it is, interesting that Mensola regarded herself as being capable of *controlling* these devils. Mensola had already been convicted and placed in prison in Rome when she was denounced for this, so it did not appear to serve any purpose for the investigation.

These three accounts are merely a sample of the many denunciations made against Mensola di Tiracoscia. Like Lucida di Canino and Pollonia di Gallo, Mensola offered assistance particularly in problems concerning her clients' love life. The allegations against her were, however, far more serious. In the first of the testimonies, Mensola had tried to use witchcraft to get rid of a woman. The account contained several elements that worried Isabella and caught the attention of the inquisitor. Mensola would use a spell to attempt to kill the captain's wife. The assumption was that Mensola could use flour and wax to create a figure that could resemble the wife. A *fattura* required special skills, and the denunciator, Isabella, did not comment on Mensola having to travel to Naples and back in a single night. We do not know how, or possibly in what form, Mensola travelled. In the third denunciation it appears that Mensola claimed to be able to take other forms – in this case, when she travelled in the form of a fly.

The example of the melancholic Domenica, who refused to live with or even see her husband, has been included to show that Mensola also had been rumoured to be able to practise counter-magic. Domenica's mother had been assisted by Mensola, because she possessed special skills to determine whether a person had been bewitched or not. She was also capable of lifting the spell. The trial against Mensola demonstrates what was commonly known in Orbetello, namely that by practising counter magic, Mensola could cause harm, as well as heal. Eventually, and probably helped on by the religious efforts in the town and most clearly by the edict of faith, Mensola's reputation for malignant witchcraft overshadowed the positive application of her skills, and this led to the many denunciations against her.

To gain or to harm

In drawing some parallels between the denunciations, accusations and allegations that came before the inquisition in Orbetello and the provincial court in Viborg, it is important to emphasize the social background against which the allegations were made. In both places, by crossing the boundaries of acceptable social behaviour, the suspects had motivated the witnesses and denunciators. In Orbetello many denunciations related to episodes familiar to the witness through town gossip, although it was always a concrete event, such as the blasphemous statement of Virginia di Leandro on the street, or watching a magical ritual being performed, that precipitated the denunciation. Generally feelings of envy and jealousy, especially in love and marriage, were essential ingredients in the allegations. In Denmark, the element of revenge was significant, and the belief that the witch would try to get her enemies back was present in practically all allegations.

In both of the areas studied, a small number of trials stood out from the rest. In Orbetello, this was especially the trial against Mensola di Tiracoscia, who without a doubt topped the magical hierarchy of the town. Mensola di Tiracoscia, Lucida di Canino and Pollonia di Gallo were clearly well known to the inhabitants of the town. All three of them were clearly old hands, not worrying about passing on their knowledge. In addition, all three were consulted on a regular basis, mostly by the women of the town, and assisted them in all kinds of problems, especially regarding matters of the heart. Ultimately all three received a harsh sentence from the inquisitor.

The Danish trials were characterized by being the fruit of an existing and burgeoning conflict between the accuser and the suspect. The trials that stand out are those in which the defendant did not succumb to the allegations but instead put up an active legal defence. Such people were not rich in terms of their wealth, but they usually possessed greater resources. Besides having a good reputation and a social network in the village, for a woman this also meant having a husband who could stand up for her in court. The next chapter will look more closely at the beliefs and values that lay behind the perceptions and the deeds of the suspects that allowed them to pose such a threat to the everyday wellbeing of the village.

8
Popular notions of witchcraft

In 1650 Jacobo Fracesso approached the inquisitor in Orbetello. Jacobo reported an episode that had taken place ten years earlier. Together with Guiseppe (Josephus) di Mariano, Jacobo had attempted to locate hidden treasure. Guiseppe had known of a certain magical practice, which involved the two men going out under cover of the night with a cane made of consecrated olive wood. On this cane were carved some mysterious letters, and the idea was that the cane would lead the two men to the right place to dig for treasure. Although Jacobo and Guiseppe believed that they had found the right spot and had started digging, they never located the treasure. When reporting the deeds to the inquisitor, Jacobo clearly followed the instructions of the confessors and the edict of the inquisition, and he applied the standard phrase, that he had come to ease his own conscience. In others words, like many others presenting themselves before the inquisitor with reports of magical rituals, Jacobo was fully aware that such a stick was forbidden in the eyes of the inquisitor and he now appeared before the inquisitor to come clean.

To anyone reading the descriptions delivered by the suspects in the court records, the uneven balance of power that existed between the suspect and the judge is unmistakeable. Jacobo's denunciation never turned into a formal trial. In the cases where denunciations led to a formal charge, the suspects generally became more aware of the gravity of their situation as the trial progressed. In Danish trials, suspects rarely gave their version until after the sentence had been pronounced, when they were interrogated under torture. That encounter between the witch and the judge is the theme of the next chapter; the focus of the present one is on the denunciation and initial questioning of witnesses and suspects, in order to investigate popular notions of witchcraft and what provided magical rituals with their effect. In the case of the inquisitorial records and the Danish lay records alike, these testimonies were constructed with the recipient in mind. They must be read both as texts of self-representation and as accounts of episodes involving evil intentions and witchcraft.[372] The representations of magic, of witchcraft and of individual suspects should be regarded as examples of popular perceptions delivered in a legal context. When the narratives of witchcraft were presented in the context of the court, their purpose was generally to benefit the speaker's own case. In this sense, such defences against allegations of witchcraft and magical rituals mirror the speaker's perceptions of these practices, but they are also constructed in accordance with what the narrator expects the judge's definition of such offences to be.

Denunciations and initial interrogations of witnesses are useful in any attempt to characterize contemporary perceptions, since these accounts are the closest we get to hearing lay illiterate people putting their beliefs into words. The Italian protocols focus predominantly on the denunciations, although they also drew upon the initial questioning of the suspects. At this stage in the trial, the suspect generally spoke freely and did not seem to feel particularly constrained by the situation. Normally the inquisitor would not tamper with these statements. Only after receiving reliable reports of suspicious acts did the inquisitor in Orbetello initiate an investigation. With Danish court proceedings being constructed in a different way, the Danish parallel to denunciation was the formal accusation, including the motivation for raising the trial. Common to the voluntary denunciation and the formal accusation is that both testimonies were constructed in such a way as to convince the judge of the rightness of the case.

The denunciations provide the closest we can get to first-hand evidence for the illiterate lay people's interpretation of the edict, since they are stories presented without the inquisitor interfering with questions.[373] Denunciations contain allegations of magic and witchcraft, but they also yield evidence of quarrels, gossip and the emotions of envy and indignation. In this sense the edict can be regarded as giving people the opportunity to tell tales on each other. Like Italian denunciations, Danish testimonies given by witnesses, including formal accusations, contain examples of allegations of actions that aroused suspicions in the minds of the illiterate lay people. Before going further into what lay people in Orbetello and northern Jutland believed gave magical rituals with their effect, I will give some examples to illustrate the kind of episode that made people address themselves to the court.

Suspicious behaviour: three denunciations of witchcraft and magic in Orbetello

The trial against Virginia di Leandro began with a denunciation by a woman named Mariana. Virginia was not the only person against whom Mariana laid information that day; her testimony also included allegations against two of the key people from the Orbetello protocols, Mensola di Tiracoscia and her daughter Lucia. As illustrated below, there was a substantial difference between the allegations against Virginia and those against Mensola and Lucia. The references to Mensola and Lucia concerned events that had taken place five years earlier. At that time Mariana and Mensola had been neighbours, and Mariana had noticed what she regarded to be a suspicious behaviour from Mensola and Lucia. On several occasions, Mariana had observed Lucia and Mensola throwing things onto the fire, and when she had confronted them with it, Lucia had admitted that the act was part of a ritual that the two women practised to make their absent husbands return home.[374] Mariana also told the inquisitor that she was aware that Mensola had helped another woman to locate her stolen money. Mariana could not provide much detail about this, but she claimed that Mensola had applied witchcraft here as well. A strong motivation behind Mariana's denunciation was clearly due to Mensola's reputation. Since she was reputed to be a witch, her actions were constantly perceived and assessed within this context.

The descriptions Mariana gave of Virginia di Leandro referred to recent events. Virginia di Leandro had arrogantly expressed a wish that the two 'wicked women' had helped her get a husband, too, and that she would gladly offer herself to the Devil, if only he would give her a husband in return. This statement must have provoked Mariana, since she now denounced Virginia to the inquisitor. Before this Mariana had reprimanded Virginia because it was 'provoking to me [Mariana] that she [Virginia] uttered such words. In marriages you need to use God and not the Devil.'[375] The denunciation of Virginia, then, was not triggered by a suspicion of her practising witchcraft, but by a blasphemous statement that caused Mariana's resentment.

In one of the late cases, from 1656, a certain signora Maria denounced her maid Giobatta Mellini. Maria's eventual approach to the inquisitor was the culmination of a lengthy course of events revolving around the infidelity of Maria's husband. He had regularly visited a prostitute, much to Maria's distress. Maria emotionally described the consequences of her husband's lifestyle to the inquisitor:

> For many months my husband, signore Francesco Tizzani, has pursued an evil [unacceptable] lifestyle to the shame of me and my home, and it has caused me great despair, and I want to find a way where he will despise [and abstain from] this scandal.[376]

Maria had shared her agony and anger with various people, and as a consequence the maid, Giobatta, had said that she knew of a man in Siena who was reputed to be a witch. He had knowledge of counter-magic that would be the solution to Maria's problems. With Maria's consent, Giobatta had established contact with the witch in Siena, who agreed to help. The witch had asked to have one of Maria's husband's dirty shirts sent to him. Using the shirt he would determine whether Maria's husband was unfaithful because he was bewitched. The Sienese witch concluded that the husband had, in fact, fallen victim to bewitchment. Still in Siena, according to

Maria's testimony, he repeatedly tried to release Maria's husband from the spell, and each time communication had gone via the girl Giobatta. When Maria complained about the lack of effect, new measures were applied. It is difficult to establish when, but eventually Maria lost faith in the powers of the Sienese witch. She ended her denunciation by underlining to the inquisitor that 'I have now learned that it was all lies and deceit, and I detest such things, and I feel compelled to report them to the 'inquisitor.'[377]

Maria had commenced her testimony by stating that she appeared before the inquisitor on the advice of her confessor. At the confession he had clearly convinced Maria that she should not put her faith in the witch from Siena. Many Orbetello denunciations refer to the inquisitorial edict as the prime mover for calling on the inquisitor. In addition to the edict, another external factor could encourage people like Maria to see the inquisitor, namely their confessor. What seems to have been the essential thing for Maria in her testimony was that the magical rituals applied by the Sienese witch had failed repeatedly; therefore he must have been an imposter. The husband appears to have continued his infidelities, because Maria seems to have shared her distress over this with her confessor and, in doing so, she had described the rituals practised by the witch in Siena.

The third Italian example concerns one of the denunciations of Girolama del Cocò, a woman of Orbetello sentenced for healing magic in 1651.[378] Girolama was originally accused by Angelica di Ascanio, who had noticed that two women had regularly called on Girolama in her home over a period of three weeks. Girolama had then explained that she had performed '*l'aperta*' (opening) on one of the women, which must have been some sort of prayer (*oratione*) with the intention of curing an illness.[379] Angelica had afterwards shared this with another local woman, whom she knew. She emphasized that she had not understood the words that Girolama had spoken in this *aperta*, and the other woman had responded by advising Angelica to go to the inquisitor.

Manifestations of evil: Danish accusations of witchcraft

Common to accounts of witchcraft in Denmark and Italy was the description of who had participated, how and where. All Danish trials also included an account of the witch's threat that evil would befall her enemy and any accident or illness that had subsequently occurred. The narratives presented to the Danish judges were constructed around this particular part of the encounter with the suspected witch.

Most allegations arose out of the accuser engaging in a quarrel with the suspected witch, during which a threat of evil was expressed. For instance, in the trial of Gunder Hanskone, a witness described a conflict between Gunder Hanskone and the mother of the witness, Anne Gundis.[380] The two women had quarrelled over some grain, and at some point Gunder

Hanskone had threatened Anne with evil. Anne Gundis had immediately fallen ill, and she had remained so until she passed away a year later. The trials of northern Jutland include numerous similar allegations. Besides such specific episodes in which threats of evil were made and were followed by illness or accident, various other kinds of suspicious behaviour could lead to accusations of witchcraft. In the trial presented in chapter 5, Sidsel Christens was formally accused by Mikkel Christensen of bewitching his wife, son and livestock. Sidsel's response to the allegations of witchcraft made against her had contributed to convincing Mikkel that she was, in fact, guilty. When Mikkel's son had fallen ill, he had called on Sidsel and, in front of many people, had accused her of being a witch and of causing his son's illness, and had threatened that, if she would not undo her evil work, he would send her to the stake. Sidsel had replied, 'You just go home, he will not die, but he will get better.'[381] Her words were regarded as an admission that she was responsible, since the boy, according to Mikkel, did get better that same night. To Mikkel this indicated that Sidsel was in control of the boy's illness.

As in Orbetello, the Danish trials include many examples of people who witnessed or experienced, more or less by accident, things that they afterwards considered to be witchcraft. When one of the two trials that sparked a whole series of cases in Aalborg 1612–1621 first came to court, the allegations against Maren Knepis revolved around a suspicious arrangement taking place in Maren's house on a St. Lucia Night in 1611. Maren Knepis was formally accused by Peder Poulssøn. One night in December he had looked through Maren Knepis' window and seen a group of women gathered around one woman who seemed to be giving birth. The women had pulled what they referred to as a thing (*tingist*) from Maren Knepis' womb. What had then happened was, according to Peder Poulssøn, so scandalous that 'it was a disgrace to describe'.[382] He had reacted by shouting through the window, and the gathering of women had then disappeared.[383] To Peder Poulssøn there was no doubt that the obscene ritual performed by the women had been witchcraft. After the incident he had gone to the bailiff in Aalborg, before whom he accused Maren Knepis of being a true witch.

Manifestations of witchcraft could also be unspoken, consisting of a mixture of personality and reputation of the suspects combined with their behaviour in specific situations. In the city of Ribe, Bodild Harchisdatter was on trial for witchcraft in 1614. Bodild's mother, Ingeborg, had been sentenced for witchcraft a few years earlier, and since then Bodild and her father had developed a growing antipathy towards the man who sent Ingeborg to the stake. During her trial, Bodild's mother had made allegations of witchcraft against Bodild and, although she had withdrawn them before she was pushed into the flames, Bodild had since borne the reputation for being a witch. In 1614 the same man formally accused Bodild of witchcraft, and a witness supported his accusation with the observations that Bodild Harchisdatter had one day entered his house and asked for 'something'.[384] When they refused to give her anything, she had left. A few days later Bodild had returned, and this time the witness and his household were in the process of brewing. Bodild did not ask for anything and left the house again without speaking a word. However, the yeast immediately failed to work and the brewing tub had been filled with bubbles.[385]

Narratives in court

The denunciations and accusations above illustrate various types of acts that could become suspicious when they were noticed in the tense atmosphere that must have prevailed when allegations of witchcraft started to fly in a small community. The Italian denunciations were in response to the inquisitor's condemnation of magical rituals and witchcraft in the edict. Still, the testimonies reflect a number of popular narratives of performers of magical rituals and witchcraft. It is not hard to identify the behaviour in the Italian testimonies above that signalled the final straw. Virginia had behaved in an arrogant and blasphemous way; Giobatta was accused of having provided the contact to a witch; and Girolama for having used unknown words and prayers in a healing ritual. In the Danish examples, the signs of witchcraft were often physical and in this way symbolized the malevolence of the defendant, since the accuser had to make a convincing point in order to win the case. Sidsel was accused of controlling the illness of the son of her accuser, when she predicted that the boy would recover; Peder Poulssøn believed that what he had seen had been proof of Maren Knepis being a witch. A similar situation happened with the accusation brought by Mariana against Mensola. Mariana did not know how Mensola had helped in recovering the money, but she was certain that witchcraft had been involved. Finally, as in the testimony from the trials against Bodild Harchisdatter, the mere presence of a person notorious for witchcraft could corroborate suspicion and in this sense support the case against the suspect.

Witnesses rarely talked explicitly about what they believed to provide the magical rituals with their effect. Still, it is possible to decode these ideas through a close reading of the narratives of magic and witchcraft provided in accusations and denunciations, such as those presented above. The witness' indignation over Virginia di Leandro's blasphemous and arrogant behaviour could be seen on the one hand as the witness expressing fear of the Devil and evil and as demonstrating respect for the Church; on the other hand, it is important to read the denunciations as texts of self-representation. The origin of the conflict Mariana had with Virginia is unknown to us, but since Mariana was complying with the inquisitorial edict, she implicitly emphasized her own obedience to the inquisition and Church. Generally, arrogant behaviour was viewed badly, and by describing Virginia as such and as blasphemous, Mariana put herself in a better light before the inquisitor.

Common people in both Denmark and Italy had a clear understanding of certain patterns of actions related to risky and often forbidden practices.

Such patterns, social relations and rumours all contributed to the individual act being interpreted in the context of witchcraft.[386] Earlier witness accounts were quite different in content and illustrate the great disparity of everyday challenges that evidently could be solved using magical rituals. But what powers did people believe provided the rituals with their effect? To ordinary people, the source of witchcraft appears to have been inseparably connected with the intention. To both the Protestant and Catholic Church, magical rituals were tantamount to witchcraft, and as such were signs of a pact with the Devil.

When Girolama del Cocò was denounced for having used her healing prayer (*oratione*), it was not because of the actual prayer uttered – it was the circumstances surrounding the recitation of the words that had aroused suspicion among onlookers. The allegations against Girolama reflect popular notions about witchcraft and what caused it to work. Being able to practise magic and witchcraft required a special combination of personality and knowledge and a command of magical powers. Nevertheless, how did people imagine that someone could acquire such talent? Where did the powers behind the rituals come from? The following paragraphs will investigate this further.

Girolama del Cocò seemed to have no intention of keeping her rituals a secret. She herself had introduced her denunciator, donna Angelica, to the prayer and how to recite it. Indeed, it was probably the words in the prayer, incomprehensible to Angelica, that drove Angelica to report Girolama del Cocò.[387] Words, sometimes incomprehensible and mumbling, figured in many rituals, and they represented a divide between the practitioner and the onlooker. This made the rituals appear secretive and mysterious despite the fact that, in Orbetello, they took place in front of others. Magical rituals were performed in secret but often before a select group of onlookers, who could either participate or remain passive.

Many witnesses were spectators to magical rituals and a clear distinction was maintained between the practitioner and the onlooker. An invisible line divided those who practised the magical rituals of witchcraft and those who watched. Angelica's testimony is an example of this imaginary line. When she denounced Girolama for using an illicit prayer with mumbling words, she reported her for doing things of which she herself had no knowledge. Lurking in the twilight zone, in the flicker of candlelight and inarticulate mutterings, in the inchoate gestures that carried no meaning except to the initiate, the unknown stirred suspicion and fear. As in the world of children, what could be felt, understood and seen carried no unpleasant surprises.

The Danish material also contains numerous examples of how mumbling, unknown words, acts and similar things were interpreted negatively. Those reputed to be witches had to be particularly careful, as they were also under special scrutiny. In the allegations against Maren Knepis, Peder Poulssøn had interpreted the strange sight that met him through the window on St. Lucia Night as witchcraft. Karen Nielsdatter testified in the same case, and she claimed to have been present with Maren Knepis that night when Peder Poulssøn had shouted through the window. Karen had, however, been sent outside the door before the 'birth' of the wax child. Despite being excluded, she had been able to watch small bits of the arrangement through a hole in the door. When the group of women had discovered Karen peeking, they had filled the hole with a piece of cloth. Karen could nevertheless add to her testimony the fact that she knew that Maren Knepis had a rod with which she beat a little black 'thing', which she kept in her chest. Karen's accusations against the women were examples from northern Jutland of how exclusion could generate suspicion towards witchcraft. In her testimony Karen mentioned nothing about what she believed the little thing to be, but from other testimonies it appears that the black thing was 'evil itself' (*den onde selv*), which Maren would regularly whip with the rod.

Mysterious behaviour came in many guises in Danish court records. Lurking around, refusing to answer or staring at people without uttering of word were just some of the behaviours which could generate suspicions. Other acts were scornful, such as in a case from 1622 against Anne Pedersdatter from Trankær. She was accused by a shoemaker of having killed his child, and the midwife supported the shoemaker's accusation. She testified that when the child was born, Anne had called on the new mother to see the baby. On that occasion, Anne had lifted up the child and spat three times on its chest. Eighteen weeks later the child had died. The shoemaker and the midwife clearly linked Anne's unnatural behaviour to the death. Anne Pedersdatter was already notorious for witchcraft, and she was convicted by the manor court as well as by the provincial court.

Origins of the secret arts

From the testimonies of witnesses, it is clear that Girolama del Cocò had a solid reputation of being able to cure illnesses.[388] She was herself aware of the fact that her rituals were not allowed by the Church. This appears from the first interrogation, in which she admitted to the inquisitor that she was aware that she was being incarcerated due to her reciting her forbidden prayers again.[389] The woman who had denounced Girolama del Cocò had gone to the inquisitor, because she had come to question the legitimacy of the use of *l'aperta*; however, she was not doubting the fact that it worked. All of the witnesses took it for granted that the rituals were working. Her motive for calling on the inquisitor was officially 'for the sake of her conscience and the love of God'.[390] Still, the ritual had made several people suspicious. In their accounts, witnesses emphasized that the ritual involved a prayer combined with reciting incomprehensible words or mumbling. The effect was certainly welcome, but the incomprehensible words and mumblings in the rituals were what made the witnesses denounce Girolama. In her healing

magic Girolama used this *aperta* and another ritual,[391] in which she filled a
glass with water and placed three pieces of coal in it. The patient was then
to drink the water. A witness, Andrea di Protanio, stated:

> [Girolama] took a glass of water and made the sign of the Cross, and she
> said the prayer [to] us, I do not know which one it was, as she said it with
> a low, mumbling voice, and finally she did the sign of the Cross again to
> us, and placed three pieces of burning coal [in the glass] and made me
> drink the water.[392]

Here, too, the ritual contained mumbling that was impossible for Andrea to
hear and understand, and Girolama in addition to this had made the sign
of the Cross over the glass of water before Andrea was to drink it. Girolama
would have seen this act being performed in church, and every parishioner
knew that this was the priest's way of blessing the congregation or an individual, and in this sense Girolama copied the rituals from the Church. The
symbolism of the water as healing and the fire as the illness is clear, and by
putting pieces of coal in the glass, she was thus of the belief that she could
add supernatural power to the water, which, once consumed by the patient,
would cast away the illness from the inside. A witness could equally report
how Girolama used another priestly gesture when she 'touched her [the
patient] where she felt sick'.[393]

Girolama's healing rituals were common and combined remedies and
actions with no evident connection to the Church, as well as Christian
institutionalized symbols and rituals. As in Denmark, people believed that,
having seen representatives of the Church perform church ceremonies, it
was possible by simply copying the act to transfer divine power from the
ecclesiastical to the personal sphere. A perception prevailed that magical
objects such as wax children or magnets possessed a power of their own, and
that adding priestly actions or symbols could enhance this.

Healing magic was mostly seen in a positive light, which came from a
belief that divine powers could contribute to the cure. Many such rituals
involved Christian effects like crucifixes, icons of saints or church candles,
and in general there was a perception that the more original the items
involved were, the greater the probability of achieving the desired outcome.
If these effects had been taken from God's own house, they must possess at
least a little of his divine power. The more symbols the objects contained
the better, since, in combination with acts of faith such as kneeling or praying, they would enhance their power. This idea is similarly reflected in the
many invocations of saints.[394] The act itself produced an effect, although the
rate of success would vary according to the person performing the ritual.
The most desirable thing would be to have a priest or a canon to practise
the ritual. People like Girolama del Cocò were also sought after for their
reputation as successful healers. The ideal was to get a cleric to perform the

ritual, and in Italy as a whole this did often occur. In Orbetello no clerics were reported, let alone convicted, for witchcraft, but in Modena, Venice and other places, clerics were involved in a large proportion of the cases regarding healing magic.[395]

Accusations against clerics for performing beneficial magic (*signen, manen*) came only rarely before the judges in the provincial court in Viborg. When these trials did appear, they were, like accusations against lay cunning folk, brought on by a reputation for being a witch along with that of practising beneficial magic. In his trial the vicar from Lønne, Jens Hansen Rusk, had been supplementing his clerical income by healing sick people, especially at the market in the nearby town of Ribe.[396] Jens Rusk did practise healing magic, but, when his cures failed, he was eventually accused of causing harm. One of his treatments consisted of the patient carrying a note with some words that the vicar had written.[397] Such sheets of paper with words or letters written on them seem to have been as common in Denmark as in Italy. In the case against Apelone Ibsdatter from Aalborg, Apelone's husband, Anders Guldsmed, had carried pieces of paper some years earlier with the names of prominent people from the city, to ensure that they dealt kindly with him. Similar practices were known from Italy, here the letters, *carte del ben voler*, contained names of saints.[398] In Venice the most regular invocation was to carry a piece of paper with the name of St. Daniele and then touch the chosen person with the paper.[399] In Orbetello magical practices, including images and medallions, were usually directed at St. Anthony. The meaning of the rituals, however, remained the same in Italy and Denmark; in both countries it was the object that possessed a power on its own, as long as it was used in the correct way. Not surprisingly, many of the healing rituals practised in Denmark paralleled Catholic practices as they had been observed before the Lutheran Reformation, and the populace did not dismiss these as witchcraft.

None of the rituals mentioned were intended to cause harm. It should also be noted that the healing rituals in the two Danish trials were not included in the formal accusation, but surfaced during the course of the trials. Instead of looking for motives, it is important to focus on the ideas that lay behind prayers such as *l'aperta* and notes with words and letters. The power of a ritual was not static. As has been seen, it would be dependent on the quality of its components, which is what lay behind getting clerics to perform the ritual. In Orbetello, the same objects, prayers and practices could be included in healing magic as in other rituals. The most common incantations involved an image or a medallion of St. Anthony. The rituals could be performed in various ways, but they all included kneeling, church candles and prayers. In some instances the practitioner would invoke God, Jesus, the Virgin Mary and so on, and sometimes even the Devil. A young woman, Columba, mentioned to the inquisitor a ritual, which she had seen performed by Elisabetta di Mancino:

she [the practitioner] took a wax candle, which she had kept in a box, and passed it to Elisabetta, who lit it and knelt in front of a figure of St. Anthony, which she had in her home, [while] she said I know not what words, as I did not hear them;
but from what this [E]Lisabetta had told me, it was the prayer to St. Anthony. [400]

In another case, against Rosa di Longone, the same ritual was meant to help Elisabetta di Jacobo get her absent lover to return to Orbetello after his regiment had left the town.[401] The same spell was used to find lost objects, as seen from the allegations against Virginia di Leandro. Depending on the purpose, similar rituals could be applied by different people and with differing results.

Common people did not believe the Devil to be the source of Girolama's magic, not least since her intention was benevolent in every respect. In Italy practitioners of benevolent magic risked being prosecuted, even though they were not suspected of performing malevolent deeds. In Denmark the court records only hold evidence of healers who were also being suspected of malevolent magic. Many cunning folk probably practised their rituals without ever being accused of evil deeds, but still they always risked being accused of witchcraft, but only if their reputation for healing became woven into accusations of malevolent magic. This was the case in the trial against Anne Jespersdatter from Gøl, a village north of the Limfjord. In court, several men blamed Anne for having stolen their potency. The man to formally accuse Anne, Mikkel Lauridsen, claimed that, some time after he had been married to his current wife, he had lost his potency and it had been gone for nearly a year. In that time, he had been 'ill and fragile' (*syg og skrøbelig*). Mikkel had then called on a cunning woman referred to as 'the cunning girl [*pige*], Uldsted Mette',[402] who had told him that Anne Jespersdatter was to blame for his impotence. Although Mikkel did not say so, he had probably mentioned to the cunning woman that he had 'bred children' with Anne and that she was infamous in the village and in the vicinity for stealing men's potency. This trial includes no further reports on Uldsted Mette.[403] It seems that Anne Jespersdatter herself was a cunning woman, since reports of rituals surfaced, although these did not really interest the judges. One witness, the wife of a blacksmith, testified that Anne had performed healing rituals on a fellow villager. The man, Svend Smed (Blacksmith) himself, was referred to as diseased. Apparently Anne, in order to cure him of his illness, had 'had him in the ground', a ritual of symbolical burial, in the couple's scullery. The testimony does not contain details about the illness the man suffered, and nor do we get any additional information about the blacksmith except that the ritual did not work and he eventually died. The ritual of putting ill people into the ground appears in several trials, and it was clearly ambiguous. The wife of the blacksmith recalled that during the practice of the ritual, she had been keeping watch by the door, so that no one would see what they were up to. This ritual seems to have been a symbolic burial with resurrection to follow, which was a kind of purification process in order to get rid of an illness. When Niels Munk at Rosborg thought his children were possessed and his wife bewitched, he sent for two cunning men to cure the children. In court one of these men testified that they had dug a small grave inside the main building (*salshuset*), and while the rest of the house had been in church, the two children were lowered into the grave, and one of the cunning men threw hallowed soil on them and read over their 'grave' before quickly raising them up again.[404] As with many other rituals referred to in the trials, the meaning and the purpose appears to have been common knowledge to people, since in most cases the ritual is simply referred to as having someone 'in the ground', without further detail.

In Orbetello, it was clear that the few accused of individual healing rituals rarely seemed to have tried their hand at explicitly malevolent magic. The grey area in Orbetello existed in magical rituals for personal gain but without intention to harm, especially in love magic, where the negative aspects were often overridden by the positive consequence that it had on the client. Mensola di Tiracoscia is the clearest example of this, but another example is the case of the scorned wife Maria, whose maid, Giobatta Mellini, was the go-between to a witch from Siena, who was to undo the spell cast over her husband.[405]

As in the trials against Mensola di Tiracoscia, Danish court records bear evidence of persons known for detecting illnesses, which was inflicted by witchcraft and for using counter-magic. The incident referred in the trial against Sidsel Christens, in which Sidsel knew whether a boy and a horse would get better, has already been mentioned.[406] In a trial of 1634, Kerstin Thamisdatter was convicted at the manor court in Storvorde, but the provincial judges later acquitted her. Thirteen years before her trial, a group of local witches had been found guilty, and Kerstin had since then borne a reputation for being a witch. When she was formally accused in 1634, a witness claimed that Kerstin had 'spoiled his milking', but when he had blamed her in public, she had promised to undo the spell, which had only made the witness more sure of his case.[407]

Expressing knowledge of whether an illness would pass or not signified that the person had special access to the supernatural, which put the person in a powerful yet fragile position. In the aforementioned trial against Anne Jespersdatter, a witness referred to him seeking the aid of the cunning woman known as Uldsted Mette. Uldsted was a village about 25 kilometres from Gøl, and in 1618, a few years before the trial against Anne Jespersdatter, Uldsted Mette (Mette Pedersdatter) had herself been convicted of witchcraft. In court Mette had confessed to various rituals of counter-magic, all of them making it clear that Mette was in control of powers not accessible to every villager. Besides helping people to get their cows to produce milk, Mette claimed that 16 years earlier she 'had been dead for three days and three nights and gone to heaven and hell'.[408] In court she testified that she had healed a widow, whom the Devil had entered, and, when Mette had conjured up the Devil, he had asked whether he could enter a specific woman of the parish instead, a request that Mette had refused. In another episode Mette had conjured evil out of a male villager, and the Devil had then returned to its sender, a woman, who had died shortly thereafter.[409] Uldsted Mette's practices reflected her awareness that her interaction with evil and control of supernatural forces combined with her reputation for identifying illnesses and practising counter-magic contributed to consolidating her position. This use of a reputation for being successful in counter-magic, combined with dropping hints of special powers and sometimes even threats, was characteristic of those convicted of counter-magic.[410]

The arrogant behaviour of some cunning folk, and their tales of contact with the supernatural aroused fear and to a certain extent respect among other villagers. In the trial against Paaske Rasmussen, a cunning man from the parish of Lem on the west coast of Jutland, about 40 people testified against him. Some of the witnesses referred to episodes that had taken place 10–15 years earlier. Paaske Rasmussen was clearly infamous.[411] The great majority stated that they had consulted Paaske with the purpose of having him heal their maladies, but at the same time it looks as if all Paaske's clients became aware that their illness might be caused by witchcraft. According to the witnesses, on many occasions the illness had disappeared, but Paaske's claims to know of the activities of suspected witches in the local area seem to have increased fear among his fellow villagers.

Many witnesses stated that Paaske had a reputation of practising 'counter magic and witchcraft' (*vise igen, trolddom og spøgeri*), and at the same time they referred to incidents in which Paaske's behaviour had been arrogant and threatening. One woman testified in court that she had called on Paaske to cure an illness, and Paaske had demanded money or other things for his services. When he heard that her poverty made it impossible for her to give him anything, he had lowered his price. Still the woman needed to borrow the money from someone else. In court the woman herself, her lender and witnesses to the illness all testified against Paaske Rasmussen. Several witnesses stated that, when revealing the client's illness to be caused by witchcraft, Paaske would sometimes offer to disclose the name of the malevolent person responsible (one's *skademand*). When it came to it, Paaske had a habit of keeping some of the information to himself, for instance by revealing that an illness was the result of a spell cast by three people, but then refusing to give up more than one name. Here Paaske may have consolidated his position as a person with special powers, who was better informed than the rest, but at the same time he was undermining his own position by keeping information from his clients. The many testimonies of incidents that could only be explained by Paaske's connection to supernatural and evil powers did not improve Paaske's standing before the judges. One witness, Christen Mortensen, recounted an incident when he and Paaske had been drinking, and at some point during the evening a light was suddenly lit in another room. Paaske had acted suspiciously by keeping quiet, so Christen had then gone in and blown out the light. Later the candle was suddenly lit again, and this had made Christen hit Paaske on the mouth, which had made him bleed, a common method to punish a witch. Afterwards Christen had suffered great loss on his cows and calves, and a few years later he had fallen seriously ill. Christen did not speak of any threats from Paaske, but given the many witnesses against Paaske, it seemed unnecessary to do so.

Compared to the narratives of healing magic and counter-magic in Orbetello trials, Danish court records included mostly counter-magic and when this was the case, it was woven into a discourse of malevolent behaviour and witchcraft. Witnesses clearly regarded people like Paaske as having some connection with evil powers. In Denmark, cunning folk on trial were usually convicted of malevolent magic. If they were sentenced according to the milder charge of 'secret arts' (*hemmelige kunster*) it was because it was not possible to prove them to be true witches. The cunning men that put Niels Munk's children in the ground were apparently not prosecuted, and, after their testimony in the trial against the suspected witch Anders Christensen, we hear no more of them.

The case concerning Paaske Rasmussen as well as the aforementioned trials of the vicar Jens Rusk and Uldsted Mette might be said to represent a Danish equivalent to the case of Mensola di Tiracoscia, although witnesses referred explicitly to Mensola as a *strega*. These people were experimenting with rituals and powers that were not entirely beneficial. In Orbetello, Mensola was the only one of her kind. If pressed for an answer by the inquisitor, healers taking smaller risks, like Girolama del Cocò, would state that divine powers were providing the power for their healing rituals and counter-magic. People could not imagine that the Devil might take part in rituals with a benevolent purpose, and in the absence of alternatives they therefore concluded that divine powers were at play. The rituals practised in Orbetello did, however, resemble those performed in northern Jutland, in the sense that heavenly powers were one out of several elements providing a ritual with its effect. The others were the physical setting, material objects involved, such as coal, fire or soil, the words and letters, and not least the person performing the ritual.

Stealing or gaining?

To the inhabitants of Orbetello, love magic was ambiguous. It could be accepted in some cases, but in others it was identified as explicitly malevolent. This depended on the circumstances. From the descriptions in the testimonies it appears that love magic with the intention of creating peace between married couples was seen as something positive. A similar perception existed for its use in attempts at catching a husband. If the man was not spoken for and did not appear to suffer physically or economically from the outcome, then people seem to have accepted the act as a kind of final option. In several cases the defence was that the use of love magic was an acceptable reaction to a miserable existence. When Lucida di Canino was charged, she explained that her motivation to attempt magical means had been her husband's mistreatment of her. Francesca di Rosata had also tried to calm her jealous husband through magical rituals.[412] Just as in healing magic, in all probability people rarely gave any thought to the origins of the powers that made these rituals effective before they came up against the Church. Instead ordinary people simply found some rituals more accepted than others. There was little attempt to articulate what the powers were that underlay these rituals, which is reflected in the following examples.

Ambiguity of motive and the need to justify actions are clearly demonstrated in the interrogation of Faustina di Leusta. Faustina had just explained how she had recited a prayer in which she had made the sign of the Cross in order to prevent her husband from causing her harm. After this she excused herself with 'I have only spoken it [the incantation] to my husband, and I did so in the belief that it was *cose di Dio* [divine things] and neither superstition nor witchcraft.'[413] Faustina clearly did not perceive this kind of love magic as the work of the Devil.

In terms of the Danish material, the court records do not show any accusations of love magic in which the magical deed has been perceived as predominantly positive. In these cases the witnesses referred to the act as stealing. The suspected witch had stolen the victim's potency or fertility, his sanity or well-being, or she had stolen the sanity of the victim's new wife. In this sense, the Danish discourse on love magic as it occurred in the trials, was simply a variety of malevolent magic, akin to stealing milk by cursing a cow, or stealing beer by spoiling the brew.[414]

To the people in Orbetello and in northern Jutland it must have been common sense to imagine the Devil as the source of malevolent magic. To theologians and to lay people, the Devil personified evil itself. Yet, from a theological perspective he also represented a powerful antithesis to God, with implications not always fully understood by lay people. It was particular true of Orbetello that witnesses and suspects would express the notion that bringing together the two supernatural powers could enhance magical rituals. According to theology, both Lutheran and Catholic, the idea that divine and satanic powers could be combined was simply inconceivable. In addition, the person of the magician was crucial to achieving the desired effect.[415]

Accounts of the Devil and evil in general were common both in Danish and Italian court records. In Orbetello the Devil was usually referred to as *il grand Demonio*, *il grand Diavolo* (the great demon or Devil) or simply *il Demonio*, and on rare occasions in plural as *diavoli*. In Danish records the Devil was named *det onde* (evil), *den onde ånd* (the evil spirit) or simply *djævelen* (the Devil). The Devil featured both in Orbetello and in northern Jutland as a force as well as a creature. When the Devil appeared, he did so in various shapes, depending on who was depicting him and at what stage of the trial.

In Orbetello as well as in Denmark, interaction with the Devil varied from trial to trial. In the Orbetello trials, it is clear that those with the most solid reputation for being witches were also those who dared to get involved in events in which the name of the Devil appeared. In Denmark, the idea of 'evil' as the generator of malevolent magic was present in all trials, although the frequency and the degree of detail with which the Devil was described varied from trial to trial. Common to the testimonies in Denmark and in Italy is a fear felt by witnesses of the Devil and of demons, and not surprisingly only few suspects from Orbetello admitted to having summoned him.

In Danish courts, the idea of evil powers underpinned all trials, but most often came to expression as 'giving evil words' or 'threatening with the Devil', referring to the witch's threat. The perception was that 'evil' was controlled by the witch, who by virtue of her relation to the Devil had the power to harm by stealing people's good fortune in milking, brewing, or draining their fertility, physical health or sanity. However, a number of trials included more information than the norm. It may seem a bit surprising that the trials in which the Devil and evil were most clearly identified were trials against cunning folk whose activities bordered on witchcraft. One example is Uldsted Mette, who claimed she had been dead for three nights and three days and during this time had been to heaven and hell. This tale was intended to convince others of her supernatural powers. When Paaske Rasmussen was convicted of witchcraft in 1618, he too had played along with the gossip about his relation to the evil powers.

If the inhabitants of Orbetello were required to articulate their idea of the Devil to the inquisitor, their answer would in all likelihood correspond to the answer that the inquisitor himself would give, namely that the ruler of Hell was a terrifying creature that no one should engage with. There is no doubt that common people regarded the Devil as the embodiment of evil. However, in magical rituals the Devil could also be counted on as a particularly powerful force, which could be harnessed by those with special knowledge, just as God's power could be by the priest. To lay people it remained difficult to understand the theological idea of the Devil as the source of all kinds of magic. The previous section emphasized that, when in direct confrontation with the inquisitor and forced to choose, lay people believed that God was the power providing magical rituals with any effect that was not explicitly malevolent. When the Devil or demons were invoked as part of the ritual, onlookers experienced a mixture of fright and indignation.[416]

In Orbetello as in northern Jutland, those reputed to control supernatural powers were subject to gossip. As a consequence, much of the information we get about the popular perception of the Devil and demons sprang from rumours and second- or third-hand accounts. The court records both from Orbetello and from the provincial court in Viborg are filled with people gossiping and voicing their indignation. Set alongside the idea that everyone ought to show fear of the Devil and the demons, talk and rumours intensified around those people suspected of involvement with the Devil, for instance by saying his name out loud. Rumours typically circulated about someone having applied a diabolical incantation for a specific purpose. The practitioner might have invoked the Devil or demons by ordering the diabolical forces to be of help, as had been the case in the extensive trial against Pollonia di Gallo. Ginerva di Pietro testified to how she had heard from another woman that Pollonia was believed to have practised several magical rituals in which the Devil's name had been included. The description of Pollonia's practices was literally without any details, as Ginerva stated: '[in] there she performed witchcraft behind closed doors and she summoned the Demon'.[417] Ginerva did, however, not know the details of the rituals, since 'Faustina [the witness] never told me what was said or invoked in this prayer.'[418] The key point in Ginerva's account was that this ritual involved an invocation of the Devil, and that Ginerva found that it required no more than her awareness of the rumour to go to the inquisitor. Pollonia di Gallo's motive had, as in most of the other episodes reported about her, been a desire for marriage.

Provincial court records from Viborg include many examples of witnesses feeling offended and indignant at someone suspected of witchcraft, and then they spiced up their testimony with references to the Devil. In Skive, on the southern coast of the Limfjord, Karen Christensdatter was accused of witchcraft in 1620, and at about the same time a trial was conducted against her and her husband for serving beer instead of being at Sunday service in church.[419] This last allegation had clearly offended many witnesses, even though this kind of offence was fairly common. In the allegation concerning witchcraft, a girl testifying against Karen stated that she knew that Karen kept a Devil. Together with her mother, Karen had beaten and torn the Devil, which had made it whine. According to the witness, the Devil was a small black thing, looking roughly like a dog or a cat. That Karen kept a devil in the shape of a black thing was confirmed by the confession made by Birgitte Engeland, who was burned at the stake the year before Karen's trial.[420] Birgitte had then denounced Karen, claiming she had a devil in the shape of a small black creature, which she whipped until it screamed. It is most probable that the maid had picked up on the gossip about Karen, which must have been flowing thick and fast following the execution of Birgitte Engeland.[421]

Generally, the depiction of the Devil as a small hairy black thing was common, but the Devil could take numerous forms in Danish trials.[422] In testimonies he could be referred to simply as 'evil' or the 'evil spirit', haunting them at night. In the trial against Anne Lundts from Skagen, a witness stated how she had been quarrelling with Anne and at some point Anne had threatened her with the Devil. Afterwards, late at night, 'evil' had come to haunt her in her house. It had first climbed on her head, and it had then moved to her mouth and tried to enter her body. This had made the woman shout to God and to make the sign of the cross over her chest. The shouting had made her husband come running and they had lit the candles and searched the room but they did not find anything.[423] That lay people perceived magic as a power that could vary in strength, is indicated by the many rituals that combined an invocation of the Devil and God. Uldsted Mette of northern Jutland had been to heaven and hell. In the trial against Anne Lumpens, a woman told the judges how a great storm had struck after she had met Anne on her way to Aalborg. At this time, the woman had already suspected Anne Pedersdatter Lumpens of witchcraft and the terrible storm on the water had confirmed her belief in Anne's control over evil powers.[424]

In northern Jutland and in Orbetello there existed a perception that the force working in a ritual could be enhanced if the magician dared to add diabolical powers. In Orbetello the common ritual of kneeling before St. Antonio could be performed only with the invocation of divine powers or by adding an invocation to the Devil or demons. The trial against the priest Stefano Tommei revolved around his invocation of all powers from heaven and hell in magical rituals.[425] As stated earlier, Stefano was accused of having read from the forbidden book of St. Daniel, and the niece Lelia recounted her experiences to the inquisitor:

> he [Stefano] knelt with a lighted wax candle in his hand, [and] I think that it was consecrated, and this priest [Stefano][...] [was] kneeling by my side; he read the invocation from the book to me, and I remember that he recited [...] blessed St. Daniel, Jesus Christ, The Virgin Mary, the entire angelic choir, and he summoned all the prophets, the angelic choir, the sun, the moon, the stars, and then started to invoke the devils one by one.[426]

According to Lelia and the other witnesses questioned, after the reading and the invocation, not least of the devils, the ritual always culminated in a violent storm and rain.[427] The bad weather must have served as a symbol of the very strong forces at play. Still, the Devil did not show himself; instead he was present as a power, as in the majority of the Danish cases.

Descriptions of encountering the Devil vary considerably, depending on whether the depiction is taken from a witness's testimony or from statements from the suspected witch. In Orbetello the Devil was mostly described as a creature summoned by the magician, who would then order him around. A similar image is presented in the Danish trials, although here the idea of the Devil as the witch's henchman is more explicit. This last part of the current chapter is dedicated to presenting some of the various shapes the Devil could take, when encountered by lay people in Orbetello and northern Jutland. In popular narratives the Devil could take various forms, but never as the fearsome creature with horns and tail.

In Orbetello, Lucida di Canino described an incantation to summon the Devil. Lucida did not give any details of his shape, but from the description a magician would not have doubts that this was, in fact, the Devil. Mensola di Tiracoscia would give more detailed accounts when interrogated. In the first couple of years of the inquisitor's presence in Orbetello, Mensola was the only one to claim that she had interacted with the Devil and demons in physical shapes. One day, for example, she had seen a large dog on the road. When it barked at her, she knew that it was the Devil himself.[428] Similarly, as described earlier, when Mensola needed to eliminate a belittled husband she was said to have summoned the Devil, who had subsequently appeared in the shape of three young, beautiful men.

In northern Jutland, many witnesses claimed they had encountered the Devil or evil itself. Accounts of the Devil usually served as proof of the witch's guilt. In Danish cases the perception of the Devil as a creature serving the witch was most evident in the witches' confessions, but the testimonies from witnesses also reflect this perception. In the trial against Jahan Knepis, a witness claimed to have watched Jahan and her fellow witches interacting with the Devil. According to the witness, he had seen three women gathered with the aim of getting the Devil to help them bewitch (*forgøre*) a co-villager. The three women had whipped the Devil, and he had been screaming 'like a howling dog'.[429] The Devil had denied being able to help the witches, since the victim was too godly and pious. This idea of the divine being able to protect people from witchcraft and evil was also seen in other trials and will be discussed further in the following chapter.

The origins of magic – a source of conflict

Perceptions of the source of witchcraft are the key to understanding the encounter between the inquisitor and illiterate lay people. Where the inquisitor had a well-defined frame of interpretation, ordinary people were interrogated about perceptions that they had hitherto not needed to explain. Interesting parallels can be drawn between the illiterate lay people's ideas in Orbetello and northern Jutland. The *intention* played a key role in attitudes towards acts of witchcraft, whether in northern Jutland or Orbetello. Central to any discussion of popular perceptions of the origins of magic is the understanding that common people did not perceive magic and witchcraft as originating from something explicitly divine or diabolical. To lay people in Orbetello as in northern Jutland, Christian dualism had little relevance. The powers at work in magical rituals came from a variety of sources. Supernatural powers, divine or diabolical, were one thing; the person performing the ritual also mattered. So did material objects, such as cloth, books or salt; actions, such as kneeling, and space all had consequences when performing a ritual. This perceived admixture of Christian doctrine and older pagan beliefs was not compatible with theological thought where everything was interpreted using the duality of good and evil, God and the Devil. To the Danish Lutheran and the Italian Catholic Church it would be unthinkable that Girolama del Cocò's pieces of coal in a glass of water or Francesca di Rosata's urine in a bowl were to have any effect at all.

Part III
Encounters in the courts

9
Honest people and wicked people

Court records clearly show how Danish trials for witchcraft perpetuated the legal practices of the Middle Ages, with the court (*tingstedet*) as a site for negotiation between two parties. Generally, a trial was instigated by prolonged enmity, which at some point culminated in yet another conflict. When the case came to court, the party with the stronger case won, and it was the judge and jury who, on the basis of testimonies given, reached this decision. The loser would be forced to pay the costs of the trial.

In Orbetello, too, what made people turn to the inquisitor would be some quarrel or conflict. They considered the arrival of the inquisitor and his instructions to report anything suspicious as the establishment of a forum, albeit a temporary one, at which they could air and settle their everyday differences. In this way their view reflected that of the Danish villagers' perception of the court (*tingstedet*). When lay people in Orbetello denounced each other, they were usually motivated by envy at certain people having something they did not have themselves, and/or indignation caused by arrogant behaviour. They blamed each other for magical offences due to concrete consequences. The inquisitorial court was not, however, a forum for solving social conflict. It was a religious court with the aim of correcting religious error, and it had the power to re-admit those who had gone astray to the flock of true believers.

An inquisitorial trial can be divided into three phases before the sentence was ultimately pronounced. The initial phase was the preliminary interrogation of witnesses, as was treated in the previous chapters. The second phase began when a defendant was incarcerated and underwent initial interrogation. The third part was the cross-examination of the defendant, one stage of which was conducted using torture. In the two last parts of the trial, the inquisitor as confessor submitted the defendant to the most blatant and intense indoctrination. When searching for a comparable encounter between Church and parishioner in the Danish courtroom, it must be remembered that before the verdict, the confrontation took place between lay persons, albeit belonging to different parts of society. The Danish trials could be divided into two phases, before and after the verdict, and clergy-men did not usually participate actively before after the sentence had been pronounced. Still, the first phase of a trial did bear the fingerprints of the Lutheran Church. In the majority of the cases, the vicar stated the suspect's living and name prior to sentencing, and in doing so acted as a kind of character witness. In addition, it was not until after the verdict, that is, during the cross-examination under torture, that the defendant herself was asked by lay and clerical authorities to respond in detail to the accusations against her.

This chapter investigates the encounter that took place in court between the judge and the person under interrogation. When a defendant or a sus-pect testified, their purpose was to convince the judge. In order to do so, it was necessary to appear to be a reliable and a sincere witness. In this sense, these testimonies reflect the norms and the behaviour that people attributed to a trustworthy person, as well as those forms of behaviours that were offensive and crossed the boundaries of social and moral norms. When reading the statements as texts of self-representation, it is possible to analyse which elements of the good citizen and the good Christian were integrated into narratives of the witch in the courtroom. Initially, the chapter identifies elements of faith that witnesses relied upon to convince the judge of their probity. What norms of moral behaviour and what perceptions of God and the Devil did people articulate before the judges in both courts?   Secondly, the chapter investigates what were the options for the suspect to defend himself or herself, and how these were applied.

The 'good Christian'

Those put on trial in Orbetello were fully aware that the inquisitor repre-sented religious authority, and in their various ways the testimonies from witnesses and suspects alike reflect how people aimed at convincing the inquisitor that they did obey the Roman Catholic faith. The answers given by the suspect and witnesses often reflected, almost copied, the leading ques-tions from the inquisitor.   At the same time, in all phases of a trial their statements can be read as nothing other than attempts to win over the judge.

Here, too, the different nature of the Danish records must be taken into consideration. Witness statements indicate that the common people drew on a narrative of the witch as a perpetrator of evil, and this perception generally dominated the course of the trial. To have a judge pass sentence on a suspected witch, the accuser had to prove that the witch had, in fact, threatened with evil and that an accident or illness had ensued. Not sur-prisingly, tales of such episodes made up the most common allegations at these trials, and here the terms 'Devil' (*Djævel*), 'the evil' (*den onde*) applied as a pronoun or 'the evil spirit' (*den onde ånd*) were used interchangeably. In many cases the witnesses and accusers reinforced this narrative by referring to a situation in which the connection between the witch and the Devil was juxtaposed against their own pious trust in God. In these examples the witness might suggest the notion of a balance of power between God and the Devil by referring to episodes in which the Devil suffered defeat at the hands of God, as occurred in the trial against Anne Lundts from Skagen. In this case, one witness testified that during a quarrel Anne had threated her that the Devil would come after her for what she did, and that night the Devil (*den onde*) had paid her a visit. By her own account, the woman had been very scared and had called out to God. Apparently this had scared the evil spirit (*onde ånd*) away, because when her husband came in, it had disappeared. The woman had been in no doubt that it was, indeed, a malevolent power at work. Afterwards she had been in a lot of pain and her arm had swollen, and soon afterwards her fingers had withered.[430] In another case, against Maren Lauridsdatter from north of the Limfjord, Anders Jensen had quarrelled with Maren, and he had called her a witch. According to Anders, Maren had responded by threatening him, saying he would get his just reward for offending her. Anders claimed that Maren had taken revenge by sending [the] evil (*den onde*) to him for three nights in a row. On the third night Maren had, too, been present. She had grabbed his feet, which had filled Anders with fear. He had called out to God, and, as he put it, this meant that '[the] evil did not get power over him'.[431] As in the case against Anne Lundts, God had come to Anders' rescue. A similar direct confrontation with the Devil occurred in Viborg one night, when a young boy had woken his parents. The boy claimed he was being chased by evil in the shape of cats. When the boy's mother had tried to lift the child into her bed, the Devil, referred to as the 'the evil fellow' (*den onde kumpan*), had grabbed her arms and tried to pull her to the floor. This had caused the husband to threaten the Devil with Jesus and, once again, the Devil showed his fear of God, this time by jumping out the window, while making a horrible noise. To underline the drama of the story, the man added that outside the window, a pack of howling dogs was waiting to accompany the Devil.[432]

The records from Orbetello do not include such evidence of encounters with the Devil. To provide their testimonies with credibility people still attempted to present themselves as good Christians by declaring to the inquisitor that they were indeed devout Christians. All the denunciators justify their appearance before the inquisitor with the standardized phrase 'to ease my conscience' (*per discarico della mia coscientia*), or 'to be honest', often adding 'for the love of God'.[433] The records, however, include further and more substantial statements of belief. Not surprisingly, none of the suspects in the Orbetello trials expressed a desire to forsake God, and in the protocols many examples are to be found of ordinary people declaring their religious dedication directly to the inquisitor. Viewed from a modern perspective, several passages carry evidence of common people, who, having previously bent Christian teachings, now tried to convince the inquisitor that they were faithful Christians after all.

They might practise illicit rituals and have an unconventional lifestyle but that did not mean they had no desire to present themselves as good Catholics.[434] Even the *strega* of Orbetello, Mensola di Tiracoscia, considered herself a devoted Catholic. She opened her testimony by declaring that she was indeed 'a sister of the Holy Cross and the illustrious Rosary'.[435] She maintained to inquisitor Pedrosa that she attended mass every week and on holy days, and that she never forgot to say her daily prayers. Afterwards Mensola revealed her knowledge of more than 30 rituals of magic and witchcraft, all of which she had practised herself.[436]

In all interrogations, both of witnesses and suspects, the inquisitor sought to clarify their practice of the faith. He made in-depth inquiries about when the witness had last confessed, had received the sacrament and had attended mass.[437] In the trial against the *donna dalla mala*, Lucida di Canino, the defendant explained that when she was young and unmarried, she had given birth to a child by a soldier.[438] She now had several sexual relationships behind her and during the last four years had at times shared her bed with an unnamed priest. Her *mala prattica* with the priest had, however, made it difficult for her to comply with her Catholic morality. She claimed herself that her only wish was to be allowed to confess and receive communion. Yet this had lately become difficult. Lucida explained:

> this previous Easter I did not receive the sacrament of the communion, as the prior at the college would not allow it. I believe the reason for this was that I lived with this priest and I behaved in such a way so I was a disgrace to my fellow citizens.[439]

The prior had also denied Lucida confession, so it had not been possible for her to atone for her sins. Lucida had continuously succeeding in getting various canons to listen to her confession, just as she maintained that she had recited her prayers every day.[440]

Like Lucida di Canino, the local church had excommunicated Virginia di Leandro. Virginia explained in a preliminary interrogation that she had neither confessed nor received communion for several years as a result of her relationship with Carlo. In a subsequent interrogation the inquisitor dealt with the topic more thoroughly in order to clarify Virginia's awareness of sin. As in the first interrogation, Virginia stated that she did not believe that she had committed any sin by living with Carlo. The two of them lived as husband and wife, and she considered the arrangement as a marriage[441]:

I, Father, do not believe that I have committed a sin in having sexual intercourse with monsignor Carlo di Luca Antonio Todi and by continuing (to keep him) company in his bed, as I see him as my husband.[442]

The inquisitor, however, did not share Virginia's perception of her sincere intentions in subduing the sinful aspect of the relationship to Carlo. He could obviously not accept a marriage without clerical blessing, and Virginia was subsequently sent to her defence lawyer.[443] After consulting him, Virginia's perception of what constituted a sin had changed significantly, and she now said: 'after having spoken to my lawyer, he [the lawyer] has brought me on the path of God' and 'I do not believe that living together with this monsignor Carlo is permitted for Christians, and [now I know] that it was a mortal offence against God.'[444]

It may appear contradictory at first glance that the suspect or witness could regard themselves as faithful Catholics while at the same time confessing to serious sins such as fornication, prostitution and witchcraft. The idea of sin preoccupied all those involved in the Orbetello trials: church authorities, witnesses and accused. People were entirely aware that a sinful life would have consequences, and the worst of these would be eternal damnation. It was therefore important to confess to these and receive absolution. Rituals of receiving communion or confession would provide people with a smattering of the sacred, just enough for them to maintain the perception of themselves as good Catholics.

Convincing the judge

As an inquisitorial trial proceeded, interrogations of witnesses became fewer and the examination of the defendant occupied increasingly greater space in the protocol.[445] During the interrogations, the defendant herself repeatedly had to account for her beliefs and for the practice of her faith. Virginia di Leandro admitted to having practised magical rituals to secure the marriage she had set her heart on. Her accuser shared this material perception of magic, and her initial accuser had denounced her out of indignation over Virginia's arrogant behaviour in the streets. In court, Virginia's relationship with Carlo, her practice of magical rituals and her unpopular behaviour towards her fellow inhabitants had been made clear to the inquisitor. When sentencing Virginia for magical offences, the inquisitor emphasized that she had believed it not to be a sin to live with Carlo. Finally, the inquisitor emphasized that for many years she had refrained from going to church and from confession. One the one hand, Virginia was convicted for having practised magical rituals and for having believed that the rituals worked. On the other, her sinful lifestyle with Carlo also became a strong reason for sentencing her. Her involvement with Carlo, her *de facto* sin of fornication and the absence of confession were offences which surfaced during the trial;

they had not featured in the original denunciations which led to formal accusation. In the interrogations Virginia repeatedly had to account for the practice of her faith and confess to her sins, and ultimately it were these statements and the sincerity of her intentions of conforming to Christian teachings that formed the basis for the verdict. In this sense it was Virginia who created the evidence against herself through her own statements. As a part of standard procedure, the inquisitor noted that through her recanting she would be absolved from the excommunication to which she had hitherto been subject.

The trial against Virginia di Leandro demonstrates that, though denunciations from neighbours may have been what initiated an inquisitorial trial in Orbetello, sentence was based on the defendant's dialogue with the inquisitor and on statements made during the cross-examinations. This is also evident from the trial against Agata di Camillo, who was first denounced for malevolent magic in 1649. Two sisters blamed her for the death of their brother, Stefano, with whom Agata had lived. According to the denouncers, Agata had cast a deadly spell on Stefano after he had expressed a wish to terminate their relationship. Several witnesses had subsequently testified to Agata's practice and knowledge of magic and witchcraft. When the inquisitor summarized the case, he emphasized the magical rituals that, according to witnesses, Agata had practised. Some people even believed her to have invoked the Devil.[446] Agata di Camillo had a motive: Stefano wanted to leave her. And she had witnesses testifying against her – as previously mentioned, the two sisters of the late Stefano, who had denounced her. Added to this, a nephew testified that Agata had quarrelled with Stefano and threatened him that he would get 'a hundred Devils in [his] body' (*cento diavoli in corpo*).[447] Agata herself had denied ever having practised malevolent magic or having had anything to do with the death of her lover. Upon the recommendation of the tribunal in Siena, inquisitor Pedrosa had sent Agata to cross-examination in the torture chamber. This did not, however, produce a full confession of malevolent magic. Agata merely admitted to having practised several incantations of love magic, all of them with the intention of 'tying' Stefano.

The allegations made against Agata were serious and they were made by those who knew her. The final sentence does, however, stand in contrast to the denunciations. The inquisitor convicted her of the lightest category of heresy,[448] and he justified the verdict by stating that Agata had 'believed and held [it to be] possible that using magical incantation the demons could violate the human will'.[449]

Agata was found guilty of believing in the efficacy of love magic, and the inquisitor overlooked the allegations that she had killed Stefano. He clearly believed these to have been based on personal grudges by Stefano's two sisters. The accusations of malevolent magic against Agata arose from the disapproval that Stefano's family felt for this amorous connection. To convince the inquisitor that she did not have evil intentions and that she had merely acted out of desperation, Agata had continuously insisted on her belief in God and had denied ever having evil intentions. She, too, was motivated by a selfish desire to retain her lover, and magical rituals became a method for achieving this. In the inquisitor's sentence, the accusations had developed into sin, namely heresy and apostasy. To the inquisitor, the ideal evidence in such cases continued to be a full confession from the defendant. Similar to Agata, the 30-year-old Faustina di Leusta denied the allegations made against her. Witnesses accused her of repeatedly having practised love magic, but she persistently rejected these allegations, although she confessed to the milder offence that on a few occasions she had recited an *oratione ad amorem*. The inquisitor categorized Faustina as 'slightly suspected of heresy'[450] and she was sentenced to the mild penalty of abjuring her heretical beliefs and standing in front of the church while mass was celebrated.[451]

These examples illustrate how the inquisitor in Orbetello regarded the practice of magical rituals as religious offences, rather than as a method for material gain, which had formed the basis of the original accusations. Equally, they demonstrate that these trials were held in a judicial system in which the judge acted as confessor with the obligation of giving absolution. The denunciations from fellow inhabitants of the town were always included in the trials, but the most crucial piece of evidence against a suspect continued to be the statements – the confession – given by the suspect herself.

Judgement in Denmark

In a Danish trial, a suspect was rarely interrogated until after the verdict, which meant that the option of conducting a defence through a dialogue with the judge was practically non-existent. Every guilty verdict notes the reputation that the accused enjoyed among co-villagers, and records whether anyone had been willing to stand up for her by defending her reputation and name (*skudsmål*). The great majority of those convicted of witchcraft in northern Jutland resembled Sidsel Christens, who, as is noted by the judges at the provincial court, did not present evidence in court of being an honest person living an honest life, which meant she could not provide witnesses swearing to her good name. In contrast to the Orbetello cases, public opinion in a village was crucial to a Danish suspect's chances of acquittal. When the judges pronounced the sentence, summarizing the accusations from co-villagers and the lack of *skudsmål*, they commonly applied the phrase 'those living in the same parish and who therefore are best acquainted with her way of life'.[452] Co-villagers, then, played a crucial part to the outcome of a trial. If the local village was willing to support the suspect, chances of acquittal increased. It is clear that in those cases where the suspect was able to present witnesses in her own defence, her chances of acquittal were significantly increased. In the trial against Anders

Christensen from Fusager, the defendant was accused alongside his wife and children. The accuser, captain Niels Munk, blamed Anders and his wife for causing the illness of Niels Munk's wife and children. During the trial, Anders Christensen presented a parish witness who confirmed that at the lower court, 24 men had stood up for him in stating that 'Anders Christensen, his wife and children had always behaved and led a Christian life'.[453] Ultimately, Anders Christensen and his wife were acquitted by the King's Court (*Kongens Retterting*). A similar course of events took place in the trial from 1620 against Karen Christensdatter from Skive. She was charged with witchcraft, and during the trial it was Karen's husband, Christen Jensen Gammelgaard, who led her defence. Gammelgaard first raised doubts about the trustworthiness of the witnesses against his wife. About a year before the trial, Karen Christensdatter had been denounced for witchcraft by a convicted witch, Birgitte Engelands. In court, Gammelgaard maintained that such a denunciation coming from an offender (*misdæder*) could not be trusted and therefore should not be considered valid by the court. Additionally, he argued that two girls who had testified against his wife were ignorant, and that a third witness, an adult man, had been drunk when he accused Karen. After refuting the credibility of the witnesses against his wife, Gammelgaard presented the testimony of 24 men, who had all given an oath on Karen Chrestensdatter's good name and reputation and avowed that no one in the parish had ever suspected her of witchcraft before Birgitte Engelands had denounced her in her confession. Gammelgaard also presented a witness confirming that 24 men had sworn always to have known Karen as an 'honest and pious *dannekvinde*'.[454] When applied to a married woman the term *dannekvinde* meant that the woman was a good wife and mistress of her household – or in other words that she had all the virtues of a Christian woman; she was loyal, honest and respectable. Gammelgaard chose a common and successful strategy to handle the Danish legal system, when he proved that the witnesses against his wife were not to be trusted, and by proving that the local community would swear to her good name. In addition, Gammelgaard had 24 men affirm that Karen was pious and sought the Church as a devoted Christian. Her *skudsmål* for being a good Christian woman was supported by the vicar of Skive, Antonius Christensen. The vicar asserted that he had always known Karen to have acted according to the faith in matters 'inside the church as well as outside'. Only when the witch Birgitte Engelands had denounced Karen, had her reputation been damaged.

The cases against Karen Christensdatter of Skive and Anders Christensen of Fusager illustrate how an active defence became included in the evidence and was therefore crucially important to the outcome of a Danish trial. In order to conduct an active defence, a female defendant needed a male guardian to present witnesses on her behalf. The trials also served to demonstrate that the witch's name and reputation were crucial in trials for witchcraft.

To acquire a good *skudsmål* and to rebut charges of witchcraft demanded a twofold strategy. First, the suspect had to present good and honest men from the local society to testify to the suspect's good name. Secondly, the person who was supposed to best know all the parishioners – the vicar – had to make a positive statement.

Only rarely was a clergyman brought in to verify that an illness had in fact been caused by witchcraft, as in the case against Inger Jensdatter from Malle near Thisted.[455] Here the vicar confirmed that the girl, whom Inger was accused of harming, was really suffering from an unnatural illness and that evil forces had possessed her. However, in most trials the vicar was called upon to comment on the reputation of the suspect. Almost every trial for witchcraft contains a written statement from clergymen. In his statement he would confirm whether the suspect was reputed to be a witch, and for how long she had had this reputation. This was the case of 'Lang' Maren Lauridsdatter from Øster Hassing. The vicar recalled that Maren had had the reputation for being a witch for as long as he could remember, and that he and many people in the village were familiar with a certain incantation she would practise against mice and rats.[456] Trials often contained the testimony of more clergymen. This was the case in the trial against the cunning man Paaske Rasmussen, sentenced for witchcraft in 1618. Three clergymen testified to Paaske's reputation, one being from Paaske's resident parish, another the dean, who also acted as vicar of the church in a neighbouring parish, and the third also from a neighbouring parish. They unanimously declared that Paaske had had a reputation for being a witch for years.

The testimonies of clergymen were fundamental in revealing the reputation of a suspect. Evidence against a suspect was gathered partly through witnesses recounting how the suspect had threatened them with evil, and partly through proving the suspect's poor reputation. The vicar was expected to know his parishioners, and in this sense the Danish lay judges were dependent on the testimony of the clergy. Although usually delivered as a written statement, the declaration by the vicar emphasizes that what mattered in a Danish trial was the accused's reputation in the neighbouring community, and to reveal this the testimony of the vicar was essential. A trial for witchcraft remained a legal contest between two individuals with the judges determining who had the better case.

Responses to popular narratives

In an inquisitorial trial, the essential part of the evidence came from the confession. This was obtained during repeated interrogation of the suspect, and following the verdict the convicted person had to recant her evil ways. As was the case with interrogations of other witnesses and suspects, these cross-examinations were recorded as exact transcripts of both questions and answers. Historians have noted the ignorance of the people on trial and the inquisitor's awareness of this. According to the Church, magicians who thought they were kneeling before God were in fact kneeling before the Devil.[457] In Orbetello a number of similar examples were seen. The most common were spells involving the practitioner having to kneel before the image of St. Anthony and holding a lit candle. Although, a number of people in Orbetello seem to have been familiar with the doctrine of free will, this did not, however, inhibit the practice of love magic.

To the inquisitor it was crucial to establish the accused's understanding of the notion of free will. Chapter 3 demonstrated how the inquisitor's condemnation of love magic came from a post-Tridentine emphasis on the doctrine of free will. The trials involving love magic expose the essential meaning of the popular perception of the will. When Mensola di Tiracoscia's sister, Deva di Tiracoscia, was questioned about her use of magnets in love magic, the inquisitor asked about her thoughts on free will, specifying whether or not she believed that demons could force human will. Not surprisingly, she replied simply to this leading question: 'I do not believe that demons have the powers to force the human will.'[458]

Suspects clearly tried to answer questions correctly, but their statements were rarely more detailed than repeating the inquisitor's leading questions. Francesca di Rosata, sentenced for love magic in 1651, was questioned by the inquisitor as to her motives. Francesca maintained that she had practised magical rituals due to fear: 'and this I did, so that this Pasquale would desire me and not end our relationship'.[459] This made the inquisitor inquire further to clarify Francesca's ideas concerning love magic and human will. When asked directly if she thought it possible that demons could coerce human will, she answered[460]:

It was never my wish or my belief that, using this urine [which had been applied in the ritual], the demons that I invoked could force either Pasquale's or anyone else's will [...] knowing too well that the Devil does not have such power.[461]

In the following passages of the interrogation, Francesca can be seen to comply with the perception of the inquisitor. She had probably never before found herself in a situation where it was necessary to conduct a theological discussion of free will. That her perception was rather shallow is also apparent later in the interrogation: 'as I said, I learned it from the said Nastasia, who told me about this and led me to believe that it was the urine incanted by this star that had the power'.[462] Francesca might have agreed with the inquisitor that the Devil did not exercise power over human will, but in her view this only meant that something else did. It must have been the urine and the star. Although Francesca denied having interacted with the Devil, the case remained serious for the inquisitor, as her ideas still came into conflict with the Church.

In the subsequent interrogation, Francesca maintained that she had explained everything that might be of interest to the inquisitor. Her perception of magical rituals as a means for acquiring something is reflected in her statements, and she seems to have believed that, by confessing to her entire repertoire of magical practices, she had satisfied the inquisitor's requirements. It was characteristic of those on trial to expect the interest of the inquisitor to be limited to the physical act performed in the rituals. Having confessed to these practices, the suspects were clearly surprised when the inquisitor continued his questioning, often by starting all over again.[463] In his preliminary interrogation, inquisitor Pedrosa must have let Francesca express her beliefs concerning human will. He had not questioned her argumentation and, by not doing so he had led Francesca to believe that her ideas were acceptable. This strategy of letting people talk was a standard method applied by the inquisitor in the first interrogation of the suspect.[464] Even when the *strega* Mensola di Tiracoscia was interrogated, she was allowed to recount her rituals without interruption from the inquisitor, except for occasional questions and requests to clarify matters. To the inquisitor this was the part of an investigation that would prepare him for the subsequent interrogations. The suspect's voluntary testimony meant that the inquisitor was able to glean information about the person and his or her actions that provided him with information on how to approach matters in the subsequent and more intense interrogations.[465] The low profile kept by the inquisitor would possibly also have encouraged the defendant to speak.

When Francesca was put before the inquisitor for questioning once more, she was again required to state her ideas concerning human free will. The inquisitor now became more direct in his questions and demanded yet again that Francesca present her ideas about magical rituals. She continued to deny any connection between her actions and the Devil, and firmly maintained that she had never professed herself to the Devil. Throughout the interrogation, Francesca clearly failed to understand the Devil's role in love magic, as it was perceived by the inquisitor. The act had been motivated solely by a desire for Pasquale to maintain his affection for her and not to abandon her. Ultimately she admitted to having been motivated by 'a dishonest wish, which I had, that Pasquale Pesci would desire me and not abandon me'.[466]

Francesca was now led to the torture chamber for the final cross-examination.[467] Before the torture got under way, she asserted once again that she did not believe that the Devil could force human will. That Francesca now refrained from mentioning her original perception of the powers of the stars seems to have been sufficient to the inquisitor, as he did not probe further into her perception of free will during the interrogation by torture. The encounter with the *strappado* apparently eradicated any lingering doubts that might have existed concerning Francesca's repentance. Clearly under extreme stress, she assured the court that she now knew that practising magical rituals was forbidden, and that she had been tempted by the Devil as a result of her dishonest desire (*desidera inhonesta*).

All of the trials of love magic show that during the course of events the suspect was required to acknowledge that the practice of love magic involved the mocking of free will. Francesca must have acquired a degree of familiarity with the doctrine of free will through her confessor, but she had not fully understood its meaning. Some witnesses, though, did show that they understood that love magic interfered with the choices open to the individual. This was expressed by an older woman, who testified in the trial against Lucida di Canino:

> I have understood, and this is publicly known, that on many occasions this donna Lucida [di Canino] has practised incantations and witchcraft to [...] get a man to marry a certain woman, even if this is only the desire of one of them.[468]

When the inquisitor posed direct questions about the perception of the accused regarding free will, the people on trial almost always gave a negative answer. An example was the case against the maid Giobatta Mellini, who was accused of having arranged the contact between her mistress and a witch in Siena with the purpose of liberating her mistress' husband of his *mala prattica* with another woman. Giobatta was asked under interrogation whether she believed that will could be forced, and she categorically stated, 'Father, I have never believed in such a thing.'[469] Such answers were typical results of the inquisitor's leading questions concerning the perception of human free will. As must be expected, none of the witnesses acted as Ginzburg's Friullan miller Menocchio and actively debated this with the inquisitor. Everyone went along with the orthodox perception of free will.[470] The perception did not seem to be more than skin-deep, however, and it did not correspond with actions in real life. Francesca di Rosata's idea of urine and the stars being able to bend free will should probably not be regarded as a well-considered theory but rather as expressing a perception that the Devil did not interfere in the ritual.

What made lay people condemn and denounce the offence to the inquisitor was a material perception of love magic. When women manipulated men into marriage, it was regarded as a dishonest method in an already tough competition. If an individual made use of diabolical means to take possession of more than their just desserts, it meant that there would be less for the righteous. None of the practitioners of love magic showed any remorse as regards the doctrine of free will. Lay people might be suspicious of the practice, but they never denied that the rituals could produce an effect. To the inquisitor it mattered less whether the rituals worked or not;

the sin lay in the violation of the doctrine of free will. In other words, it was regarded as a religious crime.

The Danish confessions

In Danish trials, everyone sentenced for witchcraft was interrogated after the verdict was pronounced, with the aim of extracting a full confession before execution. Nevertheless, the confession was not usually preserved in the trial records, and only few full accounts have been preserved.[471] It seems to have been the established procedure to read aloud the confession, possibly just before the fire was lit, in order to communicate elements of a particular confession to the spectators. The denunciations that these confessions would have elicited and the mandatory listing of fellow witches must have nourished emerging reputations for witchcraft among villagers, and formed the seedbed for the next set of accusations.[472] Numerous trials include references to confessions in which the accused had been denounced in this way. Usually these were brief quotations from what must have been lengthy confessions, though these are not preserved. Such references were often standardized notes such as, 'NN1 had denounced NN2 [the person now on trial] for this and that witchcraft, whereby she and her fellow witches had killed both people and cattle.'[473] A small percentage, less than 10 per cent of the trials from Jutland, cite confessions with detailed descriptions of malevolent deeds, and, as with fragmentary references, these descriptions are most commonly included in the trial proceedings against another suspect, who had been denounced by the convicted witch. Such references from previous confessions served as additional evidence against the accused currently on trial. Only on rare occasions was the document containing the confession attached to the trial of the witch who was actually confessing.

As stated in chapter 4, the purpose of torture was to prompt the witch to produce a full confession. In so doing she would both surrender the names of her accomplices and secure milder treatment from God in the afterlife. The circumstances surrounding the actual recording of the confession are difficult to determine. In the trial records from Ribe, those present during the torture of suspects are listed at the top of the documents. They include lay authorities as well as at least one vicar, but the trials conducted at the provincial court in Viborg do not contain this information.[474]

Some elements of folklore were always included in the confession but these varied from region to region.[475] According to the Regulation of 1617, the key element in witchcraft was that the witch had entered a pact with the Devil, and the theological argument arising from this was pursued in the cross-examination of the witch. To the interrogators the core of the offence came to the fore when the witch admitted to having abjured her faith. The confessions from Ribe in particular include information of when, where and in whose company the witch had entered into the diabolical pact. Karen Roeds from Ribe, who was sentenced for witchcraft in 1620, had been approached by a man in a chamber in her house, whom she appeared to know. Here he had 'instructed her in witchcraft'. The man's son had also been present, he being the head of their witchcraft society (*rodemester*). More commonly the abjuration took place in or around the church. Anna Lourups claimed to have renounced her baptism at the cemetery of Skast, a village near Ribe, and Bodil Harchisdatter had done so at the cemetery of St. Peter's Church in Ribe. In Aalborg, Apelone Guldsmeds had renounced her faith at St. Boel's Church, after which her servant Devil, Raggi, had been waiting for her by the southern door of the church.[476] In all of the accounts of such abjuration of God, the witch would receive her 'boy' (*dreng*) in exchange.

The idea of the witch having a boy, a kind of servant Devil, featured in all the confessions. This did not correspond to the demonological perception of the Devil as master of the witches, nor of the Devil as a deceiver tricking the witch into believing she was master of demons. Instead, the Devil encountered in the Danish witches' confessions corresponds to the image of the Devil given in the testimonies. He was summoned by the witch, who through an act of free will turned her back on God and opened herself to evil; and he would do the bidding of her and her group. The servant Devils always had a name, sometimes human names but more often reflecting attributes, such as Svarting (black), Raggi (furry, wiry) or animals and things like Ravn (Raven), Semmel Semmel (a kind of bread – and double). The Devil attended on the witch as a domestic servant, and she had the right to order him around and to punish (*revse*) him by flogging. In her confession, Apelone Guldsmeds from Aalborg had revealed that when her society was meeting the previous year, she had not been able to come herself and instead she sent her servant Devil, Raggi, ordering him to participate in all the evil deeds the other witches decided to perform. On his way to the gathering, Raggi had met 'the girl from Sæby serving at Christen Stopdrup' and this had prevented him from performing these evil deeds. Instead, Raggi cast evil in the form of an illness on the girl.[477]

Besides confessing to the witch's abjuration of God, the confessions contained detailed descriptions of the wicked and malevolent deeds the witch had been accused of in the trial. When three witches sentenced for causing illness to strike Captain Niels Munk's wife and children confessed, they recounted how together with fellow witches they had travelled through the air to Rosborg, the small manor at which the Captain lived, in the shape of birds. At Rosborg they had put down a small bag of evil to inflict illness, and they had cast away the health and fortune of Niels Munk. However, Niels Munk had never been infected with evil, since he was, according to the three witches, too firm in his belief in God. Instead, evil had been deflected and had struck his family. The motive for harming Niels Munk had been revenge on the Captain for a long-term property dispute he had been in with one of the witches. The confessions generally confirm the perception of the witch as an evil being, harming people for revenge. In the trial against Birgitte Nielskone from Varde, the confession of a convicted witch was presented. This text confirmed one of the allegations against Birgitte, namely that she had quarrelled with the owner of a shop (*krambod*) over the price of some hemp. Allegedly the disagreement had made Birgitte angry, and she had threatened the shopkeeper and afterwards cast evil on him with her 'witchcraft and their [Birgitte and her fellow witches'] boys'.[478] Similarly in Ribe, Anna Lourup's boy had capsized a boat transporting a man who had insulted Anna's honour, and in Aalborg in the 1610s, Apeloni Guldsmeds confessed that her boy placed knots and nails in the houses of her enemies, in order for 'accidents to happen to them'.[479]

Confessions of Danish witches confirm the perception of the witch adopted by the witnesses in their allegations in the initial phase of a trial. The witch was vengeful and bad-tempered and triggered fear among her co-villagers, and witchcraft was less ritualized and more verbal than in Orbetello. It is clear that it was important to have the witch admit to her turning from God and subsequently to having entered into a pact with the Devil, but other than this the presence of the Devil, in the shape of 'boys', was more in line with an indigenous narrative of wicked women controlling evil and casting it at their enemies. This is confirmed by statements from witnesses that reveal the dominant emotions in the trials were fear and anger.

Parting ways

Although there were clear differences in the magical offences brought to court in Orbetello and northern Jutland, the popular narrative of the witch/ offender as presented by witnesses drew upon similar perceptions. In both cases the suspect challenged the limits of acceptable social behaviour, and had been an obstruction to peaceful co-existence. The allegations leading to trials in Orbetello, as well as in northern Jutland, all arose from conflicts between the suspect and the accuser/denouncer. But the emotions triggered in these conflicts were diverse. In northern Jutland, witnesses referred to the suspect as evil and vengeful, and for this reason the suspect triggered fear and anger among fellow villagers. In Orbetello, the majority of suspects had triggered emotions of envy and indignation, and, in general, the suspects had challenged the perception of limited goods by using magical rituals to acquire something or someone. When witnesses tried to distance themselves from those they had denounced, the suspects' pride and arrogance seem to have been the most commonly attributed behaviours.

Both courts under both jurisdictions included dialogue about faith. In Orbetello the inquisitor always required a witness as well as a defendant to profess their relation to the Church. Appearing before the inquisitor or confronted with testimonies of their sinful acts, defendants always sought to emphasize their sincere belief in God, their good intentions, or merely their ignorance – as was the case with Virginia di Leandro justifying her cohabitation with Carlo. By stating they had received the sacraments and confessed on a regular basis, a person demonstrated they had adhered to the teachings of the Catholic Church and as such was a trustworthy person. One's relation to the Church determined if one was trustworthy. In Denmark, witnesses could underline a suspect's evil doings by providing examples of their own unshaken faith and trust in God and how they had used their faith to disrupt a witch's evil doings. In addition they implicitly underlined their own worth as good Christian people. The medieval and lay term *dannemand* or *dannekvinde* was applied to indicate a person being honourable and trustworthy. In trials for witchcraft the terms were explicitly linked to faith, to the idea of being a good *Christian* woman or man. Nevertheless, the proof of being trustworthy went through the surrounding local society. A suspect's only hope to prove their trustworthiness was by by presenting witnesses in court to swear to their good name and honest lifestyle. Without village support in court, it was hard, if not impossible, for the accused to be acquitted.

10
Conclusion: the confessor and the judge

The aim of this book was to compare how the authorities proscribed and proceeded against witchcraft, and how the prosecutions were applied locally. How did official positions on witchcraft come to have influence on the offences brought to trial, and what agency were accusers, witnesses and suspects left with? In my introduction, I presented two trials to illustrate the main differences between Roman Inquisitorial and Danish lay prosecutions of witchcraft. Stefano Tommei from Orbetello was sentenced to imprisonment and a large fine; Johanne Pedersdatter from Sejlflod was sentenced to death by burning. Both were convicted of witchcraft (*sortilegio/trolddom*), and the difference in punishments can be traced back to the two essentially different courts prosecuting the same offence.[480]

To understand the differences in the prosecutions of witchcraft, one must start by understanding the beliefs in witchcraft. Therefore, the initial part of the book concentrated on identifying the official approaches of the Danish provincial court and of the Roman Inquisition; and furthermore to analyse these in operation, in order to compare the practical handling of the cases. The second part of the book was devoted to examining the individuals on trial. It investigated the kind of actions and behaviours that led to suspicions of witchcraft, and identified the common aims of practising witchcraft and magical rituals. The final chapter examined the encounter between the suspects and the judge, and the strategies applied by both accusers and suspects when trying to convince the judge.

Instruction and reaction

As in many other European regions, cases in the present studies were sparked from below. Although it was the Roman inquisitor in Orbetello who decided whether to prosecute or not, he was rarely the prime mover of an investigation. The numerous denunciations for witchcraft indicate that the inquisitor was at no time lacking potential suspects. The wave of denunciations for witchcraft in Orbetello must on the one hand be regarded as a local response to a prohibition, that is, the edicts of faith, issued by the Roman Inquisition in Siena, and what practices and rituals the populace of Orbetello categorized as witchcraft; on the other hand, the court testimonies bear witness to what kind of people were prone to practise illicit rituals and the behaviours that were linked to these transgressors of social norms.

A similar pattern can be detected in Denmark. Here the pulpit was commonly used for communicating new regulations from lay authorities, and the Witchcraft Regulation of 1617 was no exception. As in Orbetello, the Regulation was a *carte blanche* and a seal of approval from the highest of authorities (the king) for the lower courts and villagers to launch the witchhunt that had been smouldering for at least the past decade. The wave of trials lasting the following five to six years can be characterized as hailstorms moving across Jutland. As soon as one witch was convicted, more accusations arose. It was a self-perpetuating process until something or someone broke the pattern. Either the local community had suffered from a collective shock causing them to stop the brutalities, or the judges, especially at the Provincial court, repeatedly dismissed trials or acquitted suspects, so causing the accusers to give up.

In many areas of northern Jutland, witchcraft prosecutions swept across villages and districts before moving on to the next; in some villages, prosecutions returned after decades, albeit on a smaller scale. In Orbetello, a micro-scale version of this scenario can be detected, when the inquisitor issued an edict of faith in late 1648, causing a surge of denunciations. For the first 18 months the inquisitor thoroughly investigated and sentenced several individuals, but he soon abstained from prosecution, despite the fact that new denunciations kept coming. After several years, denunciations for witchcraft started to decrease and soon faded out. The main activity of the inquisitor then became dealing with blasphemous outbursts of the populace – generally, simple swearing.

Witchcraft: gaining and harming

In Orbetello, rituals for personal gain were primarily practised to acquire a lover or achieve marriage. The suspects were poor and with only a few exceptions, women. In the 17th century, marriage was the only certain way for women to move up the ladder of social status and to eliminate the risk of social marginalization.[481] In early modern Tuscany, the age of men entering into marriage was higher than in northern Europe. This left a large proportion of Tuscan women unmarried, since many men simply died before they reached their marital age.[482] Another challenge to securing a husband was that many Italian men were affiliated with the Church or serving in the army. This was also the case in Orbetello, although, as we have seen, neither a military uniform nor canonical garb were insurmountable obstacles. Many trials involved women practising magic to have their soldier *amici* return after they were transferred to other military companies. In Denmark, marriage continued to be the common way of organizing families and communities in the 17th century.[483] Therefore, a possible reason for the lack of accusations of love magic in Denmark could be that marriage was more common. It would simply not have been 'necessary' to practise magical rituals to achieve marital status in the same way, although this is perhaps too simplified an explanation.[484]

In both regions, marriage was perceived as a secular matter. It was a functional union in relation to economy, production, emotional life and reproduction. Both in Italy and Denmark, the Churches sought to make marriage a religious matter. Despite having rejected marriage as a sacrament, Luther regarded it a divine gift and alliance between two people. In the Catholic Church, marriage continued to be a sacrament, and naturally, according to the Church, it should be overseen by ecclesiastical authorities. For the Roman Catholic as well as the Danish-Lutheran Church, marriage ceremonies in churches became an instrument in social disciplining in the 16th and 17th centuries. Love magic in Orbetello was very much connected to sexual relationships outside of or before marriage, and this was highly incompatible with the post-Tridentine ideals. By prosecuting love magic, the inquisitors and, as such, the Catholic Church, implicitly prosecuted sexual relationships outside of marriage; it was, in other words, an effective method of social disciplining the population. Still, this connection between marriage and love magic can only be a part of the explanation as to why love magic was prevalent in Orbetello and absent in Denmark.

That love magic in its non-harming form did not appear in the Danish witch trials is not that surprising considering the fact that the law prohibited malevolent magic only throughout the 16th century; however, absence of the phenomenon in the cases should not lead us to think that love magic was not a part of popular belief in early modern Denmark. Magical practices to gain fortune in love were traditionally not considered a part of the Danish discourse of witchcraft. This discourse referred to witchcraft as speech rather than rituals and it primarily contained explicit malevolent magic inflicted by evil-natured people. Rituals, spells and prayers were applied to vital parts of daily lives, such as the harvest, the brewing of beer, fertility, childbirth and marriage. A collection of old Danish spells published by the folklorist Ferdinand Orht includes eighteen spells to awaken the love of a desired person.[485] Like the Italian *orationi*, the Danish love-spells are a mix of pagan and Christian symbols and rituals; one involved chicken eggs, another one the invocation of St. Thomas Aquinas.

Honest people always speak the truth

A greater demand for love magic amongst the women in Orbetello than amongst Danish women is far from the full explanation for the difference

between northern Jutland and Orbetello. The perception of the people performing these acts, or rather, the perception of what kind of persons were *liable* to perform them, must be incorporated. From the court records we know
that in Orbetello the majority of suspects were generally poor and prostitutes, concubines or adulterous married women. In Denmark, most suspects
were also women, but usually they were married or widows, and they only
rarely belonged to the impoverished group of society. In Orbetello, Mensola
di Tiracoscia was the only person to be referred to as a witch (*strega*), that
is, as mastering inherent powers. The remaining individuals were described
by their practices, that is, they knew of *sortilegio*, and with reference to their
reputation in the town: that is. they were *donne dalla mala fama*, women of
a bad reputation. These women did not cause people to fear them; instead
they made their neighbours indignant and occasionally angry. In Denmark,
witches were described both as witches (*troldfolk*) and as those knowing of
or controlling witchcraft (*trolddom, trolddomskunst, spøgeri*).

Love magic has traditionally been linked to urban societies, whereas cases
in rural areas were predominately ones of malevolent magic.[486] In his comparative study of Valencia and Catalonia, Gunnar Knutsen has argued that
demographic diversity in the regions played a decisive role for the form of
witchcraft sentenced by the inquisitors.[487] The Catalonian tribunal treated
several cases of malevolent magic, possibly due to influence of demonological ideas brought to the region by French immigrants. The rural areas
of Valencia were mostly inhabited by Moriscos, who did not adhere to
Christian demonology; in towns, where Christians were the majority inhabitants, cases were predominately concerned with magic for personal gain.
Although Orbetello was not an urban environment like Venice or Rome, the
town did possess some of the features characteristic of urban spaces, namely
soldiers and prostitutes, and this demographic mix must have generated
fertile ground for love magic.

In Denmark, too, port towns in particular were home to a significant number of prostitutes and soldiers, although it is difficult to say anything certain
about the use of love magic. It is likely to have been commonly practised,
but it did not come up in the witch trials. The cases from Aalborg, one of
Jutland's larger port towns, and the important trading centre of Ribe provide
no evidence of love magic; here too the cases revolved around malevolent
magic. In Denmark, the presence of prostitutes and soldiers apparently did
not generate trials for love magic.

It is worth noting what kind of people were regarded as likely to practise
witchcraft. Who were the culprits in Orbetello compared to the culprits
in Jutland? By comparing the narratives of witches with the narratives of
their opposites, that is, the good Christians, it is possible to conclude that
in Jutlan people feared the witch and especially her anger and revenge.
This narrative corresponds with the argument posed by Stephen Mitchell
regarding the evil woman in Nordic folklore melding with the misogyny

of the 15th century, and thereby creating fertile ground for witch-hunts. In the 17th century, the narrative of the witch in Jutland continued to be the narrative of the evil woman feared by neighbours and villagers for her anger and vengefulness. Only in the confessions did demonological features add to this figure. The narratives presented in the confessions by the witch herself support this. As soon as the interrogators were informed of when, where and with whom the witch had renounced her faith, as well as of some incidents revealing a few details on the sabbath, the rest of the confession was basically a confirmation of the 'evil woman narrative'. Here the witch herself confessed that she was indeed vengeful and filled with anger, and that she had harmed people due to this. Ultimately this narrative was confirmed and enforced by the judges when they pronounced the sentence. In the sentence, the judges always underlined that the witch had threatened others with illnesses or accidents and that these had struck. Thus, as a rule the judges would confirm the 'evil woman narrative'.

Ideas of witchcraft within the courts

A clear difference between the two legal systems was apparent as soon as a trial began. In the inquisitional system, the inquisitor was the one assessing if an offence had been committed. The inquisitor's theological perception of witchcraft was thus decisive in determining which reports would lead to a charge. This was profoundly different in the Danish lay system, where the injured party also acted as prosecutor, and where the trial was basically a negotiation between the accuser and suspect. As long as the Danish judges continued to sentence people for witchcraft with reference to the same narrative as the accusers, it was this popular narrative of witches and witchcraft which determined what kinds of witchcraft would be brought to court.

The Catholic idea of penance as an atonement of sin was rejected in Lutheran Protestantism with the Reformation. Only God could forgive Man. The personal relationship to God was, however, interwoven with Mosaic Law. The Lutheran Church viewed God as zealous, and the king was obliged to punish all offenders in order for God not to cast his wrath on the entire kingdom. According to this system, punishment of perpetrators was effected to protect the entire community. God would deal with the individual in the afterlife, since forgiveness could not be obtained in this life but should be sought beyond. When the Danish legal system punished witches, it was thus a sanction performed on behalf of the community to demonstrate before God that the secular authorities did not tolerate offenders. The lower courts and the provincial courts became institutions carrying out this task in practice; thus executing or exiling the culprits cleansed society. The essential concern remained for society in general rather than the individual.

The rare use of the death penalty within the Italian cases symbolized the fundamental Catholic idea of penance as atonement of sin, and that through penance the individual could be readmitted into the Church. Officially, the inquisitor sanctioned for the sake of the individual. It was the offences committed against the Church that needed to be eliminated, not the people committing them. Instead, the offender needed to understand her errors and the sinful nature of her acts. The post-Tridentine inquisitor considered himself the benevolent father, who was meant to discipline his flock. The individual was thus placed at the centre, since the inquisitor in fact punished the offender out of mercy.

Epilogue: changes at the turn of the 17th century

During the second half of the 17th century scepticism towards witchcraft grew with Danish lay courts and within the Roman Inquisition.[488] In Denmark, the last guilty sentence for *trolddom* was pronounced in 1693 by the High Court in Copenhagen. In Orbetello, the last sentence for *sortilegio* was pronounced in 1660 against Giobatta Mellini, found guilty of love magic.[489]

Absolutism was established in Denmark in 1660, and it generally caused a heavier bureaucracy in official administration, as well as the continuation of the centralization of legal institutions. During the second half of the 17th century, Danish courts gradually adopted legal features known from the Roman Inquisition. Cases for witchcraft from the late 17th century distinguish themselves on essential points from the ones earlier in the century. The procedures of the early 17th century were basically a continuation of the old medieval legal system, in which the accuser was usually the offended party, and a trial was a negotiation between two parties in order for the offended party to claim compensation. At the turn of the century, legal cases in Denmark had started to become more professionalized, and the Danish system gradually moved from the dominant accusatorial features towards one entirely based on inquisition. This change was accompanied by the professionalization of the legal system which saw attorneys (*prokuratorer*) leading the cases on behalf of the offended party, and later during the 18th century on behalf of the state.

Another feature can be identified in regards to the motive for sentencing. In the 17th century the Roman Inquisition stressed the *corpus delicti*, whereas the motive for sentencing in Danish cases in the first half of the 17th century was the connection between a threat of witchcraft and an actual occurrence of illness or accident. In Denmark from 1686 onwards, all sentences for witchcraft needed to be brought to the highest legal level of the kingdom – the High Court – and this caused a shift in the main grounds for sentencing.[490] The pact with the Devil now became the core offence, and in this sense, the charge emphasized the witches' offence against God, rather than the physical harm caused.

The mandatory appeal to the High Court in Copenhagen prolonged the road from accusation to sentence geographically as well as financially. In addition, highly educated judges coming from various professions now dealt with the cases, and they did not take lightly the sentencing of witchcraft.[491] From their deliberations, we see that the offence was intensely debated, and scepticism among several of the judges can be detected.[492] When Anne Pallis from Falster was tried before the High Court in Copenhagen in 1693, she had, in fact, withdrawn her previous statements about how she had entered into a pact with the Devil. The judges, though, found her confession binding. In the present context, however, the interesting part is the internal debate between the High Court judges. In order to determine whether Anne Pallis was guilty, the discussion did not revolve around the question of whether she had indeed harmed people with witchcraft, but rather whether she had entered a pact with the Devil. Not all of the judges were convinced that it was at all possible for a human being to enter a pact with the Devil. One prominent judge, Casper Bartholin, a chief attorney (*generalprokuratør*), dismissed the idea of a pact with the Devil, but a majority of judges ultimately found Anne guilty of having entered a diabolical pact.

Anne Pallis was the last individual to be burned for witchcraft in Denmark. Before being put on the stake, she was hanged to spare her the worst pain. This act of mercy did not benefit other offenders against God in the following 50 years. An increasing focus on offences against God combined with new and harsher means of capital punishments, turned executions into dramatic performances with features of religious ceremonies in the 18th century. They bore a resemblance to the *auto da fe*, but here adding the brutal maltreatment of the culprit at the centre. Fortunately, after the Pallis execution, when passing sentence in such cases Danish judges found the belief in witchcraft to be something only for the illiterate peasantry, although as the poet and dramatist, Ludvig Holberg put it in 1748, 'so many plausible stories are told that only with difficulty can one deny the existence of witchcraft'.[493]

Notes

The following abbreviations are used:

ACDF   Archivio per la Congregazione della Dottrina della Santa Fede
NLA   Landsarkivet for Nørrejylland (The Provincial Archive for northern Jutland)

1 Introduction

1. The trial against Stefano Tommei, Archivio della Congregazione per la Dottrina della Santa Fede (ACDF), Siena, processi, 51, fols. 103r–196r.
2. From the provincial court of northern Jutland, protocols (NLA) B 24–54, fols. 212r–214r.
3. I am fully aware that the term 'Italy' can be misleading, and I use it simply as referring to the area geographically covering present day Italy.
4. In Norway, death by burning was also applied as a penalty, although many culprits were executed by sword, Knutsen, Gunnar, *Troldomsprocesserne på Østlandet. En kulturhistorisk undersøgelse* (Tingbogsprojektet: Oslo 1998), pp. 142f.
5. Johansen, Jens Chr. V., *Da Djævelen var ude...Trolddom i Danmark i det 17. århundrede* (Odense University Press: Viborg 1991), pp. 242–282. Johansen's book is still among the most important works on Danish witchcraft. Key works also include Mitchell, Stephen A., *Witchcraft and Magic in the Nordic Middle Ages* (University of Pennsylvania Press: Philadelphia 2011); Appel, Hans Henrik, *Tinget, magten og æren. Studier i sociale processer og magtrelationer i et jysk bondesamfund i 1600-tallet* (Odense University Press: Viborg 1999); Wittendorff, Alex, 'Trolddomsprocessernes ophør i Danmark' in *Historisk Tidsskrift*, 92/1 (1992), pp. 1–28 and '"Evangelii lyse dag" eller hekseprocessernes mørketid? Om Peder Palladius' historieopfattelse' in *Tradition og kritik. Festskrift til Sven Ellehøj*, Christensen, Grethe et al. (eds.) (Den Danske Historiske Forening: Copenhagen 1984), pp. 89–119, and Danish works by Gustav Henningsen, 'Anmeldelse af Da Djævelen var ude...Trolddom i det 17. århundredes Danmark' in *Historisk Tidsskrift*, 92/1 (1992), pp. 131–149, and *Heksejægeren på Rugård* (Skippershoved: Ebeltoft 1991).
6. The important works on Italian witchcraft prosecution are all linked to studies on the Roman Inquisition. The most recent monographs in English are the two volumes by Mayer, Thomas F., *The Roman Inquisition on the Stage of Italy, c. 1590–1640* (University of Pennsylvania Press: Philadelphia 2014) and *The Roman Inquisition. A Papal Bureaucracy and Its Laws in the Age of Galileo* (University of Pennsylvania Press: Philadelphia 2013); Black, Christopher, *The Italian Inquisition* (Yale University Press: New Haven 2009) and Decker, Rainer, *Witchcraft and the Papacy. An Account Drawing on the Formerly Secret Records of the Roman Inquisition* (University of Virginia Press: Charlottesville and London 2008), and Duni, Matteo, *Under the Devil's Spell. Witches, Sorcerers, and the Inquisition in Renaissance Italy* (Syracuse University Press: Florence 2007), see also Tamar Herzig's article on the Italian witchcraft prosecutions in *The Oxford Handbook of Witchcraft in Early Modern and Colonial America*, Brian P. Levack (ed.) (Oxford University Press: Oxford 2013), pp. 249–267. In Italian, the collected volume edited by Matteo Duni and Dinanora Corsi on the Roman Inquisition and witchcraft, *Non la vivere*

la malefica. Le streghe nei trattati e nei processi (secoli XIV–XVIII) (Firenze University Press: Florence 2008) and the monograph by Di Simplicio, Oscar, *Autunno della stregoneria, Maleficio e magia nell'Italia moderna* (il Mulino, Ricerca: Bologna 2005). The most comprehensive work on the Roman Inquisition is the newly published *Dizionario storico dell'Inquisizione*, by Adriano Prosperi in coll. with John Tedeschi and Vicenzo Lavenia, 4 vols. (Pisa: Edizioni della Normale 2010); essential reading also includes Del Col, Andrea, *L'inquisizione in Italia. Dal XII al XXI secolo* (Libri Editore Mondadori: Milan 2006); Prosperi, Adriano, *Tribunali della coscienza. Inquisitori, confessori, missionari* (Giulio Einaudi Editore: Torino 1996); Romeo, Giovanni, *Inquisitori, esorcisti e streghe nell'Italia della Controriforma* (Sansoni Editore: Florence 1990) and *Esorcisti, confessori e sessualità femminile nell'Italia della Controriforma* (Le lettere: Florence 1998); on the grey area of saints, witches and the Counter-Reformation, see also Gentilcore, David, *Healers and Healing in Early Modern Italy* (Manchester University Press: Manchester 1998); Jacobsen Schutte, Anne, *Aspiring Saints. Pretense of Holiness, Inquisition, and Gender in the Republic of Venice, 1618–1750* (Johns Hopkins University Press: Baltimore 2001).

7. For the local tribunals, see Black (2009), pp. 19–56.
8. The Danish legal procedures will be discussed further in chapter 3.
9. See Pihlamäki, Heikki (ed.), *Theatres of Power. Social Control and Criminality in Historical Perspective* (Matthias Calonius Society: Helsinki 1991).
10. A similar argument is posed by Knutsen, Gunnar, *Servants of Satan and Masters of Demons. The Spanish Inquisition's Trials for Superstition, Valencia and Barcelona, 1478–1799* (Brepols: Turnhout 2009), pp. 2f.
11. ACDF, Siena, processi, 51, fol. 182r.
12. The semantic field as introduced by Reinhardt Koselleck. Although I find great inspiration in conceptual historians as Koselleck and Quentin Skinner, this study does not pretend to be one. My references to Koselleck are limited to some Danish works by Nevers, Jeppe and Niklas Olsen (eds.) *Begreber, tid og erfaring* (Hans Reitzels Forlag: Copenhagen 2007); see also Nevers, Jeppe, 'Til begreberne! En skitse af to begrebshistoriske analysestrategier' in *Historiefagets teoretiske udfordring*. Hansen, Per H. and Jeppe Nevers (eds.) (University Press of Southern Denmark: Odense 2004), pp. 81–105.
13. English translation in Bloch, Marc, 'Toward a Comparative History of European Societies' in Lane, Frederick C. and Jelle C. Riermersma (eds.), *Enterprise and Secular Change. Readings in Economic History*, George Allen and Unwin: London 1928, pp. 494–522.
14. Bloch (1928), pp. 504ff.
15. Denmark lost Skåne, Halland and Blekinge in 1658, Slesvig was part of Denmark until 1864.
16. Mitchell, Stephen A. (2011); see also 'Pactum cum diabolo og galdur á Nordulöndum', Tulinius, Torfi H. (ed.) *Galdramenn: Galdrar og Samfelag a Mioldum* (Reykjavik: Hugvisindastofnun Háskóla Islands 2008), pp. 121–145 (English summary, pp. 1–17).
17. Dillinger, Johannes, *'Evil People'. A Comparative Study of Witch Hunts in Swabian Austria and the Electorate of Trier* (Charlottesville, VI: University of Virginia Press 2009).
18. Knutsen (2009), see also Norwegian historian Liv Helene Willumsen, *Witches of the North. Scotland and Finnmark* (Brill: Leiden 2013).
19. See Cameron, Euan, *Enchanted Europe. Superstition, Reason, and Religion 1250–1750* (Oxford University Press: Oxford 2010); Clark, Stuart, *Thinking with Demons. The Idea of Witchcraft in Early Modern Europe* (Oxford University Press: Oxford 1997).

20. Kieckhefer, Richard, *The European Witch Trials. Their Foundation in Learned and Popular Culture, 1300–1500* (Berkeley and Los Angeles 1976), esp. 'Introduction' and 'Distinction of Popular and Learned Tradition'; Cohn, Norman, *Europe's Inner Demons. An Enquiry Inspired by the Great Witch-Hunt* (Sussex University Press: London 1975). The earliest work inspired by anthropology is probably Trevor-Roper, Hugh, *The European Witch-Craze of the Sixteenth and Seventeenth Centuries* (HarperCollins: London 1969), see also Henningsen, Gustav, *The Witches' Advocate. Basque Witchcraft and the Spanish Inquisition* (University of Nevada Press: Reno 1980).

21. Ginzburg, Carlo, *The Night Battles. Witchcraft and Agrarian Cults in the Sixteenth and Seventeenth Centuries*, transl. by Tedeschi, John and Anne (Routledge and Kegan Paul: London 1966/1983); the micro-historical approach was unfolded in *The Cheese and the Worms*, transl. by Tedeschi, John and Anne (Johns Hopkins University Press and Routledge and Kegan Paul: New York and London 1976/1982/1992); 'L'inquisitore come antropologo', Danish translation 'Inkvisitoren som antropolog', in *Spor*, Thing, Morten (ed.) (Museum Tusculanum: Copenhagen 1999), pp. 142–151.

22. Del Col, Andrea, 'I processi dell'inquisizione come fonte: Considerazioni diplomatiche e storiche' in *Annuario Istituto storico italiana per l'eta moderna e contemporanea*, vol. 35–36 (1983/84), pp. 31–50, here esp. p. 44; see also the introduction to *Domenico Scandella Known as Menocchio. His Trials Before the Inquisition*, trans. by Tedeschi, John and Anne, (Renaissance Studies: Binghampton, NY, 1997), pp. xlv–xlix.

23. Romeo, Giovanni, 'Inquisizione, Chiesa e stregoneria nell'Italia della Controriforma: nuove ipotesi' in *Non la vivere la malefica*, pp. 53–64, see also the commented 'Stat der Forschung' by Matteo Duni in the same volume, 'Le streghe e gli storici, 1986–2006: bilancio e prosepettive', pp. 1–18; in English, see Herzig (2013).

24. Ruggiero, Guido, *Binding Passions. Tales of Magic, Marriage, and Power at the End of the Renaissance* (Oxford University Press: Oxford 1993).

25. Davis, Natalie Zemon, *Fiction in the Archives* (Stanford University Press: Stanford 1987), p. 3; see also Trouillot, Michel-Rolph, *Silencing the Past. Power and the Production of History* (Beacon Press: Boston 1995), esp. pp. 1–30.

26. Cohen, Elizabeth, 'Back Talk: Two Prostitutes' Voices from Rome c. 1600' in *Early Modern Women. An Interdisciplinary Journal*, 2 (2007), p. 95, p. 101.

27. See Jansson, Karin Hassan, 'Våld som aggression eller kommunikation? Hemfridsbrott i 1550–1650' in *Historisk Tidskrift* (Sweden), 126:3 2006, pp. 429–452, esp. 445f.; see also Österberg, Eva and Erling Sandmo, 'People Meet the Law. Introduction', in *People Meet the Law. Control and Conflict Handling in the Courts*, Sogner, Sølvi and Eva Österberg (eds.) (Universitetsforlaget: Stamsund 2000), pp. 9–26; and Sandmo, Erling, 'Volden som historisk konstruksjon' in *Nord Nytt* 1999:77, pp. 61–74.

28. The number of accused before the Siena tribunal was according to Black 6,893, compared to 5,464 in Modena and 4,400 in Venice (suggested figure due to lacunae), Black (2009), p. 135.

29. Di Simplicio, *Autunno della stregoneria*; in 2008 Decker's *Witchcraft and the Papacy* also draws on the documents in the ACDF, although not on the trials of the Siena Tribunal.

30. I have not identified trials conducted between the years 1613 and 1649.

31. It is not always clear if the notary or the inquisitor posed the questions and how much the notary interfered in an investigation; see Black (2009), pp. 64–68.

32. The Danish Archive for Folklore has a collection of photocopied trials in its collection. Extracts of trials have been published by Jacobsen, J.C., *Danske Domme*

i Trolddomssager i øverste Instans (G.E.C. Gad: Copenhagen 1966) and *Christenze Kruckow. En adelig Troldkvinde fra Chr. IV's Tid* (G.E.C. Gad: Copenhagen 1972), Grønlund, David, *Historisk Efterretning om de i Ribe Bye for Hexerie forfulgte og brændte Mennesker* (Ribe 1784). Extracts of trials can also be found in the collective volumes of published court records from the lower courts, for instance from Skast (Southwestern Jutland), Aasum (Funen) and Elsinore (Zealand).
33. For details on preservation, see Johansen (1991), pp. 15ff.
34. The formal charge of a suspect is described as it took place, by referring to how the prosecutor placed his hand on the head of the suspect and charged the suspect of being a true witch in the presence of the court.

2   Marking the limits of transgression

35. http://www.newadvent.org/cathen/13797b.htm, as seen http://www.newadvent. org/cathen/13797b.htm 24 February 2015.
36. In Kors, Alan C. and Edward Peters (eds.), *Witchcraft in Europe 400–1700: A Documentary History*, 2nd revised edition by Edward Peters (University of Pennsylvania Press: Philadelphia, 2001), pp. 44–47. Augustine on superstition has recently been discussed by Cameron (2010), pp. 79–85.
37. Baroja, Julio Caro, 'Witchcraft and Catholic Theology' in Ankarloo, Bengt and Gustav Henningsen (eds.) *Early Modern European Witchcraft. Centres and Peripheries* (Oxford University Press: Oxford 1990), pp. 24ff., and *The World of the Witches* (University of Chicago Press: Chicago, 1961/1971), pp. 42ff.
38. Tertullian (AD 160–218), the quote goes: 'The Devil is an imitator, a gifted impostor, especially in regards to acts of magic. His miracles are however illusory', in Baroja (1990), p. 25.
39. An English translation of *Canon Episcopi* (from the 12th century) can be found in the first edition of *Witchcraft in Europe, 400–1700. A Documentary History*, Kors, Alan and Edward Peters (eds.) (University of Pennsylvania Press: Philadelphia 1972, 1st edition), pp. 28–32. I would rather quote from the most recent, 2001 edition, which has a more extensive intro to *Episcopi*. *Canon Episcopi* was included in Gratian's decrees *Concordantia discordantium canonum,* also known as *Decretum Gratiani,* which are believed to have been written down between 1140 and 1151. In the Middle Ages it was thought to have been written in relation to a council in Ankara in AD 314, known as *Ancyra* at the time. The council, however, never took place. The Canon Episcopi has recently been discussed by Cameron (2010), pp. 85–88.
40. Kors and Peters (1972), p. 29.
41. *Canon Episcopi*, Kors and Peters (1972), p. 31.
42. For an online edition of this magical book, see http://www.esotericarchives.com/ solomon/ksol.htm http://www.esotericarchives.com/solomon/ksol.htm as seen 24 February 2015.
43. *Summa theologica* was meant as a sort of guidebook in theology. In it, five of the 512 posed questions focused on sorcery, witchcraft and divination. *Summa contra gentiles* was a clarification of Catholic dogmas, particularly against Muslims. Relevant paragraphs are found in an English translation in Kors and Peters (2001), pp. 90–103. On the scholastics and Thomas Aquinas, see Cameron (2010), 89–102.
44. Baroja (1990), p. 25.
45. *Summa theologica*, questions 94–96, *The assault of demons*, art. 1–5, via Kors and Peters (2001), pp. 96–103.

46. *Summa theologica*, questions 94–96, *The assault of demons*, art. 4, Kors and Peters (2001), p. 101.

47. *Summa contra gentiles*, 3 vols., pt 2, chapter 104–106, Kors and Peters (2001), p. 93, p. 96.

48. *Summa theologica*, questions 94–96, *The assault of demons*, art. 4, Kors and Peters (2001), p. 102.

49. English translation in Kors and Peters (2001), pp. 117f.; see also Peters, Edward, *The Magician, the Witch and the Law* (University of Pennsylvania Press: Philadelphia, 1978), pp. 99f.; pp. 131ff. The Papal inquisition in the medieval period consisted rather of single inquisitors and was not a centralized institution as the early modern inquisitions, see Peters, Edward, *Inquisition* (University of California Press: Berkeley 1989), pp. 67–71.

50. Nicolau Eymeric, Spanish theologian and inquisitor (1320–1399).

51. Kallestrup, Louise Nyholm, 'Francisco Peña', in *Encyclopedia of Witchcraft. The Western Tradition*, Golden, Richard M. (ed.) (ABC–CLIO eBook Collection: Santa Barbara, CA 2006), pp. 889f.

52. 'among many heretics there are found also many Christian and Jewish magicians, diviners, invokers of demons, enchanters, conjurers, superstitious people, augurs, those who use nefarious and forbidden arts [etc .]', Kors and Peters (2001), p. 153.

53. English translation in Kors and Peters (2001), pp. 177–180; see Broedel, Hans Peter, *The Malleus Maleficarum and the Construction of Witchcraft. Theology and Popular Beliefs* (Manchester University Press: Manchester 2003), Peters (1978), pp. 170ff.; excerpts found inter alia in Baroja (1961/1971), p. 94; (1989) based on Hansen, Joseph, *Quellen und Untersuchungen zur Geschichte des Hexenwahns und der Hexenverfolgung im Mittelalter* (Carl Georgi, Universität Buchdrückeri und Verlag: Bonn/Hildesheim, 1901/1963), p. 53; Wilson, Eric, 'Krämer at Innsbruck: Heinrich Krämer, the Summis Desiderantes and the Brixen Witch-Trial of 1485', in *Popular Religion in Germany and Central Europe, 1400–1800*, Scribner, Bob and Trevor Johnson (eds.) (Palgrave Macmillan: New York 1996), pp. 88ff.

54. Decker (2008), pp. 58f.; see also Tamar Herzig, *Christ Transformed into a Virgin Woman. Lucia Brocadelli, Heinrich Institoris and the defense of the faith* (Edizione di Storia e Letteratura: Rome 2013), pp. 27ff., and Michael Bailey, *Battling Demons. Witchcraft, Heresy, und Reform in the Late Middle Ages* (University of Pennsylvania Press: Philadelphia 2003), on the *Malleus Maleficarum*, esp. pp. 30f., 48f.

55. First edition 1486. See Wilson (1996), pp. 87ff.; Baroja (1961/1971), pp. 94ff. *Malleus maleficarum* can furthermore be found online in Montague Summer's (often faulty) translation, http://www.malleusmaleficarum.org, which only confirms the continued interest surrounding the work. *Malleus maleficarum* has recently been retranslated and annotated by P.G. Maxwell-Stuart (Manchester University Press: Manchester 2007) which is an abridged edition, and by Christopher Mackey, *Hammer of Witches. A Complete Translation of the Malleus maleficarum* (Cambridge University Press: Cambridge 2006/2009), which is now the standard. See also Behringer, Wolfgang, 'Malleus Maleficarum' in *Encyclopedia of Witchcraft: The Western Tradition*, Golden, Richard M. (ed.) (ABC–CLIO eBook Collection: Santa Barbara, CA 2006), pp. 718ff.

56. Martin, Ruth, *Witchcraft and the Inquisition of Venice 1550–1650* (Blackwell: London 1989), pp. 53f.; Wilson (1996), p. 88; Baroja (1961/1971), pp. 94f.; *Summis desiderantes* never had explicit influence on the prosecutions in Italy, Romeo, Giovanni, *Inquisitori, esorcisti e streghe nell'Italia della Controriforma* (Sansoni Editore: Florence 1990), p. 23. In her recent book Tamar Herzig (2013)

persuasively argues that the *Malleus maleficarum* had a larger impact on Italian witchcraft prosecutions than scholars found in the 1980s and early 1990s. For a rejection of *Malleus maleficarum* being commonly used as a guide in witch trials, see Cohn (1975); Martin (1989) specifically on Venice, pp. 58f.

57. Wilson (1996), p. 88.
58. On the Catholic and Counter Reformation, see Mullet, Michael, *The Catholic Reformation* (Routledge: New York 1984); Bireley, Robert *The Refashioning of Catholicism, 1450–1700. A Reassessment of the Counter-Reformation* (Palgrave Macmillan: Basingstoke 1999); Jedin, Hubert, *A History of the Council of Trent* (T. Nelson: London 1957–1961).
59. Excerpts in English translation in P.G. Maxwell–Stuart (2001), pp. 59f.
60. Decker (2008), p. 105.
61. Martin (1989), p. 68.
62. Duni (2007), p. 33; O'Neil (1982), p. 46, John Tedeschi and E. William Monter's examinations are difficult to apply to this purpose, due to the fact that the classification has not been made from individual years or decades. The period between 1550 and 1560 for example appears in the collective numbers for 1557–1595 in the Friulan inquisition, Monter and Tedeschi (1986, printed in Tedeschi (1991)), pp. 144ff. The only collective examination of the Siena Tribunal has been made by Oscar Di Simplicio. It is however not to much use for the early 16th century prosecutions as Di Simplicio starts in 1580. Di Simplicio (2000), pp. 22f.
63. This is verified by Prosperi (1996) by his (Prosperi's) confirmation of the inquisition's privileges two years later; where acts that had hitherto been presumed to be heretic (*praesumpta haeresis*), now had to be seen as *manifesta haeresis*, p. 391.
64. According to Decker (2008), from the second half of the 16th century and onwards about ten persons were executed for magical offences by the Roman Inquisition, pp. 134f.
65. Siena in the period 1600–1604, Di Simplicio (2000), p. 22; Modena 1591–1595, O'Neil (1983), p. 46; Venice 1589, Martin (1989), *appendix*.
66. Tedeschi, John, 'Inquisitorial Law and the Witch' in Ankarloo, Bengt and Gustav Henningsen (eds.), *Witchcraft in Early Modern Europe* (Oxford University Press: Oxford 1990/1998), pp. 87f.
67. Romeo (1990), p. 176; Martin (1989), p. 69.
68. When it came to the practical course of a trial, the inquisitors also had a number of theological counsellors, *consultori*, to draw on.
69. All three manuals circulated frequently amongst the Roman inquisitors and are a continuation of other authoritative manuals such as Nicolau Eymeric's *Directorium Inquisitorum* (1376), revised by Francisco Peña in 1578.
70. *Prattica* is attributed to the cardinal and former inquisitor Desiderio Scaglia. Not until the 1625 edition of *Sacro Arsenale* does Masini add his instructions on witches and witchcraft, for works in English see Lea, Henry Charles, *Materials Toward a History of Witchcraft*, vols. 1–3 (University of Pennsylvania Press: Philadelphia 1937/1957), pp. 950–963 and 963–966; Tedeschi, John, *The Prosecution of Heresy: Collected Studies on the Inquisition in Early Modern Italy* (Medieval and Renaissance Texts and Studies: Binghampton, NY 1991), pp. 205–259; and most recently Decker (2008), p. 122 and on the *Instructio* including references to Scaglia, pp. 113–131. Important Italian works are Prosperi (1996), esp. pp. 368–399; Turchini, Angelo, 'Il modello ideale dell'inquisitore: la Pratica del cardinal Desiderio Scaglia' in Del Col, Andrea and Giovanna Paolin *L'Inquisizione Romana. Metologia*

delle fonti e storia istituzionale. Atto del seminario internazionale Montereale Valcellina 23 e 24 settembre millenovecento99, (Università del Trieste: Trieste 1999) on Scaglia, pp. 187–199; Del Col, Andrea, *L'inquisizione in Italia. Dal XII al XXI secolo* (Libri Editore Mondadori: Milan 2006) on Masini, pp. 770f.

71. Lea (1937/1957), pp. 950–963, 963–966.
72. Decker (2008), pp. 113f., in chapter 10, pp. 113–131, Decker convincingly presents the context of the *Instructio*, which is why I refer to Decker's text for a more detailed understanding.
73. John Tedeschi has argued that in all likelihood the *Instructio* was published after the death of Pope Gregory XV in order to tone down the rhetoric of the bull *Omnipotentis Dei*. In this the Pope had ordered that anyone found guilty of apostasy to the Devil or of practising evil magic arts with fatal consequences should be executed. Gregory XV died in July 1623. The bull was published on 20 March 1623; English translation in Summers, Montague, *The Geography of Witchcraft* (Kegan Paul: New York 1927), pp. 544ff., see Tedeschi (1991), p. 206; Del Col (2006), pp. 589f., and mentioned in Lea (1937/1957), p. 951.
74. On the inquisitor needing practical not theological guidance, see Prosperi (1996), pp. 398f.
75. StStE, 5e, no. 2, fols. 22v–23r, 'Li sortilegii[ʼ], per il cui nome vengono intesi quelli che operano cose magiche e fattucchiere, et malefitÿ.' I will return to Scaglia's description of diabolical witches, *streghe*, later in this chapter.
76. StStE 5e, no. 2, fol. 25v. 'E se pure il Sant'Officio per qualche causa le conosce le suole spedire se non con monitioni, e penitenze salutari.'
77. Tedeschi (1991), p. 233.
78. StStE 5e, no. 2, fol. 25r–v. 'invocationi de Demonÿ, caratteri, e parole incognite, abuso di sacramenti, ò cose sacramentali ò in esse si fa mentione di scritture in carta Vergine, massime cò sangue ò cavando sangue ad ucelli ad animali con punto di luna crescente, ò dicrescente'. See also Lea (1937/1957), p. 964.
79. Here the term 'magic' is used in accordance with Eymeric's use of terms, see Kors and Peters (2001), p. 121; relevant excerpts have been translated and are found in the same, pp. 122–127. See also Peters, Edward, 'Editing Inquisitors' Manuals in the Sixteenth Century: Francisco Peña and the *Directorium Inquisitorum* of Nicholas Eymeric' in *The Library Chronicle*, vol. 40, 1975, pp. 95–107.
80. Turchini (1999), p. 192.
81. 'Per amore, o per morte delle persone ò per trovare tesori, o per conserver monete, acciò spese tornino in borsa, ò per dinita ò per scienza ò per altre cose', StStE5e no. 2, fol. 24v.
82. StStE5e no. 2, fol. 24v.
83. This was in accordance with Thomas Aquinas in particular: demons could not force the will, but they could influence it.
84. StStE 5e no. 2, fol. 24v, 'qualche persona s'interrogano in specie se credono, ò hanno creduto che il Demonio possa sforzare la volonta che è libera'; fol. 25r, 'si farà abiurare de formali'.
85. StStE 5e no. 2, fol. 24v 'il Demonio non possa sforzare l'humana volonta, puol bene pertubare la fantasia'. In line with Thomas Aquinas: demons had the power to create miracles, but these were not true miracles.
86. StStE 5e no. 2, fol. 24v, 'massime in quel punto che la persona che desidera l'amore della donna, si fa presente á lei'.
87. See, for example, Martin (1989), pp. 234–238, Di Simplicio (2005), p. 64, table 2.2.

88. StStE 5e no. 2, 27v 'benedicono fave con invocationi del demonio'.
89. StStE 5e no. 2, 27v 'parole incognite, ò cognite mà lascive'.
90. Scaglia specifically names St. Daniel and St. Helen, but it was also illegal to address other saints with such intentions. StStE 5e no. 2, 27v 'abusano aqua, candele benedette recitando orationi di S. Daniele ò S. Elena, et altri simili'. These were very common para-liturgical prayers: St. Martha was also very popular, see Fantini, Maria Pia, 'La circolazione clandestine dell'orazione di Santa Marta. Un episodio modenese', in Zarri, Gabriella (ed.) *Donna, disciplina, creanza Cristiana dal XV al XVII secolo. Studi e testi a stampa* (Edizioni di Storia e Letteratura: Rome), pp. 45–65; O'Neil notes that cases concerning love magic might also include examples of counter-magic (*superstitiones ad amore impedendo*). Francesco Villano (who also testified in the case) and his wife approached the accused, Margarita Chiappona, to get her to stop Francesco's love for the prostitute Barbara Grafagnina. O'Neil, Mary R., 'Magical Healing, Love Magic and the Inquisition in Late 16th Century Modena' in Haliczer, Stephen (ed.), *Inquisition and Society in Early Modern Europe* (Barnes and Noble: London and Sydney 1987), p. 102.
91. StStE5e no. 2, fol. 23r 'mà anco per il patto, che fanno cò il Diavolo [...] e sortilegio esplicitamente et implicitamente'.
92. StStE5e no. 2, fol. 23r 'prometterli la propria ò alcun anima'.
93. StStE5e no. 2, fol. 23r 'per mezzo de caratteri parole incognite di niuna significatione in qualsivoglia linguaggio, abuso di sacramento, e beneditte di parole di sacra scrittura'.
94. StStE 5e no. 2, fol. 23r 'et al incontro il Diavolo promette al sortilegio di servirlo, e sodisfarlo á i suoi desiderii ò d'amore, ò di vendetta, ò di altro'.
95. Thomas Aquinas, however, used the term 'magic' instead of 'witchcraft'.
96. *Stregoneria* literally means witchcraft, but the term holds the key elements of the diabolical witch developed during the 15th century. In Scaglia's text, the term is not to be confused with *sortilegio*.
97. The definition is: 'One of the groups amongst the magicians is the witch, both male and female. They bewitch people in various ways, either through love or death or simply by corrupting the mother's breast milk.' In the original 'Sotto i'stesso nome di sortileghi si comprendono anco le streghe, e stregoni, che malefitiano le persone in varii modi ò d'amore ò à morte, e singolarmente li fanciulli di latte', StStE 5e no. 2, fol. 27r.
98. StStE 5e no. 2, fol. 27r.
99. Eliseo Masini, Sacro Arsenale, ovvero Prattoca del Sant'Officio, (c. 1625), Stamp. Ferr. IV. 1367, also pointed out their evil intent and the damage caused by witches, see in particular P1, 16–19.
100. It can be assumed that these were letters or short words carved in the fruit's skin ('parole incognite e caratteri sopra frutti'). This passage can be found in English in Tedeschi (1991), p. 234.
101. Masini (1625/1639), P1, 16.
102. Wax figures also appeared in the Danish trials. The best known case involved a group of women from Aalborg, amongst whom the noble Christenze Kruckow.
103. StStE5e no. 2, fol. 26r, 'facendo statue di cera traffigendole cò aghi e facendole à poco à poco dileguare al fuoco'.
104. A rather broad definition of witchery StStE 5e no. 2, fol. 26r 'et in modo che alle volte le persone si consumano senz'alcuno rimedio non arrivando il medico à trovarla cagione dell'istesso modo malefitiano, anco sino a far morire per odio'.
105. Masini notes that the worship could appear as explicit and implicit (1639), P1, 17.

106. StStE 5e no. 2, fol. 27r 'condotte da lui al gioco'. The sabbath was often referred to as 'the Devil's game', and Scaglia employs this phrase as well. Because of the witch's collaboration with the Devil, the inquisitor could not regard her information on other participants in the sabbath as trustworthy. For other people seen at the sabbath, see StStE 5e no. 2, fol. 27r. For an overview of the Italian research on the sabbath, see Herzig (2013), pp. 260f.

107. Masini (c. 1625), 'vanno al ballo con il (come suol ditre) in striozzo', P1, 16.

108. For the period 1580–1666, see Di Simplicio (2005), p. 301.

109. According to Di Simplicio (2005) none of the trials at the Siena tribunal involved sexual acts with the Devil or a pact with the Devil, p. 301. The same goes for Venice, where Martin (1989) points to the populace's accusations against 'witches' as being very far from the mythological understanding of the witch, pp. 192f.

110. Martin (1989), p. 70. The spell of the angelo bianco is also condemned in *Coeli et terrae*.

111. Tedeschi (1990/1998), p. 94; for the *Instructio*, see especially Lavenia, Vicenzo, 'Anticamente di misto foro' in *Inquisizioni: percorsi di ricerca*, Giovanna Paolin (ed.) (2001); see also Romeo (2008), pp. 53–64 and Romeo, Giovanni, *L'Inquisizione nell'Italia moderna* (Laterza: Rome and Bari 2002).

112. Lavenia (2001), pp. 41–53; Tedeschi (1991), p. 211; see also dall'Olio, Guido, 'Tribunali vescovili, inquisizione romana e stregoneria: i processi bolognesi del 1559' in Prosperi, Adriano (ed.), *Il piacere del testo: Saggi e studi per Albano Biondi*, 2 vols., I (Buozoni Editrice: Rome 2001).

113. 'Experience shows clearly the gravest of errors daily committed by ordinaries, vicars and inquisitors in the trial of witches', excerpt translated in accordance with Lea (1937/1957) pp. 950–963; Tedeschi (1990/1998). For extracts on other parts of the *Instructio*, see Decker (2008), pp. 118f.

114. Among other see Prosperi (1996), Martin (1989), O'Neil (1983), Di Simplicio (2005).

115. The course of the trial according to correct procedures has been illustrated by Black (2009), pp. 57–93; on the *corpus delicti* in trials for witchcraft p. 233; Decker (2008), p. 120; Tedeschi (1991), p. 233.

116. Tedeschi (1991), p. 233.

117. StStE 5e, no. 2, fol. 26v.

118. It could also be neighbours, local clerics such as priests and confessors, depending on status and influence.

119. *Prattica*, StStE 5e, no. 2, fol. 24r–v.

120. Brown, Ralph, 'Examination of an Interesting Roman Document: Instructio proformandis processibus in causis strigum' in *The Jurist*, vol. 24/1 (1964), p. 179. The harmed person went by the term *praetensus maleficiatus*, the *presumed* bewitched/possessed.

121. Martin (1989) on Eymeric, pp. 60f. The category may seem slightly peculiar compared to modern law, seeing that it is now unthinkable to convict people of a crime they have only been suspected of committing but where the evidence has not been found sufficient.

122. StStE5e no. 2, fol. 24v 'non li fa abiurare de formali, mà de vehementi ò de levi'.

123. See, for example, Tedeschi (1991), p. 115.

124. StStE5e no. 2, fol. 28r, 'si fanno stare sù le porte della Chiesa in giorno di Festa con la candela accesa in mano [...] sin tengono in carcere formale ad tempus ò in casa seconda la qualità del delitto'.

125. StStE 5e no. 2, fol. 28v, 'Tal volta anco si frustano, mà pero è vero, che quando hanno marito ò figlie nubile il Sant'Officio per benignità si astiene da questa condanna, perche ridonna [ridonda?] in igno-minia delle figlia, che questo rispetto nò trovano mariti, et i mariti perdono l'amore alle mogli frustrate.'

3 The condemnation of witchcraft in Denmark

126. In an article from 2007 Per Ingesman discusses the documentation of two pre-Reformation trials of witchcraft on the island of Bornholm found in two registers (Bernt Knob's and Truid Ulfstand's). Ingesman, Per, 'Kirkelig disciplin og social kontrol i senmiddelalderens danske bondesamfund. En casestudy af det ærkebiskoppelige gods under Lundegård 1519–22 og Hammershus 1525–40' in *Konge, kirke og samfund*, Arnórsdóttir, Agnes, Per Ingesman og Bjørn Poulsen (eds.) (Aarhus University Press: Aarhus 2007), pp. 329–380. Furthermore, early information on witch trials are found in chancellor Claus Gjordsen's records from 1523 in a register from Holbækgård, Wittendorff (1984), pp. 106f.

127. See, for example, Andersen, Per, *Lærd ret og verdslig lovgivning Retlig kommunikation og udvikling i Middelalderens Danmark*, (DJØF Forlag: Copenhagen 2006), pp. 216–221; Gelting, Michael. 'Skånske Lov og Jyske Lov: Danmarks første kommissionsbetænkning og Danmarks første retsplejelov' in Dam, Henrik, Lise Dybdahl, Lise and Finn Taksøe-Jensen (eds.), *Jura og historie. Festskrift til Inger Dübeck som forsker*, (DJØF Forlag: Copenhagen 20030), pp. 61–67. The ruling on witchcraft in *Jyske Lov* has been reproduced in Iuul, Stig and Erik Kroman, *Danmarks gamle Love paa Nutidsdansk*, vol. II (G.E.C. Gad: Copenhagen 1945–1948), p. 224.

128. The term *forgjort* is ambiguous, as it literally means 'destroyed' and covers a wider semantic register; in this context it means 'bewitched'.

129. My translation, based on Iuul and Kroman (eds.), *Danmarks gamle Love paa Nutidsdansk*, vol. II: p. 224.

130. Jensen, Karsten Sejr, *Trolddom i Danmark 1500–1588* (Arken Tryk: Copenhagen 1982), pp. 13f.

131. Jensen (1982) , p. 14.

132. Translated from the Danish by Jacobsen, J.C., *Danske Domme i Trolddomssager i øverste Instans* (GEC Gads: Copenhagen 1966), p. 139.

133. For the church murals depicting butter witches and women allied with the Devil, see Mitchell (2008) (especially on evil women and the Devil). It should be noted that the *Landlov* also includes a differentiation between malevolent and benevolent magic. At more than one point it touches upon Roman Canonical law in trials of witchcraft and strongly indicates a consensus in the perception of witchcraft from the beginning of the 16th century to at least 1620.

134. Quote from the law that declared the kingdom Lutheran, original 'En bedre ordning og Reformation' in Wittendorff, Alex, *På Guds og herskabs nåde. Politiken and Gyldendals Danmarkshistorie*, vol. 7. Olsen, Olaf (ed.) (Gyldendalske Boghandel and Nordisk Forlag: Copenhagen 1989), p. 207.

135. For works on the Reformation in English, see Grell, Ole Peter, *The Scandinavian Reformation: From Evangelical Movement to Institutionalisation of Reform* (Cambridge University Press: Cambridge 1995); Lausten, Martin Schwarz. *A Church History of Denmark* (Ashgate: Farnham 2002).

136. The first *Tamperret* was created in Ribe in 1542; see Riising, Anne, 'Tamperrettens funktion og dompraksis' in *Festskrift til Johan Hvidtfeldt*, Iversen, Peter Kr.,

Knud Prange and Sigurd Rambusch (eds.) (Arkivvæsener, Dansk Historisk Fællesforening, Historisk Samfund for Sønderjylland, Landbohistorisk Selskab: Åbenrå, 1978), pp. 393–412.

137. The entire Ordinance has been published as *Kirkeordinansen 1539*, introduced and commented by Lausten, Martin Schwarz (Akademisk Forlag: Copenhagen 1989).

138. See also Kallestrup, Louise Nyholm, 'De besmittede og de skyldige', *Religionsvidenskabeligt Tidsskrift*, vol. 59, 2012, pp. 55–72, English revised version 'The infected and the guilty. On heresy and witchcraft in post-Reformation Denmark', forthcoming in *Contesting Orthodoxy in Medieval and Early Modern Europe*, Kallestrup, Louise Nyholm (ed.) (Palgrave Macmillan: Basingstoke and New York 2015).

139. *En visitatsbog*, translated and introduced by Lausten, Martin Schwarz (Forlaget Anis: Copenhagen 2003), p. 117.

140. *En visitatsbog*, Lausten (2003), p. 119.

141. *En visitatsbog*, Lausten (2003), p. 117.

142. Clark, Stuart, *Thinking with Demons. The Idea of Witchcraft in Early Modern Europe* (Oxford University Press: Oxford 1997), pp. 489ff.

143. 'Then no witch shall harm you' *En Visitatsbog*, Lausten (2003), p. 117.

144. *En Visitatsbog*, Lausten (2003), p. 118.

145. *En Visitatsbog*, Lausten (2003), pp. 117f.

146. *En Visitatsbog*, Lausten (2003), p. 119.

147. Tausen's pastoral letter via Jensen (1982), p. 18. In contrast to Palladius, Hans Tausen did not perceive the benevolent magic as effective, Brink, Torben, 'Niels Hemmingsens forståelse af trolddom – en nyvurdering' in *Fortid og Nutid*, hæfte 2. s (1993), p. 123.

148. 'at naar kirkenefn hafver ofversvorit nogen, som for trolddomssager er anklagit, da skal dend, som ofversvorit er, icke strax rettis, men blifve besiddendis, til saa lenge sagen indstefnis til landstinget, och landsdommerne da at dømme derpaa [...]. Dog skal dend, som ofversveris, ikke aflivis, førre domergangit til landsting, som førre et rørt', excerpt from the recess in Kalundborg, 1576, article 8, Johansen (1991), pp. 22f. The excerpt translates as: 'that when the church tribunal had convicted someone who had been accused of witchcraft, then the convicted should not immediately be punished but should remain in custody until the case can be summoned at a county court and the judges will convict accordingly [...] However, the person that has been convicted should not be executed before the trial at the county court has been conducted'. The same was instructed in regards to other convictions of dishonourable crimes (theft etc.).

149. Jensen (1982), pp. 38f.

150. For instance, the trial against Sidsel Christens from Hostrup, see chapter 5.

151. 'one [witch] will give away the other', *En Visitatsbog*, Lausten (2003), p. 117.

152. Johansen (1991), p. 22; Birkelund, Merete, *Troldkvinden og hendes anklagere. Danske hekseprocesser i det 16. og 17. århundrede* (Arusia Historiske Skrifter: Århus 1983), p. 28.

153. On torture and conviction, see Levack, Brian P., *The Witch-Hunt in Early Modern Europe* (Taylor & Francis: New York 1987/1992), pp. 76f.; on the *Carolina* and Denmark, see Jørgensen, Poul Johs. *Dansk strafferet fra Reformationen til Danske Lov. Med indledning af Ditlev Tamm and Helle Vogt* (Jurist- og Økonomforlaget: Copenhagen 2007), p. 397.

154. Jørgensen (2007), pp. 397f.

155. 'Frederick II', *Dansk Biografisk Leksikon*, vol. 5, C.F. Bricka (ed.) (Gyldendalske Boghandels Forlag: Copenhagen 1891), p. 290; the traditional perception of the king has recently been challenged by Grinder-Hansen, Poul in *Frederik 2. Danmarks renæssancekonge* (Gyldendal: Copenhagen 2013).

156. Johansen (1991), p. 22; Jensen (1982) points to the incident simply being the final straw, as similar information had reached the king in 1557–58 and 1560, pp. 39f.

157. Furthermore, Johansen emphasizes that the regulation has to be regarded in the light of the general development towards a more centralized state administration. Johansen (1991), p. 22; Jensen (1982), p. 40; Birkelund (1983), p. 28.

158. Lausten, Martin Schwarz, *Niels Hemmingsen. Storhed og fald* (Forlaget Anis: Copenhagen 2013), pp. 305–325.

159. Wittendorff (1989) , pp. 106ff.

160. For the international context, see Clark (1997), pp. 526–545.

161. Rewritten from *En undervisning aff Den Hellige Scrifft hvad mand døme skal om den store oc gruelige Gudsbespottelse som skeer med Troldom Sinelse Manelse oc anden saadan Guds hellige Naffns og Ords vanbrug. Item 33 Propositiones mot Troldom. Der til 33 Propositiones om Spaadom* (translates as: A teaching of The Holy Text on how to punish the great and terrible blasphemy that takes place with witchcraft's spells, doings and other abuses of God's holy word and name). The text is undated, but is usually estimated to c. 1570, the year of Rasmus Hansøn Reravius' priestly inauguration in Copenhagen, see among others Fink-Jensen, Morten, *Fornuften under troens lydighed. Naturfilosofi, medicin og teologi i Danmark, 1536–1635* (Museum Tusculanum: Copenhagen 2004), p. 125. *En Undervisning* consists of an index and thereafter five central questions in relation to witchcraft. They are subsequently answered. In closing, 33 *propositiones* on witchcraft spells and conjurations has been added; and, after these, 33 on divination. Parts of the present analysis of Hemmingsen has been published in Kallestrup (2012).

162. The role of Rasmus Reravius as translator of his time is discussed by Fink-Jensen in Appel, Charlotte and Morten Fink-Jensen, *Når det regner på præsten. En kulturhistorie om sognepræster og sognefolk 1550–1750* (Forlaget Hovedland: Gern 2009), p. 53.

163. The historian Karsten Sejr Jensen argued that there were three motives for publishing *En Undervisning* in 1575; Sejr Jensen (1982), p. 21; the dispute concerning the interpretation of the communion was at its highest, and publishing *En Undervisning* for a wider audience was a diplomatic move, by which attention was turned to another hot topic of the time: witchcraft. By demanding strict regulation against all kinds of witchcraft, Hemmingsen expressed the same opinion as the German Elector on the issue. The Elector had recently imposed significant restrictions in the legislation on witchcraft, amongst which was the death penalty for benevolent magic. The second reason, according to Sejr Jensen, for publishing the text was that Hemmingsen shared the beliefs of the Elector and also argued for the death penalty being imposed on practitioners of magic and witchcraft. As a third motive, Hemmingsen was in fact sending out a hidden contribution to the theological debate regarding communion. Jensen's arguments all rest on the assumption that *En Undervisning* had been published in 1575 and as such had played an active part in the communion dispute. Jensen (1982), p. 21. *Formaning om at undgå trolddom*, Brink (1993), p. 119. When Jensen published his dissertation, the research still presumed *En Undervisning* to be a translation of *Admonitio de superstitionibus magicis vitandis*. In an article from

1993, theologian Torben Brink demonstrated a confusion of the translations which went as far back as the end of the 18th century, Brink (1993), p. 119. He concluded that *En Undervisning* was a translation of the somewhat older *Historia Domini Hiesv Christi,* which was published in 1562. Morten Fink-Jensen has recently confirmed the confusion of *Admonitio* and *En Undervisning,* but has otherwise been critical towards Brink's arguments. Fink-Jensen has established that *En Undervisning* was based on three and not one of Hemmingsen's earlier texts.

164. Jensen (1982), in particular, has pointed out that Hemmingsen actually wanted the death penalty for both malevolent and healing magic, p. 21; Wittendorff, Alex, *På Guds og herskabs nåde. Politiken and Gyldendals Danmarkshistorie,* vol. 7. Olsen, Olaf (ed.), (Gyldendalske Boghandel and Nordisk Forlag: Copenhagen 1989) simply pointed to Hemmingsen wanting strict legislation on all kinds of witchcraft, p. 358.

165. Jensen (1982), p. 22.

166. Birkelund (1983), p. 30.

167. Jensen also notes that Hemmingsen wanted to make the authorities aware of its responsibilities in a few lines, but he does not pursue his argumentation further. Jensen (1982), p. 23.

168. Eschatological ideas were characteristic of the theologians of the period, Cameron (2010), pp. 174–195; Clark (1997), pp. 401ff. This can be seen at several points in the introductory section of Hemmingsen's work, e.g. on p. 16, where it is emphasized that this is a 'greater sin that people realize'.

169. Preface to *En Undervisning,* pp. 6f. This is also noted in Rasmus Reravius' preface, and further: 'When someone opposes such impiety, and says that it is a sin and a wrong, one [does indeed] know so much that this can be argued against. It is, they say, God's word: One does no man evil thereby, but helps people and cattle to regain their health', but Hemmingsen also draws attention to this, e.g. p. 39.

170. *En Undervisning,* pp. 23, 42, etc.

171. *En Undervisning,* pp. 18f.

172. *En Undervisning,* pp. 15f.

173. As in the *Canon episcopi* and other texts; Kors and Peters (1972), pp. 29ff.

174. *En Undervisning,* pp. 16f.

175. *En Undervisning,* pp. 18.

176. *En Undervisning,* p. 24.

177. *En Undervisning,* p. 27.

178. *En Undervisning,* p. 28.

179. *En Undervisning,* p. 29.

180. Apart from passages of Scripture, Hemmingsen mainly draws on the teachings of St. Augustine.

181. Desiderio Scaglia frequently applied the phrase *cose sacramentali,* see the previous chapter. See also Duni (2007), p. 136, n28.

182. *En Undervisning,* pp. 31f.

183. *En Undervisning,* pp. 33f., 35.

184. *En Undervisning,* p. 35.

185. *En Undervisning,* p. 42.

186. Hemmingsen has now already begun to answer his third question, *En Undervisning,* pp. 36ff.

187. *En Undervisning,* pp. 42ff.

188. *En Undervisning,* p. 47.

189. Book of Exodus 22:18, *En Undervisning,* p. 47.

190. Originally proposed by Bjørn Kornerup. That it is the traditional view is confirmed by Fink-Jensen (2004), p. 166; Wittendorff (1992), p. 25; Resen's role in the clash with the crypto-Calvinists has been examined by Kornerup, Bjørn, *Biskop Hans Poulsen Resen. Studier over Kirke- og Skolehistorie i det 16. og 17. Aarhundrede* (G.E.C Gad: Copenhagen 1928), vol. 1, pp. 373–492.

191. According to historian Alex Wittendorff, Hans Poulsen Resen had been successful in convincing Christian IV of the sinfulness of benevolent magic, and he had benefitted from the general enthusiasm for the jubilee to obtain support in the fight against every kind of witchcraft, Wittendorff, Alex, *Tyge Brahe* (GEC Gads Forlag: Copenhagen 1994), p. 226.

192. On the same day two separate regulations were published: 'On whether people of loose virtue should openly confess' and 'On unnecessary expenses found at weddings, funerals etc.'. All three regulations have been published in Rørdam, H.F. *Danske kirkelove samt udvalg af andre bestemmelser vedrørende kirken, skolen og de fattiges forsørgelse fra reformationen indtil Christian V's danske lov, 1536–1683* (Selskabet for Danmarks kirkehistorie, G.E.C. Gad: Copenhagen 1886), vol. 3, pp. 59–63. The directions of the regulation were repeated in the Great Recess of 1643, Johansen (1991), p. 24. It should be noted that for the Norwegian part of the Monarchy, a law against benevolent magic had been issued as early as in 1593, Knutsen (1998), pp. 40f.

193. My translation is based on Rørdam (1889:3), p. 60.

194. Wittendorff (1992), pp. 25ff.

195. Here a special direction was included for the nobility, who should be executed by the sword. This direction was as far as it is known only applied on a single occasion, this being the case against Christenze Kruckow.

196. *En Undervisning*, pp. 42ff.

197. I have gone through the most complete assessment of the trials, as found in Johansen (1991), pp. 242–283. No person was accused, charged or convicted of healing witchcraft alone. Only a few were convicted of healing magic, and these had originally been charged with malicious witchcraft.

198. See Kallestrup, Louise Nyholm, 'Knowing Satan from God: Demonic Possession, Witchcraft, and the Lutheran Orthodox Church in Early Modern Denmark' in *Magic, Ritual and Witchcraft*, vol. 6, no. 2 (2011), p. 163–182.

199. In Jutland this equals an estimated figure of approximately 420 cases, based on the statistics provided in Johansen (1991), pp. 242–282.

200. Danske Lov, online version http://bjoerna.dk/DL-1683-internet.pdf, as seen 4 November 2014.

4 Comparing Procedures against witchcraft in the Roman Inquisition and the Danish secular courts

201. Kors and Peters (2001), pp. 117f.

202. On the *denunce*, see Brambilla, E. 'Denuncia' in *Dizionario Storio dell'Inquisizione*, pp. 467ff.

203. Although this only occurred a few times in Orbetello, e.g. the trial against Lucida di Canino, ACDF, Siena, processi, 51, fols. 196r–229v.

204. As was the case with Mensola di Tiracoscia, ACDF, Siena, processi, 40, fols. 1r–107r, 42, fols. 882r–896r, 923r–977r.

205. Andersen, Per, *Lærd ret og verdslig lovgivning. Retlig kommunikation og udvikling i middelalderens Danmark* (Jurist- og Økonomforlaget: København 2006), esp. pp. 253–270.

206. Most likely because the costs of a trial, long travelling distances or if the suspect had fled.
207. Convicted by the town court in Skagen 30 September 1610, trial dismissed by the provincial court in Viborg 26 October 1610. NLA B 24–512, fols. 279r–286r.
208. Jørgensen (2007), pp. 231ff.
209. Rowlands, Alison, *Witchcraft Narratives in Germany: Rothenburg 1561–1652* (Manchester University Press: Manchester 2003), p. 15.
210. Jørgensen (2007), p. 318, the three *mark* fine seem to have been double in the sense that the slanderer had to pay 3 *mark* to the slandered person as well as to the king.
211. Danske Lov, 'Om Æresager', art. 6–21–7, art 6–21–8, online version http://bjoerna.dk/DL-1683-internet.pdf, as seen 4 November 2014. In the trials against the noble man Jørgen Arnfeldt, who at the turn of the 17th century launched his own witch hunt, the regulation was applied in the final verdict. Following a long and complicated series of trials Arnfeldt was himself sentenced for libel due to his distribution of written false testimonies. Still, Arnfeldt's punishment was reduced to an arbitrary punishment by which he was not deprived of his honour and did not loose his property. Instead he was sentenced to paying a huge fine of 1000 *rigsdaler (1 rigsdaler = 6 mark)*. Henningsen (1992), pp. 159f.
212. According to Johansen the threat of an accusation for slander was not sufficient to eradicate a reputation for witchcraft, Johansen (1991), p. 145. To my knowledge no systematic survey of these trials have yet been undetaken.
213. A parallel can be identified in the Swedish courts during the 18th century, see Van Gent, Jacqueline, *Magic, Body and the Self in Eighteenth-Century Sweden* (Brill: Boston and Leiden 2008).
214. According to the Copenhagen Reces (1547), no. 17.
215. ACDF, Siena, processi, 51, fols. 255v–256r.
216. Torture was not standard in all inquisitorial trials, see Black (2009), p. 81.
217. Duni (2007), p. 25.
218. In the trial against *Prete* Stefano Tommei, ACDF, Siena, processi, 50, fol. 177.
219. ACDF, Siena, processi, 51, fol. 255r–v.
220. Henningsen notes torture as 'standard procedure in trials for witchcraft', see Henningsen, Gustaf, 'Hekseforfølgelser' in Steensberg, Axel (ed.), *Daglig liv i Danmark i det syttende og attende århundrede* (Nyt Nordisk Forlag: Copenhagen 1969), p. 363; see also Jørgensen (2007), pp. 397f.
221. Birkelund (1983), p. 80; see the torture of Bould Ibsdatter in the trial against Hose-Mette, NLA B 24–518, fols. 453v–461r.
222. The narratives in these confessions as well as the Italian are discussed in chapter 9.
223. Birkelund (1983), p. 80, Jensen (1982), p. 44; Johansen refrains from discussing the purpose of torture and merely emphasizes that applying torture after the verdict meant fewer false confessions (1991), p. 22.
224. See reference above to Johansen (1991).
225. Jensen (1982), p. 44, with reference to Grønlund (1780) and a series of trials in Elsinore 1571–1580.
226. In the witch trials of Aalborg (1612–1621) nine people were charged, and seven ended their lives at the stake. The relations between the trials of the Aalborgesian witches are dealt with in chapter 6, and content of their confessions in chapter 8.
227. The court records of northern Jutland hold numerous similar examples. In a trial from 1634 linked to Else Jacobsdatter originally convicted in 1620, the

defendant Kerstin Thamisdatter stated how she had been known to be a witch ever since she was accused by Else Jacobsdatter for taking part in burning down the mill in Sejlflod by means of witchcraft, NLA B 24–545, fols. 122r–125v. Also in the South-Western part of Jutland, in Ribe, Ingeborg Harchis had denounced her own daughter but withdrew the accusation just before she was put on the stake. In this case the daughter, Bodil Harchisdatter, was also convicted a few years later, Kallestrup, Louise Nyholm,' 'Women, Witches, and the Town Courts of Ribe' in *Gender in Late Medieval and Early Modern Europe*, eds. Muravyeva, Marianna and Raisa Maria Toivo (Routledge: London 2013), pp. 123–136.

228. Jensen (1982), p. 50.
229. The trial of Chresten Lauridtzen, NLA B 24–524, fols. 245r–251r.
230. The content of these confessions is dealt with in chapter 9.
231. In the inquisitorial system, confession was crucial also for legal reasons.
232. *Sospetta d'heresia* was in severe cases increased to *gravemente sospetta d'heresia*. This was the case of the *donne di mala vita* discussed in the following chapters.
233. Other types of execution were used in the 16th century. In the 17th century, however the stake seems to have been the standard method of execution, Jensen (1982), p. 51.
234. Christenze Kruckow was one of the Aalborgesian witches referred to earlier in this book. She was originally charged with witchcraft in 1596 when living in Funen. Here she was accused of bewitching a noble woman, Anne Bille, making her give birth to 15 stillborn children. Christenze Kruckow managed to avoid conviction and moved to Aalborg in the Northern part of Jutland. The entire trial against Christenze Kruckow is published by Jacobsen, J.C., *Christenze Kruckow. En adelig Troldkvinde fra Chr. IV's Tid* (G.E.C. Gad: Copenhagen 1972). The special penalties for nobles were taken out of the legislation with the Danish Law of 1683.
235. See overview by Decker (2008), p. 133.
236. Mensola di Tiracoscia died from the plague before her trial was re-evaluated. ACDF, Siena, processi, 40, fols. 1–107r, 882r–887r, ACDF, Siena, processi, 42, fols. 930r–937r. The accusations and trial against Mensola di Tiracoscia is discussed in chapters 7 and 8.
237. 'carcere di arbitrato delle Santa e Suprema Inquisitione di Roma', ACDF, Siena, processi, 51, fol. 182v.
238. In his *Prattica* Cardinal Scaglia states the wide consequences of using the whip as punishment, ACDF, StStE 5e, fol. 28r–v.
239. Tørnsø, Kim, *Djævletro og folkemagi. Trolddomsforfølgelse i 1500 og 1600 tallets Vestjylland* (Aarhus University Press: Aarhus 1986), the problem is most recently discussed by Appel (1999), pp. 504f.

5 The local studies

240. Wittendorff (1989), pp. 357–359; the suspension of Niels Hemmingsen is discussed in chapter 3.
241. Scocozza, Benito, *Ved afgrundens rand. Politiken and Gyldendals Danmarkshistorie*, vol. 8, Olsen, Olaf (ed.) (Gyldendalske Boghandel and Nordisk Forlag: Copenhagen, 1989), pp. 136–138.
242. The number of *len* varied, but by 1660 there were 49.
243. In Danish *herredsting* or *birketing*, for the Danish legal system, see Jørgensen (2007).

244. A similar privilege is known from other contemporary towns, including Ribe, see Kallestrup, Louise Nyholm, 'Women, Witches, and the Town Courts of Ribe' in Muravyeva, Marianna and Raisa Maria Toivo (eds.), *Gender in Late Medieval and Early Modern Europe* (Routledge: London 2013), pp. 124–136.

245. Since 1873 named Porto Azzurro.

246. Piombino was already under Spanish rule in 1557. For the founding of the presidios, see Tognarini, Ivano, 'Orbetello. I presìdi di Toscana e il Mediterraneo. Il destino di un territorio tra Cosimo de'Medici, Bernardo Tanucci e Napoleone' in *Orbetello e The presidios*, Guarducci, Anna (ed.) (Centro Editoriale Toscano: Florence and Pontassieve 2000), pp. 114–117.

247. For English works, see *Spain in Italy, Politics, Society, and Religion 1500–1700*, Dandelet, Thomas and John Marino (eds.) (Brill: Leiden and Boston 2007).

248. The political argument for establishing the presidios is treated in Marrara, Danilo, 'I presidi feudo imperiale' in Guarducci (2000), pp. 59–64; and Tognarini (2000).

249. In the period that followed, 1707–1737, the area was under Austrian rule, as part of the Austrian dominance of Naples; between 1737 and 1800 it was under Naples/Sicily and finally it became part of Tuscany in 1801.

250. Symcox, Geoffrey, 'The political world of the absolute state in the seventeenth and eighteenth centuries' in *Early Modern Italy*, Marino, John (ed.) (Oxford University Press: Oxford 2002), pp. 104–122.

251. 'before, under or after the siege'. The siege went on from 9 May until 18 July 1646. The Neapolitan general Della Gatta launched a counter-attack with the Spanish fleet and on 13 June another naval battle was fought off the coast of Argentario. The Spanish armies received reinforcements and ammunition from Naples and the French were forced to retreat. They finally left the area on 18 July 1646.

252. My focus in this book has been on the cases from the mid-17th century. I have not yet had the possibility of studying the earlier cases in their proper context. My further research will hopefully provide more information on the connection between the early cases and the cases from 1648 to 1660. ACDF, Siena, processi, 24 and 25, the cases against Theodora Cona, Caterina Zenina and Madalena Roncone of Orbetello.

253. In the following referred to simply as 'inquisitor' and the inquisitor in Siena as 'inquisitor general'; for the local tribunals in Siena, see Di Simplicio (2005), pp. 31–44; see also Black (2009), p. 29.

254. Examples of such edicts are reproduced in Di Simplicio (2005), pp. 32ff.; Canosa, Romano, *Storia dell'Inquisizione in Italia dalla metà del cinquecento alla fine del settecento*, vols. 1–5 (Sapere: Rome 2000), pp. 168ff.

255. Causing the historian Oscar Di Simplicio to describe the reaction amongst the inhabitant as a 'mass-psychosis', Di Simplicio (2005), p. 37.

256. The trials are briefly mentioned by Del Col (2006), p. 766.

257. Ginatempo, Maria, *Crisi di un territorio. Il popolamento della Toscana senese alla fine del medioevo* (Olschki: Florence 1988), demographic map, p. 449; Beloch, Karl Julius, *Storia della popolazione d'Italia*, reprinted in 1994 (Le Lettere: Florence 1937–1961), p. 337. In his major demographic work *Storia della Populazione d'Italia* Karl Julius Beloch states that he could not calculate numbers for the garrison in Orbetello. It was, however, possible to document that in 1740 another garrison town in the area, Porto Longone, housed a garrison of 2577 soldiers. According to Beloch, 765 civilian inhabitants were found in the town at the same time. It has likewise been difficult to find information on the number of inhabitants in Orbetello. From a monograph on the population crisis in Tuscany

in the Middle Ages, it appears that Orbetello was to have 600–800 inhabitants in 1532. A reasonable estimate would probably be that there were about 1,000 inhabitants around 1650. Beloch lists the population of Orbetello and its surrounding areas to be approximately 2,900 in 1784.
258. Guarducci (2000).
259. For a general introduction to daily life in the 16th century, see Cohen, Elizabeth S. and Thomas V. Cohen, *Daily life in Renaissance Italy* (Greenwood Press: Westport and London 2001).
260. As in the words of a witness, 'he [the suspect] is poor like the rest of us', testimony from a witness, given in defence of the accused Stefano Tommei. ACDF, Siena, processi, 51, fol. 161v.
261. Maremma had been drained and cultivated in antiquity, but the area eventually reflooded and in the early modern period was the hide-out of robbers and others outside of the law. The land was not cultivated until the end of the 19th century.
262. Tognarini (2000), pp. 120ff.
263. Ciuffoletti, Zeffiro and Leonardo Rombai,'Saggio introduttivo: La storiografia dei presidios e le problematiche geostoriche dell'assetto territoriale', in Guarducci (2000), pp. 10ff.
264. The case of Virginia di Leandro, ACDF, Siena, processi, 51, fols. 297r–326v.
265. The case of Sidsel Christens, NLA B, 24–556, fols. 258r–262v.

6 Constructing an accusation of witchcraft for the court

266. Johansen (1991), Birkelund (1983).
267. Di Simplicio (2005), pp. 57–89.
268. Di Simplicio (2005), p. 57.
269. Tedeschi (1991), p. 233.
270. Carlo Ginzburg's arguments on the populace's clear distinction between good and evil magic has to be regarded as definitively rejected. O'Neil did this directly as early as in her dissertation: O'Neil, Mary R., 'Discerning Superstition. Popular Errors and Orthodox Response in Late Sixteenth Century Italy', PhD. dissertation (Stanford University 1982), p. 67.
271. This will be further explored in the following chapters.
272. Which poses another parallel to Modena in the second half of the 16th century, O'Neil (1982), p. 115f.
273. *Meretrice* in the sense of women of loose living, in line with Martin (1989), pp. 234f. O'Neil (1982), p. 133, defines them as prostitutes in the modern sense; this is similar to Di Simplicio (2005), pp. 295ff., especially p. 297, who lists an example of a group of prostitutes, who were accused of *stregoneria* and whose profession had been clearly stated. The same author underlines the marginalized role of the prostitutes in local society.
274. In the protocols referred to as *meretrice, donne di mala fama* or *donne della mala forza*, see for instance the case of Faustina di Leusta, ACDF, Siena, processi, 51, fols. 253r, 254.
275. An example is the accusations brought against the witches of Aalborg, who were accused of blowing through keyholes, giving birth to and baptizing a wax-child. This will be treated further in the following chapter.
276. O'Neil, Mary R., 'Magical Healing, Love Magic and the Inquisition in Late 16th Century Modena' in Haliczer, Stephen (ed.), *Inquisition and Society in Early Modern Europe* (Barnes and Noble: London and Sydney 1987), p. 99.

277. The few of whom a profession is given are soldiers; a single captain and a couple of priests.
278. Henningsen (1991), p. 22 (1992), pp. 147f. The concept of 'limited goods' has been discussed in relation to the Swedish cases of the 18th century by Van Gent (2008), pp. 116f.
279. The case of Madalena di Maura, ACDF, Siena, processi, 50, fols. 287r–292r; in Denmark in a case from north of the Limfjord, a woman named Anne Jespersdatter was suspected of stealing her lover's manhood out of revenge, NLA B 24–515, fols. 231v–235v.
280. Di Simplicio (2005), pp. 168ff.
281. Di Simplicio (2005), p. 169, Di Simplicio argues that *una personalità positiva* (a well-liked person) had a major influence on whether the person was liable to acquire the reputation for being a witch.
282. As an example, Nastasia di Cannicciati was denounced by Francesca di Rosata, but the Orbetello records do not contain records of any case brought against her, ACDF, Siena, processi, 51, fol. 349r. Caterina di Angelo Occhioni was denounced by several persons, both convicted and denounced, and the inquisitor initiated a case against her on 17 March 1650. A sentence was, however, never passed, ACDF, Siena, processi, 51, fol. 437r–v.
283. Appel (1999), esp. p. 511; Birkelund (1983), pp. 91f., pp. 138ff.; Johansen (1991), pp. 68ff., 80ff.
284. The case of Pollonia di Gallo, ACDF, Siena, processi, 51, fols. 11r–48v.
285. The interrogation of Faustina di Leusta, ACDF, Siena, processi, 51, fols. 12r–15v.
286. ACDF, Siena, processi, 51, fols. 22r–25r.
287. Pollonia was however probably already in the custody of the inquisition around 11 April. It seems that the practice in Orbetello was to gaol the suspect 5–7 days before the interrogation commenced. Based on ACDF, Siena, processi, fols. 40, 42, 51, 52.
288. The list of the denunciations against Pollonia is long. The case contains several sections that have been poorly preserved, which makes it impossible to exclude that the number might have been higher. Here stated in random order: Ipolita di Goro, Lucida di Canino, Faustina di Leusta, Agata di Camillo di Stremera, Francesca di Niccolò Semplice, Caterina di Matteo Schiacchi, Sabetta di Artenga, Mensola di Tiracoscia, Girolama d'Angolieri, Lucia di Guiseppone, Meca di Angelo Occhioni, Caterina di Angelo Occhioni.
289. For instance. the trial of Ingeborg Harcis of Ribe. Ingeborg had originally denounced her daughter, Bodild, but before her execution in 1610, she withdrew this. Bodild was later sentenced for witchcraft and burned. For the trials of Ribe, see Kallestrup (2013), pp. 121–136.
290. The 'boys' are treated in chapters 8–9.
291. The trial of Johanne Pedersdatter, Sejlflod, 1620, NLA B 24–54, fols. 212r–214r; identical to the sentenced witch presented in the Introduction.
292. The trial of Else Jacobsdatter, Storvorde, 1620; NLA B 24–54, fols. 214r–215v; Anne Jensdatter, Romdrup, 1620; NLA B 24–54, fol. 331r–v.
293. Else Lauritzdatter, Sejlflod, 1620, NLA B 24–54, fol. 239r–v.
294. As defined legally in the Witchcraft Regulation of 1617.
295. Christenze Kruckow was, as far as we can tell from the preserved court records, the only noble woman convicted of witchcraft in Denmark. Some of the cases have been published in Jacobsen, J.C., *Christenze Kruckow. En adelig Troldkvinde fra Chr. IV's Tid* (G.E.C. Gad: Copenhagen 1972); see also Tvede-Jensen, Lars

and Gert Poulsen, *Aalborg under krise og højkonjunktur. Aalborgs Historie*, vol. 2 (Aalborg Kommune: Aalborg 1988). Another group of cases against Mette Kongens et al., which also included explicit diabolical characteristics, took place in eastern Jutland. These cases have been treated in Johansen (1991), pp. 71ff.

296. Maren Nielsdatter Knepis, Jacobsen (1972), pp. 37–45; NLA 24–511, fols. 58r–64r.
297. That is, the evening before St. Lucy's day 13 December.
298. As already mentioned, Maren Knepis and Mette Pedersdatter (NLA B 24–511, fols. 83r–86v) were convicted in 1612. The sentence on Apelone Ibsdatter was passed in 1619, for the initial case, see NLA B 24–511, fols. 163v–168v, for the case leading to her final sentence, see NLA B 24–53, fols. 228v–231v, see also Jacobsen (1972), pp. 52–56.
299. Maren Pedersdatter withdrew her denunciation of Jens Andersen's wife.
300. Klitgaard, C., 'Den Store Nordjyske Hekseforfølgelse' in *Fra Himmerland og Kjær Herred*, 1915–1917, pp. 165ff.; Apelone Ibsdatter might not have had the reputation for being a witch herself, but in 1604 her husband had been suspected of witchcraft, Christensen, Poul Erik and Dorthe Skadhauge, *Kvinder og hekseforfølgelser i det 16.og 17. århundrede* (Aalborg University 1983), p. 178; Tvede-Jensen, Lars og Gert Poulsen, *Aalborg under krise og højkonjunktur fra 1534 til 1680. Aalborgs Historie*, vol. 2 (Aalborg Kommune: Aalborg 1988), p. 149.
301. I will return to the motivation for denouncing in the following chapters.
302. For further discussion of significance of the concept of honour in villages, see Appel (1999), pp. 506–525; Sandmo, Erling, *Voldssamfunnets undergang, Om disiplinering av Norge på 1600-tallet* (Universitetsforlaget, Oslo, 1999/2002), pp. 97–149.
303. Numerous variations of this can be found in the court records, the most prominent being the trial against the burgher woman Maren Splids, executed in Ribe in 1641. When her husband did not manage to clear her name after she had been accused of witchcraft for the first time in 1637, this initial accusation was presented as evidence against her in the second trial. For the Ribe trials, see Kallestrup, Louise Nyholm, 'Trolddomsforfølgelser' in *Ribe Bys Historie*, vol. 2, Christensen, Søren Bitsch (ed.) (Esbjerg Kommune and Dansk Center for Byhistorie, 2010), pp. 294–305, the case is also briefly discussed in Kallestrup, Louise Nystrop,'Knowing Satan from God: Demonic Possession, Witchcraft, and the Lutheran Orthodox Church in Early Modern Denmark', *Magic, Ritual and Witchcraft*, vol. 6/2 (2011), pp. 177f.
304. See also Appel (1999), pp. 525–531.

7   From allegation to formal accusation

305. The ambiguity of magic has been emphasized by several scholars, most recently by Van Gent, Jacqueline, *Magic, Body and the Self in Eighteenth-Century Sweden*, (Brill: Boston and Leiden 2008), pp. 159–192.
306. For more on this in a the Danish context see Kallestrup (2013), pp. 125f., Virginia di Leandro, ACDF, Siena, *processi*, 51, fols. 297r–327r.
307. No rule without an exception. When the young Bartolomeo Bartoletti was convicted, it was to achieve the consent of women to engage in sexual relationships without marriage, ACDF, Siena, processi, 51, fols. 784r–791r.
308. The trial of Stefano Tommei, commenced on 25 April 1649 and concluded on 7 October 1650, ACDF, Siena, processi, 51, fols. 103r–176v.

309. Bernardino was a priest or possibly just a canon, ACDF, Siena, processi, 51, fol. 131r. He is referred to as *prete*, which means priest, but the term was also applied to simple clerics. That Bernardino should, in fact, have been bound by celibacy is not discussed further, and he may perhaps had taken just minor orders and was not bound by the vow of celibacy.
310. The same emerges from the few trial records preserved from medieval Scandinavia, Mitchell (2011), p. 197.
311. The trial against Johane (Jahan) Jensdatter, NLA B 24–516, fols. 397r–400r.
312. The trial of Francesca di Rosata, ACDF, Siena, processi, 51, fols. 445r–462v; first collection of denunciations and testimonies against Pasquale Pesci, ACDF, Siena, processi, 51, fols. 467r–478v; second collection of denunciations and testimonies against Pasquale Pesci, ACDF, Siena, processi, 51, fols. 508r–509v; denunciations of Francesca's husband Francesco referred to both as Francesco di Fenio and Francesco Bocchino, ACDF, Siena, processi, 51, fols. 495r–496v.
313. The meaning is confirmed by O'Neil (1982), pp. 122f.; p. 133.
314. ACDF, StStE 5e, n. 2, among others fol. 25v.
315. It cannot be excluded that the young Angela, who reported Francesca to the inquisition, was identical with *la Tosa*. This would explain why Francesca's husband Francesco Bocchino would hold a grudge against her. The supporting argument is that in the trial against Agata di Camillo, she is listed as Angela di Paolo and the woman whom Francesco was chasing was the daughter of Paolo Fornaro. ACDF, Siena, processi, 51, fols. 446ff. The argument is however fragile both because Paolo was a common name and because it may be presumed that under such circumstances the inquisitor would have treated the case as threats against a witness. Two witnesses in the case against Pasquale Pesci also speak about incidents with Francesco Bocchino. One of the witnesses, Constantinus [Costantino] di Justis, specifically spoke about the incident in the church, ACDF, Siena, processi, 51, fol. 470v.
316. The first hearings of witnesses took place at the beginning of May. The next witnesses in the case were heard on 3 June 1650, ACDF, Siena, processi, 51, fols. 471–475v.
317. ACDF, Siena, processi, 51, fols. 508r–510v.
318. There are numerous examples of witnesses who gossiped about other people's love lives, about marital relationships and break-ups. See amongst others the following case against Agata di Camillo or the cases against Lucida di Canino, Pollonia di Gallo and Madalena di Maura.
319. Priest or canon. The trial against Agata di Camillo commenced on 2 April 1649, ACDF, Siena, processi, 51, fols. 68r–79r.
320. In the following discussion of the Italian trials, witchcraft refers to the Italian *sortilegio*, unless something else is specified.
321. These two women were Pollonia di Gallo and Lucida di Canino.
322. Agata herself testifies on disputes with Pollonia di Gallo, ACDF, Siena, processi, 51, fol. 72v; this dispute is confirmed by Catherina di Tegnazzi, fol. 74r–v, see note above for quotation, and Vittoria di Antonio, fols. 74v–75r; for inquisitorial norms on this, see Black (2009), p. 71.
323. 'We sentence you to stand publicly, with your face unveiled with a candle in hand on Sundays and holidays at the entrance to the Church of Saint Francesco di Paola, while the Holy Mass is celebrated', ACDF, Siena, processi, 51, fol. 79r.
324. The trial against Mensola di Tiracoscia commenced 1649 and concluded with the death of Mensola in 1656. ACDF, Siena, processi, 40, fols. 1r–107r; 882r–887r; 930r–977v.

325. Or *donne di mala fama*, meaning women of evil repute.
326. At least for the period studied. The trial against Mensola di Tiracoscia was the most extensive trial in Orbetello, divided into two *faldone* in the Siena-archive, processi, 40, 42. In these two *faldone* the trials against Mensola's daughter Lucia di Tiracoscia and the sister Deva di Tiracoscia are also located.
327. The trial against Pollonia di Gallo, also known as Appollonia/Apollonia di Gallo, ACDF, Siena, processi, 51, fols. 11r–48v.
328. In his manual, Desiderio Scaglia lists these remedies as typical along with magnets, sacred candles, holy water, herbs and beans, pieces of paper, blood, ACDF, StStE 5e, n2, fols. 23r, 25r, 27v.
329. Pollonia gave the names of a number of people who had either witnessed her magic or 'bought' magical rituals from her. It has not been possible to document whether these people were convicted by the inquisition in Orbetello.
330. The inquisitor's systematic approach is clearly demonstrated in the case, as the individuals involved were called upon to give testimony one by one. ACDF, Siena, processi, 51, fols. 18r–22r, 25r–26r.
331. It was customary for the inquisition to question persons on regarding cases other than just their own. There are several cases, therefore, in which the inquisitor questions especially Mensola di Tiracoscia, Lucida di Canino and Pollonia di Gallo.
332. ACDF, Siena, processi, 51, fol. 13r.
333. In the court records spelt *incantesmo*.
334. Excerpt from the incantation. The text is difficult to decipher and the translation is rudimentary. 'Terra Madre Terra il Core di Pietro ti/si consumi come il Marito Sotto Terra, che nò possi gire ne stare bere ne mangiare si à me non viene à trovare', ACDF, Siena, processi, 51, fol. 13v. O'Neil (1987) has quoted a similar incantation for the same purpose from Modena, p. 102; see also O'Neil (1982), p. 148. The incantation was quite common in love magic and appeared in numerous variations. A common feature of all of them, however, was that 'the victim' would not feel well before he was with the person who recited the incantation.
335. Rosa di Longone, ACDF, Siena, processi, 349r–353r, accused on 16 November 1649.
336. Meca, also called Domenica, daughter of Caterina and Angelo Occhioni. Caterina di Angelo Occhioni, is referred to in several testimonies. Divination through palm-reading was widespread amongst the women in Orbetello, but it does not appear to have held any significance to the inquisition.
337. The trial against Lucida di Canino, ACDF, Siena, processi, 51, fols. 196r–232v.
338. Lucida was arrested during the evening. According to witnesses, the time was around 10pm, ACDF, Siena, processi, 51, fols. 210r–211r; 211r–212r; 212r–212v. This would have been in line with inquisitorial procedures, as they are presented in Eliseo Masini's manual *Sacro Arsenale*, Tedeschi (1991), p. 132.
339. Quotation is referenced, ACDF, Siena, processi, 51, fol. 23v.
340. Besides Pollonia di Gallo, Lucida denounced Faustina di Leusta, ACDF, Siena, processi, 51, fol. 22v and Emilia di Baldo fol. 23r. I have only located a denunciation of Emilia di Baldo, 28 March 1649. ACDF, Siena, processi, 51, fols. 60–61v.
341. The trial against Faustina di Leusta, ACDF, Siena, processi, 51, fols. 242r–261v. The allegations by Lucida di Canino ACDF, Siena, processi, 51, fol. 216r; by Pollonia di Gallo ACDF, Siena, processi, 51, fol. 28v.
342. For instance by Beratrice di Martiale Modesti about Faustina di Leusta, fol. 253r 'I have always regarded her as an honest person of good parentage', and

concerning Pollonia and Lucida 'Lucida and Pollonia I have always seen as having a bad reputation'. Additionally, the testimony delivered by Dianora Giusti also mentions the animosity between Lucida and Faustina, and here Lucida was characterized as a 'donna di mala', fols. 253v–254r.

343. The interrogation of Faustina di Leusta under torture, ACDF, Siena, processi, 51, fols. 255r–257r.

344. There is a coincidence of dates in Lucida's testimony in Pollonia's trial and her reporting on Emilia di Baldo, 28 March 1649, fols. 60r–64r.

345. The trial against Pollonia di Gallo, ACDF, Siena, processi, 51, fol. 23r.

346. ACDF, Siena, processi, 51, fol. 201r.

347. ACDF, Siena, processi, 51, fol. 196r. Duni's (2007) and O'Neil's (1982) studies on Modena confirm that the mentioned sentence was exceptionally harsh in an inquisitorial context. It should be noted that O'Neil''s use of the term 'prostitutes' appears to have the modern meaning, whereas the use of the term 'prostitutes' (*meretrici*) in the Orbetello trials primarily concerns loose women, this being women who engaged in sexual relationships with men outside of marriage. As already mentioned, there is no mention in the records that money or goods were exchanged between the women and their *amici*, although it cannot be ruled out either, O'Neil (1982), pp. 126f.; O'Neil suggests that the penalty may even have been regarded by the authorities as a way of controlling prostitution as much as it was a punishment for witchcraft.

348. As mentioned in the presentation of the trial against Virginia di Leandro, Di Simplicio (2005) has a reference to Lucida di Canino, where she is listed as *malefica*, p. 414.

349. ACDF, Siena, processi, 51, fols. 210r, 211v.

350. ACDF, Siena, processi, fol. 206r.

351. The trial of Kiersten Nielsdatter, 1627, NLA B 24–542, fols. 1r–3r.

352. The trial of 'Lang' Maren Lauridsdatter, NLA A 24–515, fols. 77r–81v; Jyske Tegnelser, 1620, 12/2, fol. 46.

353. NLA B 24–515, fol. 81v.

354. See Kallestrup (2011), pp. 170–175; Christensen, Christen Villads, 'Besættelsen på Rosborg' in *Samlinger til Jysk Historie og Topografi* (1909), pp. 228–247.

355. The trials from Aarhus are treated in Birkelund (1983), extracts of the trials from Aalborg are published by Jacobsen (1972).

356. From the total of 1,604 witness statements delivered at the Jutlandic trials, 1,544 of them contained accusations of explicitly malevolent magic. The remaining 60 are spread out on 13 for demonic possession; 23 for healing magic; 4 for love magic; the last 23 were unspecified. The calculation has been made from Johansen's (1991) compilation of the content of the testimonies by witnesses, pp. 202–207.

357. NLA B 24–54. fols. 212r–214r.

358. NLA B 24–54, fols. 214r–215v.

359. NLA B 24–534, fols. 194r–201v.

360. Madalena di Maura, reported the first time on 6 August 1649, ACDF, Siena, processi, 51, fols. 287r–293r.

361. The protocol does not state exactly when Giovanna had arrived in Orbetello; Madalena di Maura, ACDF, Siena, processi, 51, fol. 287r.

362. Amongst others, the case against Mensola di Tiracoscia, where Madalena accused Mensola of having offered to help her in getting the captain to marry her, ACDF, Siena, processi, 40, fols. 53r–54r.

363. The trial against Mensola di Tiracoscia, the allegation was made by Appollonia Giovanni Pisciatesse. ACDF, Siena, processi, 40, fol. 88r.
364. The trial against Anne Jespersdatter, NLA B 24–515, fols. 77r–81v.
365. A man testified that Anne had shouted at her and that he had lost his potency after this. Anne was further accused of having caused harm to livestock.
366. Van Gent (2008) has explored this notion further on the basis of Swedish trials of the 18th century, esp. chs. 2 and 3.
367. For the case of Christenze Kruckow, see chapter 6.
368. See, for example, the questioning of the witness Dianora Giusti, fols. 253v–254r, and the questioning of Venera Zordazzi, fols. 205r–206r. The line must have been a fine one, however, as Pollonia di Gallo is referred to in a single place as *strega* together with Mensola; see the questioning of Caterina Branelli, fols. 208v–209r, whereas the two women are distinguished in the questioning of Caterina di Benedetti, fols. 68r–68v. The gendered aspect of the trial against Mensola di Tiracoscia is explored further in Kallestrup, Louise Nyholm, 'Fra klog kone til kætter" in *Kvinders magt og magtens kvinder i tidlig moderne Europa* (*Den Jyske Historiker*, vol. 125, 2010), pp. 73–92.
369. The trial against Agata di Camillo, ACDF, Siena, processi, 51, fol. 68v.
370. The exact procedure of this part of the ritual is difficult to decipher as the document has been damaged by damp.
371. The argument for her not having gone to the inquisition earlier was that she knew that Mensola had been convicted. Angela thus believed that now when Mensola had already been punished, further testimonies against her would be of no relevance. ACDF, Siena, processi, 40, fol. 86v. What made Angela change her mind is uncertain.

8 Popular notions of witchcraft

372. See also Davis, Natalie Zemon, *Fiction in the Archives* (Stanford University Press: Stanford 1987), p. 3.
373. See also Martin (1989), p. 81.
374. What exactly the two women threw on the fire has not been specified further here 'sentendo buttare tutto il giorno nel suo focolire', but it was most likely salt; 'ad effetto di far venir il Marito che era fuora di Orbetello', ACDF, Siena, processi, 51, fol. 298r.
375. 'bravata da me, che non dicesse queste parole, perche bisogneva riccorre a Dio nelli matrimonÿ e non al Diavolo'.
376. 'Essendo che il Signore Francesco Tizzani mio marito gia molti mesi con grande scandalo di tutti mia Casa habbia preso una cattiva prattica per la quale mi ritrovo in grandissima tribulatione e desiderosa di trovar modo accio lui detesta da uno scandolo cosi notorio', ACDF, Siena, processi, 51, fol. 892r. Several places also referred to as *mala prattica*.
377. 'hora pero conosco esser il tutto bugia et inganni e come tali li detesto, e questo e quanto mi occorre deporre avanti V.P.', ACDF, Siena, processi, 51, fol. 893r.
378. Her punishment consisted of imprisonment and a threat of flogging if she was to attempt something similar again, ACDF, Siena, processi, 51, fols. 353r–365r.
379. Several witnesses subsequently testify of Girolama's healing powers, amongst others the young Domenico di Rafaello who was cured of a headache by Girolama. *L'aperta* is not reproduced in the trial, as it is usually seen in inquisition trials. ACDF, Siena, processi, 51, fol. 257r–v.

380. NLA B 24–556, fol. 359r.
381. NLA B, 24–556, fol. 260v.
382. Via Jacobsen (1972), p. 39.
383. Peder Poulssøn's witness statement published in Jacobsen (1972), pp. 38f.
384. Desired things are not always specified in the testimonies.
385. Grønlund, David, *Historisk Efterretning om de i Ribe Bye for Hexerie forfulgte og brændte Mennesker* (Ribe 1784), pp. 61f.
386. As will be discussed further in chapter 9, the difference lay in what meaning the social conflict between the individuals had to the judges.
387. 'Lei [Girolama] diceva l'aperta à detta Gallerana non intesi però che parole si dicesse, però meglio di me lo potra dire à V.P. la moglie di Berto la quale stà sotto di lei di casa', ACDF, Siena, processi, 51, fol 355r, my underlining.
388. For example, the witness Antonio Guadagnino, who visited Girolama so that she could cure him of his erysipelas on his leg (*risipola in una gamba*) 'mandai a chiamare Girolama detta del Cocòm la quale era publica voce e fama che sapesse dire dell'oratione per guarire molti male', ACDF, Siena, processi, 51 fol. 360r.
389. 'che lei sa che è carcerata per haver detto certi orationi dell'aperta mal d'occhio, ripreso [...] et mandato il nostro Cancelle che nò dicessi [dicesse?], ma io perche pensavo che non fosse peccato l'ho detto, et per l'avvenire prometto che nó li diro piu', ACDF, Siena, processi, 51, fol. 361v. This is confirmed by the witness Gallerana di Michele, who was to have been treated by Girolama 'et essa Gieronima disse che non mi poteva dire oratione nessuno perche haveva la pena della frusta dal santo Officio in dire simili orationi', Siena, processi, 51, fol. 357r.
390. For instance, ACDF, processi, 51, fol.21r, '*della mia conscientia et ad honore di Dio et nò ad altro*'.
391. It is a bit unclear whether the ritual with the coal was a part of Girolama's '*l'aperta*'.
392. 'Piglio una tazza d'aqua senza la quale fece il segno della Croce et ci disse l'oratione quale fosse questa oratione io non sentÿ perche la diceva submissa voce, et all'ultimo ci fece un altro segno di Croce et ci pose dentro tre carboni accesi [...] et mi fece bere l'aqua', ACDF, Siena, processi, 51, fol. 359r.
393. 'Gieronima [Girolama] toccò detta Gallerana dove si sentiva male', ibid.
394. In other parts of Italy it was primarily St. Martha, St. Helen and St. Daniel who were used in the love magic rituals, O'Neil (1987), pp. 102, 104; Martin (1989), pp. 108, 176.
395. In the period examined 1648–1685. The priest Stefano Tommei was accused of witchcraft, which he had practised 15 years earlier, and before he became a priest. The material contains several accusations against clerics, but all of these concern blasphemy. Mary O'Neil has explained this part of her study in her chapter 'Sacerdote Ovvero Strione: Ecclesiastical and Superstitious Remedies in 16th Century Italy' in Kaplan, Steven (ed.), *Understanding Popular Culture, Europe From the Middle Ages To the 19th Century* (Walter de Gruyter: Berlin 1984), pp. 53–84; this has been supported by more recent studies on Milan in De Boer, Wietse, *The Conquest of the Soul. Confession, Discipline, and Public Order in Counter-Reformation Milan* (Brill: Boston and Leiden 2001), pp. 309–312; See also Gentilcore (1998) and Jacobson Schutte, Anne, *Aspiring Saints: Pretense of Holiness, Inquisition, and Gender in the Republic of Venice, 1618–1750* (Johns Hopkins University Press: Baltimore 2001).
396. The trial has been featured by several Danish scholars, most recently by Appel (1999); the protocol from the provincial court in Viborg for the year Jens Hansen Rusk was convicted is not preserved.

397. This treatment was prescribed to lift a bewitchment that Kristen Hansen believed had been inflicted upon him in 1595. His belief originated in him suffering such severe pains in his body that no 'natural' explanation could be the cause.
398. Ruggiero (1993), pp. 43ff.
399. Martin (1989), p. 135.
400. '[Elisabetta] presi un pezzo di candela benedetta che haveva in casa et mandatosila detta Elisabetta la quale accesa da lei et posta inginocchioni innanzi ad una figura di s. Antonio che havevo in Casa disse non sò che cose piano che non sentivo ma per quello detta lisabetta mi riferi haveva detto l'oratione di s. Antonio', the intention had been that Columba could marry her loved one, a Spanish soldier. ACDF, Siena, processi, 51, fol. 342r.
401. 'comprare una candela che voleva accendere à santo Antonio e dire il suo oratione, e quello detto spiritu santo', ACDF, Siena, processi, 51, fol. 349v.
402. NLA B 24–515, fol. 232r.
403. Uldsted Mette herself was prosecuted in 1618, NLA B 24–514, fols. 113r–114v.
404. RA, Herredagsdombog 1640, fols. 500r–511v.
405. This is complemented by O'Neil's examinations of Modena, where all magic was perceived as potentially dangerous by the Church. O'Neil (1982), p. 67, and especially pp. 112f.
406. When her accuser, Mikkel Christensen, became convinced that Sidsel was to blame for the illness of his son, due to her prediction that the son would get better.
407. The trial of Kerstin Thamisdatter, NLA, B 24–545, fols. 122r–125v.
408. The trial of Mette Pedersdatter, NLA B 24–514, fol. 113v.
409. The trial of Mette Pedersdatter, NLA B 24–514, fols. 113r–114v.
410. In these cases, the judges always emphasized the reports of malevolent magic. I will return to this in the following chapter.
411. The trial of Paaske Rasmussen, NLA B 24–557, fols. 163r–174v.
412. The interrogation of Lucida di Canino, ACDF, Siena, processi, 51, fol. 213r–v.
413. 'solo l'ho [the ritual] detto per Marito come ho detto penzando [pesando], che fossero cose di Dio e non superstitiosi ne incantesmi', ACDF, Siena, processi, 51, fol. 250v.
414. As emphasized in the previous chapter. Van Gent (2008) has documented a similar perception in Sweden by drawing on the 18th century court cases of magic.
415. Referred to by Jacqueline Van Gent as 'the self', Van Gent (2008), see esp. pp. 59–87.
416. For instance, Madalena di Antonio 'Elisabetta d'Artiaga haveva fatto non sò che incantesmi nel suo Astrico, et li era corparro il Demonio'. The questioning of sponte comparente Madalena di Antonio in the trial against Lucida di Canino, ACDF, Siena, processi, 51, fol. 202v.
417. 'li faceva certi incantesmi con serrare la porta fù chiamava il Demonio', ACDF, Siena, processi, 51, fol. 26r.
418. 'che cosa si dicesse in quello che chiamava oratione detta Faustina non me lo disse', ACDF, Siena, processi, 51, fols. 106r–184r.
419. The trials of Karen Christensdatter, NLA B 24–515, fols. 149v–150r, 283v–292v.
420. The trial of Birgitte Jensdatter 'Engeland', NLA B 25–53, fols. 164r–165r.
421. From other areas in Jutland we know that the witches' confessions were read out loud, probably in the last minutes before the execution. For instance, in the trial of Paaske Rasmussen when Paaske had told a woman to go and listen to the confession of a convicted witch to learn who had killed her horse, NLA B

24–557, fols. 163r–174v. In an article in the forthcoming volume of AKIH (eds. Behringer, Wolfgang, Johannes Dillinger and Iris Gareis, 2015), I explore further the topic of the Devil in the Danish context; in Danish see Kallestrup, Louise Nyholm, 'Djævelen' in Duedahl, Poul and Ulrik Langen (eds.), *Nattens Gerninger* (Gads Forlag: Copenhagen, 2015).

422. As discussed earlier, Maren Knepis of Aalborg also kept the Devil in this shape.
423. The trial of Anne Lundts, NLA B 24–512, fols. 279v–286r, esp. 282r.
424. The trial of Anne Pedersdatter Lumpens, NLA B 24–514, fols. 239r–245v.
425. ACDF, Siena, processi, 51, fols. 106r–184r.
426. 'stando io inginocchioni con una candela accesa [...] e credo, che fosse benedetta et detto Prete senza cappello inginocchioni parimente con esso me, mi leggeva l'Incantesmo di deto libro il quale per quello che mi ricordo diceva [...] il glorioso S. Dianello, il Gesu Xpno la Vergine M. a Tutti li Chori dell'Angeli chiamava tutti li patriarche profeti, Chori dell'Angeli, il Sole, la luna li stelle, e poi cominciò à chiamare li Diavoli ad uno ad uno', ACDF, Siena, processi, 51, fol. 112v.
427. on angels in love magic, see Ruggiero (1993), p. 119, see also pp. 46f.
428. 'Che apparsoli il Diavolo in forma di un Cane grosso', ACDF, Siena, processi, 40, fol. 91v.
429. As part of the trial against Jahan Knepis, Christensen (1908–10), pp. 15f.

9 Honest people and wicked people

430. NLA A, 24–512, 1616, fols. 279v–286r.
431. NLA B 24–515, fols. 77r–81v.
432. Christensen (1908–10), p. 8.
433. See also Black (2009), p. 71.
434. A similar point has been stressed by Cohen (2007), pp. 95–126.
435. 'Io son sorella della Compagnia di santa Croce, et dell'Illustrissimo Rosario, [et ci ne quando posso]', ACDF, Siena, processi, 40, fol. 32v.
436. O'Neil (1983) lists a case in which the accused, Antonio Correggi, quickly assumed the inquisitor's term *superstitione*. From the interrogations it appears that Antonio Correggi still did not share the same perception as the inquisitor, as he saw *superstitione* as a general synonym of harming others through witchcraft, pp. 78ff.
437. As an example, see the interrogation of Domenica di Paula di Giuliano Alessi 'Interrogata an semil in anno salto se communicat, et sacramentaliti confitialj. Respondit: Mi sono communicata questa Pasqua prossima passata, et mi Communio tre, ò Quattro volte l'anno et alter tanto mi confesso', ACDF, Siena, processi, 50, fol. 94r.
438. The first interrogation of Lucida di Canino, Siena, processi, 51, fols. 212r–218r. She had subsequently managed to get married. Lucida's husband, Miliano, must have been identical with the man who had abused her. As mentioned earlier, she testified against Pollonia by telling the inquisitor that she wanted Pollonia's help, so that Miliano would treat her well (*volesse bene*), ACDF, Siena, processi, 51, fols. 24r–25r.
439. 'queste Pasqua prossima passata non mi sono Communicata perche il Signore Priore della Collegiata non mi la volsuto Communicare la cuasa credo sia stata perche stavo casa di detto Prete, che io mi tenevo, che ero scandalo à questo popolo', ACDF, Siena, processi, 51, fol. 213r.

440. 'Io mi dico il Rosato della R.V.M ogni giorno, la Corona della Madonna et dell Signore et odo la messa ogni giordi', ACDF, Siena, processi, 51, fol. 213r.
441. See also Ruggiero (1993), p. 59.
442. 'Io Padre credo non haver fatto peccato stare con monsignore Carlo di Luca Antonio Todi in atto Venero [venereo], et in compagnia sua nell'istesso letto stò anno continui perche l'ho tenuto come per mio Marito', ACDF, Siena, processi, 51, fol. 313v.
443. ACDF, Siena, processi, 51, fol. 314r. It is not immediately evident who the solicitor was, but in accordance with the guidelines of the inquisition, for example of the *Sacro Arsenale* via Tedeschi (1991), p. 96 anyone who could not afford to hire a defence should have a solicitor appointed. Usually only the inquisitor and the notary were present, but legal counsel appears in a number of cases, and in the aforementioned trial against Faustina di Leusta a doctor was summoned to determine if she would be able to be interrogated under torture, as she was halfway through her pregnancy, ACDF, Siena, processi, 51, fols. 255v–256r.
444. 'doppo haver parlato con il mio advocato, il quale me la messo per la strada di Dio' and furthermore 'credo che quello stare con detto monsignore Carlo non era lecito ne da Christiana, e che offendava Iddio mortalmente', ACDF, Siena, processi, 51, fol. 314r.
445. The inquisitor was also regularly corresponding with his superior in Siena regarding incarceration and later about carrying out torture.
446. Amongst other things Agata was, like Francesca di Rosata, accused of having practised a ritual in which she urinated in a *pignatello* (a kind of bowl) and said a prayer to the stars, in order to maintain her lover's interest.
447. ACDF, Siena, processi, 51, fol. 70r.
448. 'levemente sospetta di heresia et Apostasia'. *Levemente* must correspond to the official term *de levi*, meaning the mildest form of renunciation in line with cardinal Scaglia's *Prattica*, StStE 5e nr. 2, fol. 28r.
449. 'creduto, et tenuto, che li demoni per mezzo di magici incantesmi possino violentare la volontà del homo', my underlining, ACDF, Siena, processi, 51, fol. 78v2, the page is unnumbered, but follows fol. 78v. The argument for the conviction continues: 'e farli fare, quello che essi vogliano in particolare di rimovere il volere d'altri e fare matrimonij benche la persona non voglia accensentirei'.
450. 'Leggermente sospetta di heresia', ACDF, Siena, processi, 51, fol. 255v.
451. A warning that, if she should again be reported for witchcraft, she would be flogged and banished, was added. ACDF, Siena, processi, 51, fol. 256r.
452. The present quote is from the trial of Sidsel Christens, NLA B 24–556, fol. 262v.
453. Herredagsdombog, RA, fol. 504r–v; Anders Christensen was convicted at the provincial court in Viborg, he brought the case to the King's Court (*Kongens Retterting*), where he was eventually acquitted.
454. It is not stated in this case, nor in other cases whether the first 24 witnesses are identical to the next 24 men.
455. The trial of Inger Jensdatter, NLA B24–517, fols. 350r–354v.
456. 'Lang' Maren Lauridsdatter, NLA B 24–515, fols. 77r–81v.
457. Among others, see Martin (1989), pp. 89ff. Despite spanning half a century or more, the ideas that are expressed in the Orbetello protocols correspond with the findings of Duni (2007), O'Neil (1987) from Modena and Martin (1989) from Venice.
458. 'Io non credo che li demoni habbino [abbiano?] potesti di forzare la volonta del homo', ACDF, Siena, processi, 42, fol. 905r.

459. 'et questo lo feci ad effetto che d. Pasquale mi volesse bene et non si partisse dalla mia amicitia', ACDF, Siena, processi, 51, fol. 449r.
460. The sentence was 'An credat et crediterit dicta urina sic incantata Demones potuisse violentare hominis volutate ad inhonesta amores ab [ad] ipsa pretenses' in line with the applied ritual containing urine. ACDF, Siena, processi, 51, fol. 449v.
461. 'Io non ho inteso ne credo mai che li Demonÿ per mezzo di quella orina che io incantai potessero forzare la volunta ne di Pasquale ne di altro a venire da ne [me?] sapendo [text is poorly preserved] che il Demonio non ha questa potenza', ACDF, Siena, processi, 51, fol. 449v.
462. 'mi fu insegnato da la detta Nastasia la quale mi diede ad intendere che l'orina incantato per mezzo di quella stella come ho ditto [detto] haveva questa forza', ACDF, Siena, processi, 51, fol. 449v.
463. A similar reaction is seen in almost all multiple interrogations of suspects.
464. The Venetian example treated by Martin (1989) confirms the fact that the inquisitor remained passive in the preliminary interrogation, see in particular, pp. 83ff.
465. A similar practice is referenced in Martin (1989), p. 83.
466. 'un desiderio inhonesto che io havevo, che Pasquale Pesci mi volesse bene et non mi abbandonasse', ACDF, Siena, processi, 51, fol. 450v.
467. 30 July 1650, ACDF, Siena, processi, 51, fols. 454r–455v.
468. 'Io ho inteso, et è cosa publica che detta Donna Lucida fatti molti incantesmi, et sortilegi ad effetto che V.P. [inquisitore] mi domanda di fare pigliare l'homini per moglie à qualche Donna benche sia con la loro volonta almeno di una delle due parte', testimony delivered by Venera Tordazzi, ACDF, Siena, processi, 51, fol. 205r.
469. 'Padre io nò ho mai creduto tal cosa', ACDF, Siena, processi, 51, fol. 896v.
470. A variation on this is found in one of the first interrogations of Mensola di Tiracoscia, when she was confronted with the interpretation of free will: 'Padre questo io ho fatto quelli sortilegi et Incantesmi ho creduto sempre et Tenuto che li Demoni potessero forzare le volonti delli homini à pigliar per Moglie quelle persone che io desideravo', ACDF, Siena, processi, 40, fol. 42v.
471. Hardly any research has been conducted into the Danish confessions, and this section must be regarded as merely introductory. In an article in the forthcoming volume of AKIH, I explore further the topic of the witches' confessions and their demonological features in a Danish context.
472. In the trial against Paaske Rasmussen, a witness refers to a certain episode, where two men discuss whether or not to go and listen to the confession of Else Huskone, a convicted witch, NLA B, fols. 163r–174v.
473. Extract from the trial against Sidsels Christens. The full reference reads, 'Dernæst fremlagde tvende bekendelser, den første Kirsten Poulsdatter født i Kilst af Vester Herredsting år 1614, den. 8. januar, den anden Maren, Christen Nissens hustru, i Thoffuis af Skads herredsting samme år 18. juni udgangen, formeldendes dem iblandt andet at have udlagt forne Sidsel Christens for trolddomskunster, så hun med hendes medbrødre havde taget livet både af folk og kreatur', NLA B, 24–556, fol. 262r.
474. As with the Roman Inquisition, all confessions needed to be confirmed by the witch when she was out of torment and free (*upint og løs*). Sometimes several confessions were edited into one document, Henningsen (1991), pp. 110f.

475. For the regional varieties of the confessions from Ribe, see Kallestrup (2013). Due to the limited number of confessions preserved by the Provincial Archive in Viborg, this section draws on the confessions of the witches from Ribe. See also my forthcoming article.
476. Jacobsen (1972), pp. 52–56.
477. The confession of Apelone Guldsmeds, in Jacobsen (1972), pp. 52–56. In the confessions of the Ribe witches, obtained by the court at the Town Council and not the provincial court in Viborg, the witch and her servant Devil entered into a pact similar to a marriage, see Kallestrup (2013), Kallestrup (2015).
478. NLA B 1617, fol. 253r.
479. Confession of Apeloni Guldsmeds, in Jacobsen (1972), p. 53.

10   Conclusion: the confessor and the judge

480. ACDF, Siena, processi 51, fol. 103r–196r; NLA B 24–54, fols. 212r–214r.
481. Gijswijt-Hofstra, Marijke, 'Witchcraft After the Witch Trials' in *The Eighteenth and Nineteenth Centuries. The Athlone History of Witchcraft and Magic in Europe*, vol. 5, Ankarloo, Bengt and Stuart Clark (eds.) (Athlone and University of Pennsylvania Press: London and Philadelphia 1999), p. 134.
482. Herlihy, David, 'The Tuscan Town in the Quattrocento: A Demographic Profile' in *Medievalia et Humanistica*, New series I (1970), pp. 93–95.
483. Johansen (1991) supports this by stating that priests as late as the end of the 17th century still "found [...] it to be odd if people remained unmarried', p. 66.
484. Richard Kieckhefer noted this possible connection, but refrained from pursuing the argument further, Kieckhefer, Richard, *European Witch Trials: Their Foundations in Popular and Learned Culture, 1300–1500*, (University of California Press: Berkeley and Los Angeles 1976), p. 57.
485. Historians have so far more or less neglected this collection, Ohrt, F., *Danmarks Trylleformler* (Nordisk Forlag: Copenhagen 1917), pp. 382–387.
486. For an overview and bibliographical references on urban and rural witchcraft, see the two articles by Di Simplicio, Oscar, 'Urban Witchcraft', pp. 1148–1151, and 'Rural Witchcraft', pp. 977–950 in Golden, Richard M. (ed.), *Encyclopedia of Witchcraft: The Western Tradition* (ABC-CLIO eBook Collection: Santa Barbara, CA 2006).
487. Knutsen (2009); see also chapter 1 of this book.
488. Such a tendency that can be detected in most of Western Europe. For overview pieces, see Monter, William, 'Witch Witch Trials in Continental Europe.1560–1660', in Ankarloo, Bengt, Stuart Clark and William Monter, *Witchcraft and Magic in Europe. The Period of the Witch Trials* (University of Pennsylvania Press: Philadelphia 2002), pp. 49ff., for Western Europe in general; on Italy, see Lavenia, Vicenzo, 'Stregoneria, Italia' in *Dizionario storico dell'Inquizione*, p. 1529; Norway, Sweden and Finland experienced severe regional hunts in the late 17th century, for an overview on Scandinavia, see Ankarloo, Bengt, 'Witch Trials in Northern Europe. 1450–1700' in Ankarloo, Clark and Monter 2002), pp. 75–96.
489. ACDF, Siena, process, 52, fols. 891r–909v; the Roman Inquisition in Siena continued to prosecute clusters of trials for superstition and magic into the 18th century, Di Simplicio (2000), pp. 22f.
490. This regulation was motivated by a series of scandalous trials led by the nobleman Jørgen Arenfelt, see Henningsen (1991), esp. pp. 143–164; Krogh, Tyge,

Oplysningstiden og det magiske. Henrettelser og korporlige straffe i 1700-tallets første halvdel, (Museum Tusculanum: Copenhagen 2000b), p. 121.

491. In the High Court in 1686 there were 18 judges sentencing, compared to two or three judges at a time at the provincial court. Not all of the judges were intellectuals; they came from very different professions, such as professors of law and one of botanics, theologians, a doctor and a historiographer as seen in the trials against Jørgen Arenfelt et al., 1686, Henningsen (1991), pp. 150f.

492. Henningsen (1991), pp. 156f.; Krogh (2000), p. 121.

493. Via Henningsen (1991), p. 102.

Archives/sources

Archivio per la Dottrina della Santa Fede
Siena, processi, 25
Siena, processi, 29
Siena, processi, 40
Siena, processi, 42
Siena, processi, 51
Siena, processi, 52
StStE, 5e, nr. 2, Desiderio Scaglia, Prattica per procedere nelle cause del San'Officio,

Biblioteca Apostolica Vaticana
Eliseo Masini, Sacro Arsenale, ovvero Prattoca del Sant'Officio, (c. 1625), Stamp. Ferr. IV. 1367.

The Royal Library, Copenhagen
Niels Hemmingsen, *En undervisning aff Den Hellige Scrifft hvad mand døme skal om den store oc gruelige Gudsbespottelse som skeer med Troldom Sinelse Manelse oc anden saadan Guds hellige Naffns og Ords vanbrug. Item 33 Propositiones mot Troldom. Der til 33 Propositiones om Spaadom* (Undated)

Danish Archive for Folklore
Trolddomsprocesser ved Det Nørrejyske Landsting, 2003/002
I: Nørrejyske landstingsdomme i hekseprocesser. Fotokopier, kronologisk ordnet.
III B: Hekse. Navneregister til kopisamlingen fra Det Nørrejyske Landsarkiv.

Printed primary sources

Theological works
Canon Episcopi, 1140, Kors and Peters (1972), pp. 29–31.
St. Augustin, *On Christian Teaching*, book 395–398, 426, in Kors and Peters (2001), pp. 44–46.
Thomas Aquinas, *Summa contra gentiles*, 3rd book, part 2/104–106, in Kors and Peters (2001), pp. 90–95.
—— *Summae theologiae*, The Demons Tempt Man, 2:2, quest. 94, art. 1–5, in Kors and Peters (2001), pp. 97–102.

Papal regulations and bulls
Summis desiderantes affectibus, Innocent VIII (1484), in Kors and Peters (2001), pp. 177–180.
Coeli et terrae, Sixtus V (1586), extracts in P.G. Maxwell-Stuart (1999), pp. 59f.
Omnipotentis Dei, Gregory XV (1623), extracts in Summers (1927), pp. 544–546.

Manuals and guidelines
Institoris, Heinrich (and Jacob Sprenger), *Malleus maleficarum* (1486), English translation by Christopher S. Mackey, Cambridge University Press: Cambridge 2009.
Francesco Maria Guazzo, *Compendium maleficarum* (1608), English translation by Montague Summers, Dover Publications: New York 1929/1988.

Instructio pro formandis in causis strigum, extracts published Lea (1937/1957), pp. 950–963.

Peder Palladius, *En visitatsbog*, translated and introduced by Lausten, Martin Schwarz, Forlaget Anis: Copenhagen 2003.

Stimmen gegem die Hexenprozesse, Dettling, Alois (1907), pp. 42–55.

Danish law codes

Jyske lov, in Iuul, Stig and Erik Kroman, *Danmarks gamle Love paa Nutidsdansk*, vol. II, G.E.C. Gad: Copenhagen 1945–1948, p. 224.

Kirkeordinansen (1539), introduced and commented by Lausten, Martin Schwarz, Akademisk Forlag: Copenhagen 1989.

Københavnske Reces (1547), extracts in Johansen (1991), pp. 21f.

Kalundborgske Reces (1576), extracts in Rørdam (1886), vol. II, p. 269.

Forordning om Troldfolk og deris Medvidere (1617), in Rørdam (1886), vol. III, pp. 59–61.

Trials and extracts of trials

Bæksted, Anders, *Besættelsen i Tisted 1696–98*, 2 vols., Ejnar Munksgaard: Copenhagen 1959.

Grønlund, David, *Historisk Efterretning om de i Ribe Bye for Hexerie forfulgte og brændte Mennesker*, Ribe 1784.

Jacobsen, J.C., *Danske Domme i Trolddomssager i øverste Instans*, G.E.C. Gad: Copenhagen 1966.

—— *Christenze Kruckow. En adelig Troldkvinde fra Chr. IV's Tid*. G.E.C. Gad: Copenhagen 1972.

Ohrt. F., *Da signed Krist – Tolkning af det religiøse Indhold i Danmarks Signelser og Besværgelser*, Gyldendal Nordisk Forlag: Copenhagen 1927.

—— *Danmarks Trylleformler*, Nordisk Forlag: Copenhagen 1917.

Bibliography

Alberigo, Guiseppe, 'The Councel of Trent' in *Catholicism in Early Modern History: A Guide to Research*, O'Malley, J.W. (ed.), Center for Reformation Research: St. Louis 1988, pp. 211–226.

Andersen, Per, *Lærd ret og verdslig lovgivning Retlig kommunikation og udvikling i Middelalderens Danmark*, DJØF Forlag: Copenhagen 2006.

Ankarloo, Bengt, *Satans raseri. En sannfärdig berättelse om det stora häxoväsendet i Sverige och omgivande länder*, Ordfront Förlag: Stockholm 2007.

Ankarloo, Bengt and Stuart Clark (eds.), *Witchcraft and Magic in Europe. The Eighteenth and Nineteenth Centuries*, University of Pennsylvania Press: Philadelphia 2002.

Ankarloo, Bengt, Stuart Clark and William Monter, *Witchcraft and Magic in Europe. The Period of the Witch Trials*, Ankarloo, Bengt and Stuart Clark (eds.), University of Pennsylvania Press: Philadelphia 2002.

Ankarloo, Bengt and Gustav Henningsen (eds.), *Early Modern European Witchcraft. Centres and Peripheries*, Oxford University Press: Oxford 1990.

Appel, Charlotte, *Læsning og bogmarked i 1600-tallets Danmark*, Museum Tusculanum: Copenhagen, 2001.

Appel, Charlotte and Morten Fink-Jensen, *Når det regner på præsten. En kulturhistorie om sognepræster og sognefolk 1550–1750*, Forlaget Hovedland: Gern 2009.

—— *Da læreren holdt skole. Dansk skolehistorie*, vol. 1, Aarhus University Press: Aarhus 2013.

Appel, Hans Henrik, *Tinget, magten og æren. Studier i sociale processer og magtrelationer i et jysk bondesamfund i 1600-tallet*, Odense University Press: Viborg 1999.

Bailey, Michael D., 'The Age of Magicians: Periodization in the History of European Magic' in *Magic, Ritual, and Witchcraft*, 3 (2008), pp. 1–28.

—— 'The Meaning of Magic' in *Magic, Ritual, and Witchcraft*, 1 (2006), pp. 1–24.

—— *Battling Demons. Witchcraft, Heresy, and Reform in the Late Middle Ages*, University of Pennsylvania Press: Philadelphia 2003.

Bang, Gustav, *Kirkebogsstudier. Bidrag til dansk Befolkningsstatistik og Kulturhistorie i det 17. Aarhundrede*, Selskabet for Udgivelse af Kilder til Dansk Historie: Copenhagen 1906/1976.

Baroja, Julio Caro, 'Witchcraft and Catholic Theology' in Ankarloo, Bengt and Gustav Henninsen (eds.), *Early Modern European Witchcraft. Centres and Peripheries*, Oxford University Press: Oxford 1990/1998, pp. 19–45.

—— *The World of the Witches*, University of Chicago Press: Chicago, 1961/1971.

Barry, Jonathan, 'Keith Thomas and the Problem of Witchcraft (Introduction)' in Barry, Jonathan, Marianne Hester and Gareth Roberts (eds.),*Witchcraft in Early Modern Europe. Studies in Culture and Belief*, Cambridge University Press: Cambridge 1996, pp. 1–48.

Behringer, Wolfgang, *Witches and Witch-Hunts. A Global History*, Cambridge University Press: Cambridge 2004.

—— *Witchcraft Persecutions in Bavaria. Popular Magic, Religious zealotry and Reason of State in Early Modern Europe*, Cambridge University Press: Cambridge 1997.

—— *Hexenverfolgung in Bayern: Volksmagie, Glaubesefer und Staatsräson in der frühen Neuzeit*, Oldenbourg Verlag: München 1987.

189

Beloch, Karl Julius, *Storia della popolazione d'Italia*, reprinted in 1994, Le Lettere: Florence 1937–1961.

Bireley, Robert, *The Refashioning of Catholicism 1450–1700. A Reassessment of the Counter Reformation*, Palgrave Macmillan: Basingstoke 1999.

Birkelund, Merete, *Troldkvinden og hendes anklagere. Danske hekseprocesser i det 16. og 17. århundrede*, Arusia Historiske Skrifter: Århus 1983.

Black, Christopher F., *The Italian Inquisition*, Yale University Press: New Haven and London 2009.

—— *Early Modern Italy: A Social History*, Routledge: London 2001.

Bloch, Marc, 'Toward a Comparative History of European Societies' in Lane, Frederick C. and Jelle C. Riermersma, (eds.), *Enterprise and Secular Change. Readings in Economic History*, George Allen and Unwin: London 1928, pp. 494–522.

Bornstein, Daniel, 'Women and Religion in Late Medieval Italy: History and Historiography' in Bornstein, Daniel and Robert Rusconi (eds.), *Women and Religion in Medieval and Renaissance Italy*, University of Chicago Press: Chicago and London 1992/1996, pp. 28–47.

Borromeo, Agostino, 'The Inquisition and Inquisitorial Censorship' in Ozment, Steven (ed.), *Catholicism in Early Modern History: A Guide to Research*, Center for Reformation Research: St. Louis 1988, pp. 253–273.

Bossy, John, *Christianity in the West 1400–1700*, Oxford University Press: Oxford 1984.

Boyer, Paul and Stephen Nissenbaum, *Salem Possessed. The Social Origins of Witchcraft*, Harvard University Press: Cambridge, MA 1974.

C.F. Bricka (ed.), *Dansk Biografisk Leksikon*, 19 vols., Gyldendalske Boghandels Forlag: Copenhagen 1887–1905.

Briggs, Robin, *The Witches of Lorraine*, Oxford University Press: Oxford, 2008.

—— *Witches and Neighbors. The Social and Cultural Context of European Witchcraft*, Penguin Books: New York 1996/1998.

—— '"Many Reasons Why": Witchcraft and the Problem of Multiple Explanation' in Barry, Jonathan, Marianne Hester and Gareth Roberts (eds.), *Witchcraft in Early Modern Europe. Studies in Culture and Belief*, Cambridge University Press: Cambridge, 1996, pp. 49–64.

—— *Communities of Belief. Cultural and Social Tension in Early Modern France*, Clarendon Press: Oxford 1989.

Brimnes, Niels, 'Sammentræf og hybriditet. To nøglebegreber i postmodernismens komplekse verdenshistorie' in *Historisk Tidsskrift*, vol. 102/2 (2002), pp. 419–433.

—— 'Pragmatisk konstruktivisme – betragtninger om konstruktivisme og studiet af kultursammenstød' in *Den Jyske Historiker*, vol. 88 (2000), pp. 92–117.

Brink, Torben, 'Niels Hemmingsens forståelse af trolddom – en nyvurdering' in *Fortid og Nutid*, vol. 2 (1993), pp. 119–134.

—— *Den teologiske forståelse af trolddom i Danmark indtil midten af det17. århundrede*, Aarhus Universitet 1992.

Broedel, Hans Peter, *The Malleus Maleficarum and the Construction of Witchcraft. Theology and Popular Beliefs*, Manchester University Press: Manchester 2003.

Brown, Ralph, 'Examination of an Interesting Roman Document: Instructio pro formandis processibus in causis strigum' in *The Jurist*, vol. 24/1 (1964), pp. 169–192.

Brunsmand, Johan, *Køge huskors*, 1674, introduced and annotated by Anders Bæksted, Ejnar Munksgaard: Copenhagen 1953.

Burke, Peter, 'The Comparative Approach to Witchcraft' in Ankarloo, Bengt and Gustav Henningsen (eds.), *Early Modern European Witchcraft. Centres and Peripheries*, Oxford University Press: Oxford 1990/1998.

—— *The Historical Anthropology of Early Modern Italy*, Cambridge University Press: Cambridge 1987/1994.

—— *Popular Culture in Early Modern Europe*, Cambridge University Press: Cambridge 1978/1994.

—— *The Italian Renaissance, Culture and Society in Italy*, Polity Press: Cambridge 1972/1987.

—— 'A Question of Acculturation?' in Paola Zambelli (ed.), *Scienze, credenze occulte, livelli di cultura*, Olschki: Florence 1982, 197–204.

Burke, Peter and Roy Porter (eds.), *The Social History of Language*, Cambridge University Press: Cambridge 1987/1992.

Bæksted, Anders, *Besættelsen i Tisted 1696–98*, 2 vols., Ejnar Munksgaard: Copenhagen 1959.

Cameron, Euan, *Enchanted Europe: Superstition, Reason, and Religion 1250–1750*, Oxford University Press: Oxford 2010.

Canosa, Romano, *Storia dell'Inquisizione in Italia dalla metà del cinquecento alla fine del settecento*, vols. 1–5, Sapere 2000: Rome 1999.

Christensen, Chr. Villads, 'Besættelsen på Rosborg' in *Samlinger til Jysk Historie og Topografi*, 3rd series/2 (1899–1900), pp. 225–260.

—— 'Hekseprocesserne i Midtjylland' in *Samlinger til Jydsk Topografi og Historie*, 3. rk, bd. 5, Copenhage 1908–10.

Christensen, Poul Erik and Dorthe Skadhauge, *Kvinder og hekseforfølgelser i det 16. og 17. århundrede*, Aalborg University 1983.

Cifres, Alejandro, et al., *L'apertura degli archivi del Sant'Uffizio romano*, Atti dei convegni Lincei, 22 January 1998, 142, Accademia Nazionale dei Lincei, Rome 1998.

Ciuffoletti, Zeffiro and Leonardo Rombai, 'Saggio introduttivo: La storiografia dei presidios e le problematiche geostoriche dell'assetto territoriale' in Guarducci, Anna (ed.), *Orbetello e i presidios*, Centro Editoriale Toscano: Florence and Pontassieve 2000, pp. 9–27.

Clark, Stuart (ed.), *Languages of Witchcraft. Narrative Ideology and Meaning in Early Modern Europe*, Macmillan: Basingstoke 2001.

—— *Thinking with Demons. The Idea of Witchcraft in Early Modern Europe*, Oxford University Press: Oxford 1997.

Cochrane, Eric, *Italy 1530–1630*, Longman: London and New York 1988/1999.

Cohen, Elizabeth S., 'Back Talk: Two prostitutes voices from Rome c. 1600' in *Journal of Early Modern Women: An interdisciplinary journal*, 2 (2007), pp. 95–126.

—— 'To Pray, to Hear, to Speak: Women in Roman Streets c. 1600' in Riita Laitinen and Thomas Cohen (eds.), *Cultural History of Early Modern Streets*, Brill: Boston and Leiden 2008, pp. 95–118.

Cohen, Elizabeth S. and Thomas V. Cohen, *Daily life in Renaissance Italy*, Greenwood Press: Westport and London, 2001.

—— *Words and Deeds in Renaissance Rome. Trials before the Papal Magistrates*, University of Toronto Press: Toronto 1993.

Cohen, Thomas V., *Love and Death in Renaissance Italy*, University of Chicago Press: Chicago and London 2004.

Cohn, Norman, *Europe's Inner Demons. An Enquiry Inspired by the Great Witch-Hunt*, Sussex University Press: London 1975.

Cowan, Alexander, 'Gossip and Street Culture in Early Modern Venice' in Riita Laitinen and Thomas Cohen (eds.), *Cultural History of Early Modern Streets*, Brill: Boston and Leiden 2008, pp. 119–140.

Dall'Olio, Guido, 'The Devil of Inquisitors. Demoniacs and Exorcists in Counter-Reformation Italy' in Raiswell, Richard with Peter Dendle (eds.), *The Devil in Society in Pre-Modern Europe*, Centre for Reformation and Renaissance Studies: Toronto 2012, pp. 511–536.

——' Chiamata a me di me stesso testimonio. Infamia e disonore nei processi d'inquisizione' in Bordin, Michele and Paolo Trovato, *Lucrezia Borgia. Storia e mito*, Olschki: Florence 2006, pp. 195–207.

—— 'Tribunali vescovili, inquisizione romana e stregoneria: i processi bolognesi del 1559' in Prosperi, Adriano (ed.) *Il piacere del testo: Saggi e studi per Albano Biondi*, 2 vols:, I, Bulzoni Editore: Rome 2001, pp. 63–82.

Dandelet, Thomas, 'Politics and the state system after the Habsburg-Valois Wars' in Marino, John A. (ed.), *Early Modern Italy 1550–1796*, Oxford University Press: Oxford 2002, pp. 11–29.

—— *Spanish Rome 1500–1700*, Yale University Press: Harrisonburg 2001.

Dandelet, Thomas and John Marino (eds.), *Spain in Italy*, Brill: Leiden and Boston, 2007.

Darnton, Robert, *The Great Cat Massacre and Other Episodes in French Cultural History*, Penguin Books: London 1984/1988.

Davidson, Nicolas, 'Rome and the Venetian Inquisition in the Sixteenth Century', *Journal of Ecclesiastical History*, vol. 39/1 1988, pp. 16–37.

Davis, Natalie Zemon, *Fiction in the Archives*, Stanford University Press: Stanford 1987.

—— *The Return of Martin Guerre*, Harvard University Press: Cambridge, MA 1983.

—— 'From "Popular Religion" to "Religious Cultures"' in Ozment, Steven (ed.), *Reformation Europe: A Guide to Research*, Center for Reformation Research: St. Louis 1982, pp. 321–341.

De Blécourt, Willem, 'Sabbath Stories: Towards a New History of Witches' Assemblies' in Levack, Brian, *The Oxford Handbook of Witchcraft in Early Modern and Colonial America*, Oxford University Press: Oxford 2013, pp. 84–101.

De Boer, Wietse, *The Conquest of the Soul. Confession, Discipline, and Public Order in Counter-Reformation Milan* Brill: Boston and Leiden 2001.

Decker, Rainer, *Witchcraft and the Papacy. An account drawing on the formerly secret records of the Roman Inquisition*, University of Virginia Press: Charlottesville and London 2008.

Dedieu, Jean Pierre, 'The Archives of the Holy Office of Toledo as a Source for Historical Anthropology' in Henningsen, Gustav and John Tedeschi, in ass. with Charles Amiel, *The Inquisition in Early Modern Europe. Studies on Sources and Methods*, Northern Illinois University Press: Dekalb 1986, pp. 158–189.

Del Col, Andrea, *L'inquisizione in Italia. Dal XII al XXI secolo* Libri Editore Mondadori: Milan 2006.

—— 'Le strutture territoriale e l'attività dell'inquisizione romana' in Borromeo, Agostino (ed.), *L'inquisizione; atti del Simposio internazionale, Citta del Vaticano, 29–31. ottobre 1998*, Biblioteca Apostolica Vaticana: Vatican City 1998, pp. 345–381.

—— *Domenico Scandella Known as Menocchio. His Trials Before the Inquisition*, Medieval and Renaissance Texts and Studies: Binghamton, NY 1997.

—— 'I processi dell'inquisizione come fonte: Considerazioni diplomatiche e storiche' in *Annuario Istituto storico italiana per l'eta moderna e contemporanea*, vol. 35–36 (1983/84), pp. 31–50.

Delumeau, Jean, *Catholicism between Luther and Voltaire. A New View of the Counter-Reformation*, Westminster Press: Philadelphia 1977.

Dillinger, Johannes, *'Evil People'. A Comparative Study of Witch Hunts in Swabian Austria and the Electorate of Trier*, University of Virginia Press: Charlottesville 2009.

Di Simplicio, Oscar, *Autunno della stregoneria. Maleficio e magia nell'Italia Moderna*, il Mulino, Ricerca: Bologna 2005.

—— *Inquisizione, stregoneria, medicina. Siena e il suo stato (1580–1721)*, Il Leccio: Siena 2000.

—— 'L'Inquisizione di Siena e le accuse di maleficio' in Del Col, Andrea and Giovanna Paolin (eds.), *Metodologia delle fonti e storia istituzionale*, Edizioni Università di Trieste: Trieste 1999, pp. 256–273.

Duni, Matteo, 'I dubbi sulle le streghe' in *I vincoli della natura. Magia e stregoneria nel rinascimento*, Ernst, Germana and Guido Giglioni (eds.), Carocci Editore: Rome 2012, pp. 203–221.

—— Le streghe e gli storici, 1986–2006: bilancio e prosepettive' in Duni, Matteo and Dinanora Corsi (eds.), *Non la vivere la malefica. Le streghe nei trattati e nei processi (secoli XIV–XVIII)*, Florence University Press, Florence 2008, pp. 1–18.

—— *Under the Devil's Spell. Witches, Sorcerers, and the Inquisition in Renaissance Italy*, Syracuse University Press: Florence 2007.

Duni, Matteo and Dinanora Corsi (eds.), *Non la vivere la malefica. Le streghe nei trattati e nei processi (secoli XIV–XVIII)*, Florence University Press: Florence 2008.

Fantini, Maria Pia, 'La circolazione clandestine dell'orazione di Santa Marta. Un episodio modenese' in Zarri, Gabriella (ed.) *Donna, disciplina, creanza Cristiana dal XV al XVII secolo. Studi e testi a stampa*, Edizioni di Storia e Letteratura: Rome, pp. 45–65.

Fink-Jensen, Morten, *Fornuften under troens lydighed. Naturfilosofi, medicin og teologi i Danmark, 1536–1635*, Museum Tusculanum: Copenhagen 2004.

Firpo, Massimo, *Riforma protestante ed eresie nell'Italia del Cinquecento*, Laterza: Rome-Bari, 1993/1997.

Frandsen, Henrik, 'Niels Hemmingsen – armianismens åndelige fader' in *Dansk Teologisk Tidsskrift*, 51/1 (1988), pp. 18–35.

Gamrath, Helge, *Roma Sancta Renovata. Studier i romersk byplanlægning i det 16. århundredes anden halvdel med særligt henblik på Sixtus V's pontifikat (1585–1590)*, Danmarks Lærerhøjskole: Copenhagen 1986.

Gentilcore, David, *Healers and Healing in Early Modern Italy*, Manchester University Press: Manchester 1998.

—— 'The ethnography of everyday life' in Marino, John A. (ed.), *Early Modern Italy 1550–1796*, Oxford University Press: Oxford 2002, pp. 188–208.

Gelting, Michael, 'Skånske Lov og Jyske Lov: Danmarks første kommissionsbetænkning og Danmarks første retsplejelov' in Dam, Henrik, Lise Dybdahl, Lise and Finn Taksøe-Jensen (eds.), *Jura og historie. Festskrift til Inger Dübeck som forsker*, DJØF Forlag: Copenhagen 2003, pp. 43–80.

Gibson, Marion. 'Understanding Witchcraft? Accusers Stories in Print in Early Modern England', in Stuart Clark (ed.), *Languages of Witchcraft. Narrative, ideology and Meaning in Early Modern Culture*, Palgrave Macmillan: Basingstoke, 2001, pp. 41–54.

Ginatempo, Maria, *Crisi di un territorio. Il popolamento della Toscana senese alla fine del medioevo*, Olschki: Florence 1988.

Ginzburg, Carlo, *Spor*, Thing, Morten (ed.), Museum Tusculanum: Copenhagen 1999.

—— *Ecstasies: Deciphering the Witches´ Sabbathh*, University of Chicago Press: Chicago 1992.

—— 'The Dovecote Has Opened Its Eyes: Popular Conspiracy in 17th Century Italy' in Henningsen, Gustav and John Tedeschi (eds.),*The Inquisition in Early Modern Europe, Studies in Sources and Methods*, Northern Illinois University Press: Dekalb 1986, pp. 190–198.

—— 'The Witches' Sabbath: Popular Cult or Inquisitorial Stereotype?' in Kaplan, Steven (ed.), *Understanding Popular Culture, Europe From the Middle Ages To the 19th Century*, Walter de Gruyter: Berlin 1984, pp. 39–51.

—— *The Cheese and the Worms*, Torino 1976, transl. by John and Anne Tedeschi, Johns Hopkins University Press and Routledge and Kegan Paul: New York and London 1976/1982/1992.

—— *The Night Battles, Witchcraft and Agrarian Cults in the Sixteenth and Seventeenth Centuries*, transl. by Tedeschi, John and Anne, Routledge and Kegan Paul: London 1966/1983.

Gijswijt-Hofstra, Marijke, 'Witchcraft After the Witch Trials' in Ankarloo, Bengt and Stuart Clark (eds.), *The Eighteenth and Nineteenth Centuries. The Athlone History of Witchcraft and Magic in Europe*, vol. 5, Athlone and University of Pennsylvania Press: London and Philadelphia 1999, pp. 95–189.

Givry, Grillot de, *Witchcraft, Magic and Alchemy*, transl. by J. Courtenay Locke, Houghton Mifflin Company 1931, Dover Publications Inc.: New York, 1971.

Golden, Richard M. (ed.), *Encyclopedia of Witchcraft: The Western Tradition*, ABC-CLIO eBook Collection: Santa Barbara, CA 2006 (ebook edition).

Grell, Ole Peter *The Scandinavian Reformation: From Evangelical Movement to Institutionalisation of Reform*, Cambridge University Press: Cambridge 1995.

Grell, Ole Peter and Bob Scribner, *Tolerance and Intolerance in the European Reformation*, Cambridge University Press: Cambridge 1996.

Grendler, Paul, *The Roman Inquisition and the Venetian Press 1540–1605*, Princeton University Press: Princeton 1977.

Grinder-Hansen, Poul, *Frederik 2. Danmarks renæssancekonge*, Gyldendal: Copenhagen 2013.

Grønlund, David, *Historisk Efterretning om de i Ribe Bye for Hexerie forfulgte og brændte Mennesker*, Ribe 1784.

Guarducci, Anna (ed.) *Orbetello e The presidios*, Centro Editoriale Toscano: Florence and Pontassieve 2000.

Hagen, Rune Blix, *Dei europeiske trolldomsprosessane*, Samlaget: Oslo 2007.

Hansen, Joseph, *Quellen und Untersuchungen zur Geschichte des Hexenwahns und der Hexenverfolgung im Mittelalter*, Carl Georgi, Universität Buchdrückeri und Verlag: Bonn and Hildesheim 1901/1963.

Heiberg, Steffen, *Christian 4. – en europæisk statsmand*, Gyldendalske Boghandel and Nordisk Forlag: Copenhagen 1988/2006

Henningsen, Gustav, 'Anmeldelse af Da Djævelen var ude...Trolddom i det 17. århundredes Danmark' in *Historisk Tidsskrift*, 92/1 (1992), pp. 131–150.

—— *Heksejægeren på Rugård*. Skippershoved: Ebeltoft 1991.

—— 'The Ladies From the Outside: An Archaic Pattern of the Witches' Sabbath' in Henningsen, Gustav and Ankarloo, Bengt (eds.), *Early Modern European Witchcraft: Centres and Peripheries*, Oxford University Press: Oxford 1990/1998, pp. 191–219.

—— *The Witches' Advocate: Basque Witchcraft and the Spanish Inquisition*, University of Nevada Press: Reno 1980.

—— 'Hekseforfølgelse efter hekseprocessernes tid. Et bidrag til dansk etnohistorie' in *Folk og Kultur* (1975), pp. 98–151.

—— 'Hekseforfølgelser' in Steensberg, Axel (ed.), *Daglig liv i Danmark i det syttende og attende århundrede*, Nyt Nordisk Forlag: Copenhagen, 1969, pp. 353–376.

Henningsen, Gustav and Contreras, Jaime (1986), 'Forty-Four Thousand Cases of the Spanish Inquisition (1540–1700): An Analysis of a Historical Data Bank' in Henningsen, Gustav and John Tedeschi (eds.), *The Inquisition in Early Modern Europe, Studies in Sources and Methods*, Northern Illinois University Press: Dekalb, pp. 100–129.

Henningsen, Gustav, Jens Chr. V. Johansen and Ditlev Tamm, '16.000 jyskedomme. En sagtypologisk analyse af Hofman Bangs regest til Viborg landstings dombøger 1569–1805' in *Historie*, vol. xxviii (1979), pp. 240–271.

Henningsen, Gustav and Tedeschi, John, 'The Inquisition in Early Modern Europe. Studies on Sources and Methods (*intro.*)' in Henningsen, Gustav and John Tedeschi (eds.), *The Inquisition in Early Modern Europe, Studies in Sources and Methods*, Northern Illinois University Press: Dekalb 1986, pp. 3–12.

Herlihy, David, 'The Tuscan Town in the Quattrocento: A Demographic Profile' in *Medievalia et Humanistica*, New series I (1970), pp. 81–109.

Herskovits, Melville J., 'African Gods and Catholic Saints in the New World Negro Belief' in *The American Anthropologist*, xxxix (1937), pp. 635–643.

Herzig, Tamar, *Christ Transformed into a Virgin Woman. Lucia Brocadelli, Heinrich Institoris and the defense of the faith*, Edizione di Storia e Letteratura: Rome 2013.

—— 'Witchcraft Prosecutions in Italy' in *The Oxford Handbook of Witchcraft in Early Modern and Colonial America*, Levack, Brian P. (ed.), Oxford University Press, Oxford 2013, pp. 249–267.

Horsley, Richard, 'Who were the Witches? The Social Role of the Accused in the European Witchtrials' in *Journal of Interdisciplinary History*, vol. 9 (1979), pp. 689–715.

Hudon, William V., *Marcello Cervini and Ecclasiastical Government in Tridentine Italy*, Northern Illinois University Press: DeKalb 1992.

Hunt, Lynn and Aletta Biersack (eds.), *New Cultural History*, University of California Press: Los Angeles and London 1989.

Iggers, Georg G., *Historiography in the Twentieth Century. From Scientific Objectivity to the Postmodern Challenge*, Wesleyan/University Press of New England: Hanover 1997.

Ingesman, Per, 'Kirkelig disciplin og social kontrol i senmiddelalderens danske bondesamfund. En casestudy af det ærkebiskoppelige gods under Lundegård 1519–22 og Hammershus 1525–40' in Arnórsdóttir, Agnes, Per Ingesman and Bjørn Poulsen, *Konge, kirke og samfund*, Aarhus University Press: Aarhus 2007, pp. 329–380.

Iuul, Stig, 'Den gamle danske strafferet og dens udvikling indtil slutningen af det 18. århundrede' in Beckman, Leif (ed.), *Kampen mod forbrydelsen*, vol. 1, Wiene: Copenhagen 1951.

Iuul, Stig and Erik Kroman, *Danmarks gamle Love paa Nutidsdansk*, vol. II, G.E.C. Gad: Copenhagen 1945–1948.

Jacobson Schutte, Anne, 'Religion, spirituality, and the post-Tridentine Church' in Marino, John A. (ed.), *Early Modern Italy 1550–1796*, Oxford University Press: Oxford 2002, pp. 125–143.

—— *Aspiring Saints: Pretense of Holiness, Inquisition, and Gender in the Republic of Venice, 1618–1750*, Johns Hopkins University Press: Baltimore 2001.

Jacobsen Schutte, Anne,Thomas Kuehn, Silvana Seidel Menchi (eds.), *Time, Space, and Women's Lives in Early Modern Europe*, Truman State University Press: Missouri 2001.

Jacobsen, J.C., *Danske Domme i Trolddomssager i øverste Instans*, G.E.C. Gad: Copenhagen 1966.

—— *Christenze Kruckow. En adelig Troldkvinde fra Chr. IV's Tid.* G.E.C. Gad: Copenhagen 1972.

Jansson, Karin Hassan, 'Våld som aggression eller kommunikation? Hemfridsbrott 1550–1650' in *Historisk Tidskrift (Sweden)*, 126:3, 2006, pp. 429–452.

—— *Kvinnofrid. Synet på våldtäkt och konstruktionen av kön i Sverige 1600–1800*, Uppsala Universitet, 2002.

Jedin, Hubert, *A History of the Council of Trent*, T. Nelson: London 1957–1961.

Jedin, Hubert, E. Iserloh and J. Glazik, et al., *History of the Church, Reformation and Counter Reformation*, vol. 5, Burns and Oates: London 1980.

Jensen, Karsten Sejr, *Trolddom i Danmark 1500–1588*, Arken Tryk: Copenhagen 1982.

196   *Bibliography*

Jobe, Patricia, 'Inquisitorial Manuscripts in the Biblioteca Apostolica Vaticana: A Prelimenary Handlist' in Henningsen, Gustav and John Tedeschi (eds.), *The Inquisition in Early Modern Europe, Studies in Sources and Methods*, Northern Illinois University Press: Dekalb 1986, pp. 33–53.

Johansen, Hans Christian, 'Danmarks folketal omkring år 1700' in *Historie*, new series, vol. 12/3–4 (1978), pp. 360–375.

Johansen, Jens Chr. Vesterskov, 'Tinget, magten og æren' in *Historisk Tidsskrift*, vol. 99/1 (1999), pp. 231–236.

—— 'Denmark: The Sociology of Accusations' in Ankarloo, Bengt and Gustav Henningsen (eds.), *Early Modern European Witchcraft. Centres and Peripheries*, Oxford University Press: Oxford 1990/1998, pp. 339–367.

—— *Da Djævelen var ude...Trolddom i det 17. århundredes Danmark*, Odense University Press: Viborg 1991.

—— 'Tavshed er guld...En historiografisk oversigt over amerikansk og europæisk heksetros-forskning 1966–1981' in *Historisk Tidsskrift*, vol. 81 (1981), pp. 401–423.

Johansen, Jens Chr. Vesterskov, Kenneth Johansson, Hans Eyvind Næss and Ditlev Tamm 'The Law and the Judicial System' in Österberg, Inger and Sogner, Sølvi (eds.), *People Meet the Law. Control and Conflict Handling in the Courts*, Universitetsforlaget: Stamsund 2000, pp. 26–56.

Jolly, Karen, Catharina Raudvere and Edward Peters, *Witchcraft and Magic in Europe. The Middle Ages*, Athlone History of Witchcraft, vol. III, Ankarloo, Bengt and Stuart Clark (series eds.), University of Pennsylvania Press: Philadelphia 2002.

Jørgensen, Poul Johs., *Dansk strafferet fra Reformationen til Danske Lov*, Ditlev Tamm and Helle Voigt (eds.), Jurist- og Økonomforbundets Forlag: Copenhagen 2007.

Kallestrup, Louise Nyholm, 'Djævelen' in Duedahl, Poul and Ulrik Langen, *Nattens Gerninger*, Gads Forlag: Copenhagen 2015, pp. 173–191.

—— 'Women, Witches, and the Town Courts of Ribe' in Muravyeva, Marianna and Raisa Maria Toivo (eds.), *Gender in Late Medieval and Early Modern Europe*, Routledge: London 2013, pp. 124–136.

—— 'De besmittede og de skyldige' in *Religionsvidenskabeligt Tidsskrift*, vol. 59 (2012), pp. 55–72

—— 'Knowing Satan from God: Demonic Possession, Witchcraft, and the Lutheran Orthodox Church in Early Modern Denmark' in *Magic, Ritual and Witchcraft*, vol. 6/2 (2011), pp. 163–182.

—— 'Trolddomsforfølgelser' in Christensen, Søren Bitsch (ed.), *Ribe Bys historie*, vol. 2, Esbjerg Kommune and Danish Center for Urban History: Aarhus 2010, pp. 294–305.

—— 'Fra klog kone til kætter' in *Kvinders magt og magtens kvinder i tidlig moderne Europa, Den Jyske Historiker*, vol. 125 (2010), pp. 73–92.

Kamen, Henry, *Inquisition and Society in Spain in the Sixteenth and Seventeenth Centuries*, Indiana University Press: Indiana 1985.

Kieckhefer, Richard, 'Witchcraft, Necromancy and Sorcery as Heresy' in Osteorero, Martine, Georg Modestin and Kathrin Utz Tremp (eds.), *Chasses aux sorcières et démonologie. Entre discours et pratique (XVIᵉ – XVIIᵉ siècles)*, Edizioni del Galluzzo: Florence 2010, pp. 133–153.

—— *Magic in the Middle Ages*, Cambridge University Press: Cambridge 1989/2000.

—— *European Witch Trials: Their Foundations in Popular and Learned Culture, 1300–1500*, University of California Press: Berkeley and Los Angeles 1976.

Klitgaard, C, 'Den Store Nordjyske Hekseforfølgelse' in *Fra Himmerland og Kjær Herred*, 1915–1917, pp. 90–218.

Knutsen, Gunnar, *Servants of Satan and Master of Demons. The Spanish Inquisition's Trials for Superstition, Valencia and Barcelona, 1478–1799*, Turnhout: Brepols 2009.

—— 'Norwegian Witch Trials. A reassesment' in *Continuity and Change*, 18:2, 2003, pp. 185–200.

—— *Trolldomsprocessene på Østlandet. En kulturhistorisk undersøgelse*, Tingbogsprosjektet, Oslo, 1998.

Koch, Hal and Bjørn Kornerup (eds.), *Den Danske Kirkes Historie*, vol. IV, Gyldendalske Boghandel and Nordisk Forlag: Copenhagen 1959.

Koefoed, Nina Javette, *Besovede kvindfolk og ukærlige barnefædre*, Museum Tusculanum: Copenhagen 2008.

—— 'Sekularisering og sædelighed – Religion som politisk argument' in *Den Jyske Historiker*, vol. 105 (2004), pp. 35–52.

Kornerup, Bjørn, *Biskop Hans Poulsen Resen. Studier over Kirke- og Skolehistorie i det 16. og 17. Aarhundrede*, 2 vols., G.E.C. Gad: Copenhagen 1928.

Kors, Alan C. and Peters, Edward (eds.), *Witchcraft in Europe 400–1700. A Documentary History*, second and revised edition by Edward Peters, University of Pennsylvania Press: Philadelphia 2001.

—— *Witchcraft in Europe 1100–1700, A Documentary History*, University of Pennsylvania Press: Philadelphia 1972.

Krogh, Tyge, 'Henrettelsens fascination – Om selvmordsmord og statsreligiøsitet i 1700-tallet' in *Den Jyske Historiker*, vol. 105 (2004), pp. 19–35.

—— *Det store natmandskomplot. En historie om 1700-tallets kriminelle underverden*, Samleren: Viborg 2000a.

—— *Oplysningstiden og det magiske. Henrettelser og korporlige straffe i 1700-tallets første halvdel*, Museum Tusculanum: Copenhagen 2000b.

Kaae, Bue (1956). 'Lønnepræsten Jens Hansen Rusk' in *Ribe Amts årbog*, vol. 15, 1960–63.

Larner, Christina, *Witchcraft and Religion. The politics of Popular Belief*, Blackwell: London 1984/1987.

Lavenia, Vincenzo, 'Stregoneria e inquisizione' in *I vincoli della natura. Magia e stregoneria nel rinascimento*, Ernst, Germana and Guido Giglioni (eds.), Carocci Editore: Roma 2012, pp. 185–201.

—— '"Anticamente di mist foro": Inquisizione, stati, e delitti di stregoneria nella prima età moderna' in Paolin, Giovanna (ed.), *Inquisizioni: Percorso di ricerca*, Trieste, 2001, pp. 41–53.

Lausten, Martin Schwarz, *Niels Hemmingsen. Storhed og fald*, Forlaget Anis: Copenhagen 2013.

—— *Johann Bugenhagen. Luthersk reformator i Tyskland og Danmark*, Forlaget Anis: Copenhagen 2011.

—— *Peder Palladius. Sjællands første lutherske biskop*, Alfa: Frederiksberg 2006.

—— *A Church History of Denmark*, Ashgate: Farnham 2002.

—— *Reformationen i Danmark*, Forlaget Anis: Copenhagen 1987.

Le Roy Ladurie, Emmanuel, *Montaillou. En middelalderlandsby og dens mennesker*, trans. Jacques Berg, Gyldendal: Copenhagen 1975/1986.

Lea, Henry Charles, *Materials Toward a History of Witchcraft*, vols. 1–3, University of Pennsylvania Press: Philadelphia 1937/1957.

—— *A History of the Inquisition in Spain*, Vols. 1–4, Macmillan: New York 1906–1907.

Levack, Brian P., *The Witch-Hunt in Early Modern Europe*, Taylor & Francis: New York 1987/1992.

Liliequist, Jonas (ed.), *A History of Emotions 1200–1800*, Pickering and Chatto: London/Vermont 2012.

Macfarlane, Alan, *Witchcraft in Tudor and Stuart England. A Regional and Comparative Study*, 2nd edition, Routledge: London 1991/1999.

Macy, Gary, 'Nicolas Eymeric and the Condemnation of Orthodoxy' in Ferreiro, Alberto (ed.), *The Devil, Heresy and Witchcraft in the Middle Ages. Essays in Honor of Jeffrey B. Russell*, Brill: Boston and Leiden 1998, pp. 369–381.

Mackey, Christopher, *Hammer of Witches. A Complete Translation of the Malleus maleficarum*, Cambridge University Press: Cambridge 2006/2009.

Maggi, Armando, *In the Company of Demons. Unnatural Beings, Love, and the Identity in the Italian Renaissance*, University of Chicago Press: Chicago and London 2006.

Mangio, Carlo, 'L'assedio di Orbetello e l'occupazione francese di Porto Longone e di Piombino: Un episodio italiano della Guerra dei Trent'Anni' in Guarducci, Anna (ed.), *Orbetello e i presidios*, Centro Editoriale Toscano: Florence and Pontassieve 2000, pp. 201–211.

Marrara, Danilo, 'I presidi feudo imperiale' in Guarducci, Anna (ed.), *Orbetello e i presidios*, Centro Editoriale Toscano: Florence and Pontassieve 2000, pp. 59–64.

Martin, John, 'Popular Culture and the Shaping of Popular Heresy in Renaissance Italy' in Haliczer, Stephen (ed.), *Inquisition and Society in Early Modern Europe*, Barnes and Noble: London and Sydney 1987, pp. 115–128.

Martin, Ruth, *Witchcraft and the Inquisition of Venice 1550–1650*, Blackwell: London 1989.

Maxwell-Stuart, P.G., *Witchcraft in Europe and the New World, 1400–1800*, Palgrave Macmillan: London 2001.

Mayer, Thomas F., *The Roman Inquisition on the Stage of Italy, c. 1590–1640*, University of Pennsylvania Press: Philadelphia 2014.

Midelfort, H.C. Erik, *Witch Hunting in South Western Germany. The Social and Intellectual Foundations*, Stanford University Press: Stanford 1972.

Mitchell, Stephen A., *Witchcraft and Magic in the Nordic Middle Ages*, University of Pennsylvania Press: Philadelphia 2011.

—— 'Pactum cum diabolo og galdur á Nordulöndum', Tulinius, Torfi H. (ed.) *Galdramenn: Galdrar og Samfelag a Mioldum*, Reykjavik: Hugvisindastofnun Háskóla Islands 2008, pp. 121–145 (English summary, pp. 1–17).

Monter, E. William, *Ritual, Myth and Magic in Early Modern Europe*, Ohio University Press: Ohio 1984.

—— 'Scandinavian Witchcraft in Anglo-American Perspective' in Ankarloo, Bengt and Gustav Henningsen (eds.), *Early Modern European Witchcraft. Centres and Peripheries*, Oxford University Press: Oxford 1990/1998, pp. 425–434.

Muchembled, Robert, 'Satanic Myth and Cultural Reality' in Ankarloo, Bengt and Gustav Henningsen (eds.), *Early Modern European Witchcraft. Centres and Peripheries*, Oxford University Press: Oxford 1990/1998, pp. 139–161.

—— *Popular Culture and Elite Culture in France, 1400–1750*, trans. by Lydia Cochrane, Louisiana State University Press: Louisiana 1985.

Mullet, Michael, *The Catholic Reformation*, Routledge: New York 1984.

Murray, Margaret, *The Witch-Cult in Western Europe*, Clarendon Press: Oxford 1921.

Nalle, Sara T., 'Inquisitors, Priests, and the People during the Catholic Reformation in Spain' in *Sixteenth Century Journal*, vol. 18/4 (1987), pp. 557–588.

Nevers, Jeppe and Niklas Olsen (eds.), *Begreber, tid og erfaring*, Hans Reitzels Forlag: Copenhagen 2007.

Nevers, Jeppe, 'Til begreberne! En skitse af to begrebshistoriske analysestrategier' in *Historiefagets teoretiske udfordring,*. Hansen, Per H. and Jeppe Nevers (eds.), University Press of Southern Denmark: Odense 2004, pp. 81–105.

Nielsen, Knud, 'Lidt om Engebølle og lidt mere om Niels Hemmingsen' in *Lokalhistorisk årsskrift*, 1991, pp. 31–33.

Næss, Hans Eivind, *Trolldomsprosserne i Norge på 1500–1600-tallet. En retts- og Sosialhistorisk undersøkelse*, Universitetsforlaget: Oslo 1982.

Ohrt. F., *Da signed Krist – Tolkning af det religiøse Indhold i Danmarks Signelser og Besværgelser*, Gyldendal Nordisk Forlag: Copenhagen 1927.
—— *Danmarks Trylleformler*, Nordisk Forlag: Copenhagen 1917.
O'Malley, John, *Trent and All That. Renaming Catholicism in the Early Modern Era*, Harvard University Press: Cambridge, MA 2002.
O'Neil, Mary R., 'Tall Tales, Sober Truth and Storytellers before the Inquisition' in *Æstel*, vol. 3. 1995, pp. 1–19.
—— 'Missing Footprints: Maleficium in Modena' in *Acta Ethnographica Hungary*, vol. 37, 1991/1992, pp. 123–143.
—— 'Magical Healing, Love Magic and the Inquisition in Late 16th Century Modena' in Haliczer, Stephen (ed.), *Inquisition and Society in Early Modern Europe*, Barnes and Noble: London and Sydney 1987, pp. 88–114.
—— 'Sacerdote Ovvero Strione: Ecclesiastical and Superstitious Remedies in 16th Century Italy' in Kaplan, Steven (ed.), *Understanding Popular Culture, Europe From the Middle Ages To the 19th Century*, Walter de Gruyter Berlin 1984, pp. 53–84.
—— 'Discerning Superstition. Popular Errors and Orthodox Response in Late Sixteenth Century Italy', PhD dissertation, Stanford University 1982.
Österberg, Eva and Erling Sandmo, 'People Meet the Law. Introduction' in *People Meet the Law. Control and Conflict Handling in the Courts*, Sogner, Sølvi and Eva Österberg (eds.), Universitetsforlaget: Stamsund 2000.
Ørberg, Paul G., 'De ældste folketællinger i Aalborg og Nibe. Et bidrag til dansk folketællings-historie' in *Fra Himmerland og Kær Herreder*, vol. 37 (1976), pp. 87–107.
Ørnbjerg, Jakob, 'Mod en ny tid? Studier over det aalborgensiske rådsaristokratis økonomiske, politiske, sociale og kulturelle udvikling, 1600–1660', PhD dissertation, Aalborg University 2011.
—— *Jens Bang – en købmand i 1600-tallets Aalborg*, Aalborgbogen, Selskabet for Aalborgs Historie: Aalborg 2005.
Österberg, Eva and Sølvi Sogner (eds.), *People Meet the Law. Control and Conflict Handling in the Courts*, Universitetsforlaget: Stamsund 2000.
Palladius, Peder, *En visitatsbog*, translated and introduced by Lausten, Martin Schwarz, Forlaget Anis: Copenhagen c. 1540/2003.
Pastor, Ludvig von, *Geschichte der Päpste seit dem Ausgang des Mittelalters*, Herder: Berlin 1925–1933.
Petersen, Viggo, *Aalborg og Limfjordslandet*, Aalborgbogen 1993, Selskabet for Aalborgs historie: Aalborg 1993.
Peters, Edward, *Inquisition*, University of California Press: Berkeley 1989.
—— *The Magician, the Witch and the Law*, University of Pennsylvania Press: Philadelphia 1978.
Peters, Edward, 'Editing Inquisitors' Manuals in the Sixteenth Century: Francisco Peña and the *Directorium Inquisitorum* of Nicholas Eymeric' in *The Library Chronicle*, vol. 40, 1975, pp. 95–107.
Pihlamäki, Heikki (ed.), *Theatres of Power. Social Control and Criminality in Historical Perspective*, Matthias Calonius Society: Helsinki 1991.
Prosperi, Adriano, *L'inquisizione romana. Letture e ricerche*, Edizione di storia e letteratura: Rome 2003.
—— *Il Concilio di Trento. Una introduzione storica*, Giulio Einaudi Editore: Torino 2001.
—— *Tribunali della coscienza. Inquisitori, confessori, missionari*, Giulio Einaudi Editore: Torino 1996.
Prosperi, Adriano, Vicenzo Lavenia and John Tedeschi (eds), *Dizionario storico dell'inquisizione*, 4 vols., Scuola Normale Superiore: Pisa 2010.

Purkiss, Diane, *The Witch in History: Early Modern and Twentieth-Century Representations*, Routledge: New York and London 1996.

Rasmussen, Poul, *Viborg Landstings Dombøger 1617A. Udtog af dommene*, Landsarkivet for Nørrejylland: Viborg 1971.

Raveggi, Pietro, *Orbetello antica e moderna*, reprinted 2004, Biblioteca Comunale Orbetello: Orbetello 1933.

Riising, Anne, 'Tamperrettens funktion og domspraksis' in *Festskrift til Johan Hvidtfeldt*, Iversen, Peter Kr., Knud Prange and Sigurd Rambusch (eds.), Arkivvæsenet: Åbenrå 1978, pp. 393–412.

Romeo, Giovanni, 'Inquisizione, Chiesa e stregoneria nell'Italia della Controriforma: nuove ipotesi' in *Non la vivere la malefica. Le streghe nei trattati e nei processi (secoli XIV-XVIII)*, Duni, Matteo and Dinanora Corsi (eds.), Florence University Press, Florence 2008, pp. 53–64.

—— *L'Inquisizione nell'Italia moderna*, Laterza: Rome and Bari 2002.

—— *Esorcisti, confessori e sessualità femminile nell'Italia della Controriforma*, Le lettere: Florence 1998.

—— *Inquisitori, esorcisti e streghe nell'Italia della Controriforma*, Sansoni Editore: Florence 1990.

Roper, Lyndal, *The Witch in the Western Imagination*, University of Virginia Press: Virginia 2012.

—— *Witch Craze: Terror and Fantasy in Baroque Germany*, Yale University Press: New Haven and St. Edmunsbury Press: Bury St Edmunds 2004.

—— *Oedipus and the Devil. Witchcraft, Sexuality and Religion in Early Modern Europe*, Routledge: New York and London 1994/2002.

—— *The Holy Household. Women and Morals in Reformation Augsburg*, Clarendon Press: Oxford 1991.

Rowlands, Alison, 'Witchcraft and Popular Religion in Early Modern Rothenburg ob der Tauber' in Scribner, Bob and Trevor Johnson (eds.), *Popular Religion in Germany and Central Europe, 1400–1800*, St. Martin's Press: New York 1996, pp. 101–119.

Ruggiero, Guido, *Binding Passions. Tales of Magic, Marriage, and Power at the End of the Renaissance*, Oxford University Press: Oxford 1993.

Russell, Jeffrey B., *A History of Witchcraft. Sorcerers, Heretics and Pagans*, 2. revised edition, Thames and Hudson: London 2007.

Rørdam, H.F. *Danske kirkelove samt udvalg af andre bestemmelser vedrørende kirken, skolen og de fattiges forsørgelse fra Reformationen indtil Christian v's danske lov, 1536–1683*, Selskabet for Danmarks kirkehistorie, vol. 2+3, G.E.C. Gad: Copenhagen 1886.

Sabean, David Warren, *Power in the Blood. Popular Culture and Village Discourse in Early Modern Germany*, Cambridge University Press: Cambridge 1984/2003.

Sanders, Hanne, 'Sekularisering – Et relevant begreb for historisk forskning?' in *Den Jyske Historiker*, vol. 105 (2004), pp. 5–19.

Sandmo, Erling, *Voldssamfunnets undergang, Om disiplinering av Norge på 1600-tallet*, Universitetsforlaget, Oslo, 1999/2002.

—— 'Volden som historisk konstruksjon' in *Nord Nytt* 1999:77, pp. 61–74.

Sarpi, Paolo, *Sopra l'officio dell'inquisizione*, 1613, published in *Scritti Giurridizionalistici* (1958).

Schjerning, Camilla, *Følelsernes fællesskaber. Moralske følelser og sociale relationer i København 1771–1800*, University of Copenhagen, 2013.

Schulte, Rolf, *Man as Witch. Male Witches in Central Europe*, Palgrave Macmillan: Basingstoke, 2009.

—— *Hexen Vervolgung in Schleswig-Holstein 16.-18. Jahrhundert*, Verlag Boyens & Co.: Heide, 2001.

Scocozza, Benito, *Ved afgrundens rand, 1600–1700*, Gyldendal og Politikens Danmarkshistorie, vol. 8. Gyldendal and Politiken: Copenhagen 1989.

Scribner, Bob and Trevor Johnson (eds.), *Popular Religion in Germany and Central Europe, 1400–1800*, St. Martin's Press: New York 1996.

Scribner, Bob, Roy Porter and Mikulás Teich (eds.), *The Reformation in National Context*, Cambridge University Press: Cambridge 1994.

Sharpe, James, *Instruments of Darkness: Witchcraft in Early Modern England*, University of Pennsylvania Press: Philadelphia 1997.

Semerano, Martino, *Il tribunale del Santo Officio di Oria. Inediti processi di stregoneria per la storia dell'inquisizione in età moderna*, A. Giuffrè: Milano 2003.

Sluhovsky, Moshe, *Believe Not Every Spirit. Possession, Mysticism and Discernment in Early Modern Catholicism*, University of Chicago Press: Chicago, 2007.

Skadhauge, Dorthe, 'Kvindefællesskaber og troldkvinder', *Kvindefællesskaber, Hæfter for Historie*, vol. 1. (1985), pp. 79–99.

Steensberg, Axel (ed.), *Dagligliv i Danmark, vol. 1, 1620–1720*, Nyt Nordisk Forlag Arnold Busck: Copenhagen 1969, 2nd edition 1981.

Summers, Montague, *The Geography of Witchcraft*, Kegan Paul: New York 1927.

Symcox, Geoffrey, 'The Political World of the Absolute State in the Seventeenth and Eighteenth Centuries' in Marino, John (ed.), *Early Modern Italy 1550–1750*, Oxford University Press: Oxford 2000, pp. 104–122.

Tangherlini, Timothy, 'How do you know she's a witch? Witches, Cunning Folk and Competition in Denmark' in *Western Folklore* 59, 2000, pp. 279–303.

Tauber, E., in ass. with A. H. Nielsen, *Personal-historiske notitser om Embeds- og Bestillingsmænd i Aalborg i Fortid og Nutid*, Jydsk Historisk-Topografisk Selskab Aalborg 1879–1880.

Tedeschi, John, *The Prosecution of Heresy: Collected Studies on the Inquisition in Early Modern Italy*, Medieval and Renaissance Texts and Studies: Binghamton, NY 1991.

—— 'Inquisitorial Law and the Witch' in Ankarloo, Bengt and Gustav Henningsen (eds.), *Witchcraft in Early Modern Europe*, Oxford University Press: Oxford 1990/1998, pp. 83–120.

Thomas, Keith, *Religion and the Decline of Magic. Studies in Popular Beliefs in Sixteenth and Seventeenth Century England*, Oxford University Press: Oxford and New York 1971/1997.

Tognarini, Ivano, 'Orbetello. I presidios di Toscana e il Mediterraneo. Il destino di un territorio tra Cosimo de'Medici, Bernardo Tanucci e Napoleone' in Guarducci, Anna (ed.), *Orbetello e I presidios*, Centro Editoriale Toscano: Florence and Pontassieve 2000, pp. 105–189.

Trevor-Roper, Hugh, *European Witch Craze in the Sixteenth and Seventeenth Century*, Collins: London 1969.

Troels-Lund, Troels, *Dagligliv i Norden i det sekstende århundrede*, vols. 1–14, cd rom edition, LFL's Bladfond 1908–1910.

Trouillot, Michel-Rolph, *Silencing the Past. Power and the Production of History*, Beacon Press, Boston 1995.

Turchini, Angelo, 'Il modello ideale dell'inquisitore: la Pratica del cardinal Desiderio Scaglia' in Del Col, Andrea and Giovanna Paolin *L'Inquisizione Romana. Metologia delle fonti e storia istituzionale. Atto del seminario internazionale Montereale Valcellina 23 e 24 settembre millenovecento99*, Università del Trieste: Trieste 1999.

Tvede-Jensen, Lars and Gert Poulsen, *Aalborg under krise og højkonjunktur fra 1534 til 1680. Aalborgs Historie*, vol. 2, Aalborg Kommune: Aalborg 1988.

Tørnsø, Kim, *Djævletro og folkemagi. Trolddomsforfølgelse i 1500 og 1600 tallets Vestjylland*, Aarhus University Press: Aarhus 1986.

Valente, Michaela, 'Per uno stregone che si vede, se ne veggono dieci milla donne'. Caccia alla streghe e questioni di genere' in *I vincoli della natura. Magia e stregoneria nel rinascimento*, Ernst, Germana and Guido Giglioni (eds.), Carocci Editore: Roma 2012, pp. 239–252.

Van Gent, Jacqueline, *Magic, Body and the Self in Eighteenth-Century Sweden*, Brill: Boston and Leiden 2008.

Vespasiani, Gioia, http://www.presidios.it/stato-dei-presidi/breve-storia/3 October 2014.

Waite, Gary K., *Heresy, Magic, and Witchcraft in Early Modern Europe*, Palgrave Macmillan: Basingstoke 2003.

Weber, Max, *Den protestantiske etik og kapitalismens ånd*, Nansensgade Antikvariat: Copenhagen 1920/1995.

Willumsen, Liv Helene, 'Seventeenth-Century Witchcraft Trials in Scotland and Northern Norway', PhD dissertation, University of Edinburgh 2008.

Wilson, Eric, 'Krämer at Innsbruck: Heinrich Krämer, the Summis Desiderantes and the Brixen Witch-Trial of 1485' in Scribner, Bob and Trevor Johnson (eds.), *Popular Religion in Germany and Central Europe, 1400–1800*, Palgrave Macmillan: New York 1996, pp. 87–101.

Wittendorff, Alex, 'Tinget, magten og æren. Om mikrohistorie, kulturteori, og ortodoks teologi i anledning af en disputats' in *Historisk Tidsskrift*, vol. 99/1 (1999), pp. 211–230.

—— *Tyge Brahe*, GEC Gads Forlag: Copenhagen 1994.

—— 'Trolddomsprocessernes ophør i Danmark' in *Historisk Tidsskrift*, vol. 92/1 (1992), pp. 1–28.

—— *På Guds og herskabs nåde. Politiken and Gyldendals Danmarkshistorie*, vol. 7. Olsen, Olaf (ed.), Gyldendalske Boghandel and Nordisk Forlag: Copenhagen 1989.

—— 'De danske reformationer og den folkelige bevidsthed' in Bøgh, Anders, Jørgen Würtz Sørensen and Lars Tvede-Jensen, *Til kamp for friheden: Sociale oprør i nordisk middelalder*, Aalborg universitetsforlag: Aalborg 1985/1988, pp. 215–232.

—— '"Fire stolper holder et skidehus". Tidens forestillingsverden' in *Christian IV's verden*, Sven Ellehøj (ed.), Nyt Nordisk Forlag Arnold Busck: Copenhagen 1988, pp. 214–249.

—— *Rejsen mod Virkeligheden. Den europæiske forestillingsverden fra reformationen til nutiden*, Aschehoug: Copenhagen 1986.

—— '"Evangelii lyse dag" eller hekseprocessernes mørketid? Om Peder Palladius historieopfattelse' in *Tradition og kritik. Festskrift til Sven Ellehøj*, Christensen, Grethe et al. (eds.), Den Danske Historiske Forening: Copenhagen 1984, pp. 89–119.

Index

Printed and bound by CPI Group (UK) Ltd, Croydon, CR0 4YY